JOB CREATION
IN
AMERICA

JOB CREATION

— IN —

AMERICA

How Our Smallest Companies Put the Most People to Work

David L. Birch

THE FREE PRESS
A Division of Macmillan, Inc.
NEW YORK

Collier Macmillan Publishers
LONDON

The Free Press
A Division of Macmillan, Inc.
866 Third Avenue, New York, N.Y. 10022

Collier Macmillan Canada, Inc.

Printed in the United States of America

printing number
1   2   3   4   5   6   7   8   9   10

Library of Congress Cataloging-in-Publication Data

Birch, David L.
    Job creation in America.

    1. Small business—United States—Employees.
2. Job vacancies—United States. I. Title.
HD2346.U5B47   1987   331.12′4′0973   87–8523
ISBN 0–02–903610–0

To my wife,
LOUISA

Contents

Acknowledgments

This book draws on twelve years of research, massive amounts of data, and a large number of people who worked hard to make it possible. There is no pretense of this being a solo effort.

In the early days Peter Allaman, Elizabeth Martin, and Mike Luby helped lay the foundation for what followed. They developed the first software that permitted us to examine the history of 15 million businesses in a reasonably efficient manner. They also established the initial framework in which we analyzed those millions of companies.

The technical work was picked up by Sheryll Weber and William Parsons. Sheri has struggled mightily to keep our data bases current and to improve significantly the process by which we analyze them. Bill has focused on the models required to forecast job growth and economic change, the results of which are found in Chapters 5, 6, and 7.

I have had the great privilege of working with Susan Mac-Cracken on several of the analyses that followed our initial findings. Sue and I have studied (and written together about) the processes by which corporations evolve and about the special role played by high-technology firms—and innovative firms in general. Sue's ideas and contributions are very much a part of Chapters 1, 2, and 3, and are present in general terms throughout. In the last stages she was joined by Sarah Hammond, who produced many of the final tables appearing in the book.

We have learned a great deal about job creation in America by contrasting it with the processes by which jobs are created in other nations—particularly the United Kingdom, Sweden, and Canada. Colin Gallagher at the University of Newcastle upon Tyne was one of the first to take an active interest in our research, and to undertake a comparable project in the United Kingdom. Torgny Nandorf became a partner, through his firm Consultus, in our efforts in Sweden and helped to build a Swedish data base. Rudy Oldenburg and Nancy Chinfen of the Canadian Department of Regional Industrial Expansion undertook the Canadian analysis. Each person, and organization, worked diligently to overcome the obstacles to creating complex data sets in totally different environments, mastered the analytical techniques involved, and made considerable contributions to our understanding of how different cultures go about creating jobs for themselves.

Much of our research has been based on data provided by Dun and Bradstreet. Throughout this effort, we have received a great deal of cooperation from D & B as they have carefully explained their data collection procedures and accommodated our sometimes unusual requirements. Properly used and understood, Dun and Bradstreet's DMI file offers a unique and powerful tool for understanding the dynamics of economies here and abroad, and we are greatful to Dun and Bradstreet for taking the effort to make our research possible. Special thanks go to Dennis Jacques, who, over the years, has been our constant liaison with Dun's Marketing Services, figuring out over and over again how to do what had never been done before within his organization.

Our style of research is demanding of the organizations for which we work. We need computers and specially equipped rooms and employers who are tolerant of our erratic schedules and the need for hunks of time to write and to think. The Massachusetts Institute of Technology has been a most supportive employer throughout, providing the facilities and flexibility and administrative help we needed to undertake a long-term effort. Michael Joroff, director of MIT's Laboratory of Architecture and Planning, in which we worked, has been with us during this entire period, and we are especially grateful to him. I also appreciate the support of Cognetics, Inc.—a spinoff from MIT with which several of the research team are now affiliated, and which has made its computers and staff available to me to complete the book. Of particular help have been Marian Constantine and Lynn Freedman, who patiently and accurately translated my yellow-paper scribbles into a finished manuscript.

Robert Sobel has played a special role. As a business historian, thoughtful observer, and skillful writer, Bob has turned a somewhat dry initial manuscript into the better illustrated, more easily read book you are now holding. Bob's contribution has gone well beyond that of editor. He has served much more as a co-writer, turning raw material and text into a smoothly flowing finished product. If you find this book a pleasure to read, it is because of Bob, and I am grateful to him for his help.

Spouses can play a very important role in sustaining a research tradition of the sort represented by this book, and my wife Louisa is the best example I know of. My dedication of this book to her is a woefully inadequate way of acknowledging twelve years of consultation, advice, critical reaction to earlier and current writings, many lonely nights, and endless tolerance of all that goes with a husband engulfed in research.

Introduction

The economy is like the weather, talked about incessantly, understood marginally, and predicted poorly. Yet, what happens in the economy is usually more important than what the weather might be. An umbrella can shield us against the rain, but when the untoward appears in the workplace there is often no equivalent protection.

Some 20 million Americans leave their jobs every year, half of them involuntarily—they are either fired or laid off with little warning. About 10 million American workers change their careers each year for a wide variety of reasons; again some of their own volition, more involuntarily. They go from schoolteacher to insurance agent, textile worker to elevator repairman. Some do it without changing employers; most have to switch employers, sometimes moving across the country looking for work.

All that is frightening. One day there is a job, the next there is none. We often know why the jobs have gone—either the product or service is no longer needed or can be provided less expensively in another part of the country or of the world. Finding out where replacement jobs will come from is a more difficult exercise, since it involves exploration into the innards of capitalism at work. But the personal questions remain, the most important of which being "What can I do to prepare for the best and the worst?"

Part of the problem is that no one has looked carefully into how jobs are created and destroyed. Far too many economists seem to think of the economy as consisting of huge blocks—consumption, investment, government spending, exports, and so forth—that can be moved around by a relatively few "economic crowbars," among them the money supply, interest rates, government programs, and

1

tax policies. If good news is not immediately forthcoming, the pundits tell us not to worry; in time, the pressures will produce desired accommodation, in somewhat the same way orthodontic procedures can shift teeth.

It isn't that simple. Of late the big blocks haven't moved where they were supposed to, or at the rate that prevailed in the past. We face huge deficits (domestic and international) and continued sharp rises and declines in the unemployment rate, and no one seems to know how to alleviate either situation without causing grave harm to the economy. The old rules no longer seem to apply. Economists of all persuasions, from laissez-faire libertarians to Marxists, struggle for explanations and for nostrums to cure our ailments. Yet when the blocks fall in the wrong way, literally millions of workers each year are crushed.

Why is this so? What can be done about it?

Start off by realizing that the economy is *not* comprised of these blocks. The "steel industry" is an abstraction, and so are the "service" and "manufacturing" sectors. We can't define "money" with any degree of precision, so those money-supply figures are of limited use. No one reading this book works for an industry. Rather, jobs are supplied by a specific company or, perhaps, a division of a company, or by themselves.

There are some 7 to 8 million companies in the United States, along with a large and unknown number of partnerships and self-employed individuals, which collectively employ the 85 million nongovernment workers in America. This does not take account of the so-called underground economy, which simply cannot be measured. No one sticks up his or her hand when asked who is working off the books.

Most of these enterprises have little or no direct interest in what the government does. They do not pay much attention to where the crowbars are positioned as they go about their business. The run-of-the-mill companies simply are trying to make ends meet, take in more revenue than they have expenses, locate more customers, work out better deals with suppliers, get as much as they can out of their workers, come up with a new or improved way to do what they do.

This book deals with just that—the processes by which the millions of companies create jobs, grow or decline, expand or go out of business. While we consider partnerships and sole proprietorships in general terms, most of the analysis focuses on companies.

Our companies have been examined individually, one at a

time, part by part, and then fitted into a conceptual framework. The basic research was done at the Massachusetts Institute of Technology, where a staff of researchers has been tracing and tracking the histories of some 12 million individual business establishments since 1969. All of the generalizations made in this book are based on this empirical research.

The raw data on establishments were acquired from Dun and Bradstreet. Most of these establishments are single-unit, stand-alone companies—a store or a small plant or a law firm. A relatively few are parts or divisions of larger companies. Collectively, in 1986 the establishments in our files employed about 95 percent of all nongovernment workers in the United States.

Dun and Bradstreet keeps track of the employment rolls, age, and location of each establishment (as well as what kind of business it's in) on a regular basis—usually once or twice a year. We—the MIT staff and I—acquired complete Dun and Bradstreet files at regular intervals between 1969 and 1986, usually two years apart. We then hooked the records together over time to form histories for each individual establishment—some 12 million of them. We also hooked together the parts of more complex corporate families to form "family trees." Along the way, we checked for clerical and reporting errors and eliminated records that looked suspicious.

When we were all done, we had created an economic microscope through which we could see the economy, not as big blocks, but as a collection of small units living out what for some will be very short lives. There are drug stores and shoe repair shops, General Motors and American Express. A few companies could be classified as high technology, like IBM and Lotus, or like that small components firm in a low-lying building you might pass every day, but most are pretty low tech. Some are old; most are young and will never reach maturity. Some are growing rapidly; most do so sluggishly, and then under pressure.

By tracking the individual companies over time we have learned how the behavior of each creates and then destroys jobs. We will learn in Chapters 1 and 2 that this corporate population is enormously turbulent, that it is not by accident so many workers move on each year. We will learn that millions of enterprises are formed each year and that a significant number of them grow—so much so that the formation and growth of fairly small firms now accounts for virtually all of our job growth.

Why is this happening? Why are smaller firms dominating job

creation? Chapter 3 explores the context in which this basic shift is taking place. In the United States, fewer companies and workers are taking materials from the ground or the fields and shaping them into cars, missiles, cloth, and food. A greater proportion are using manufactured products to create better ways of doing their work—to distribute parcels, conduct medical procedures, move people from one place to another, create and exchange information—and are selling the better ways (along with the physical objects making that possible) abroad.

The United States is running a deficit in foreign trade for visible things, such as machine tools and autos. We have a sizeable export trade, however—some $144 billion in 1985—in what usually are deemed services. "The fastest growing area of world trade is invisible," said Henry Eason of the U.S. Chamber of Commerce. "You can't load it on a ship or stack it on a display shelf," he noted, going on to say, "We call it services."* And it is the area in which the United States leads the world.

This fundamental shift in the structure of the economy has fostered an era of great innovation. As we look through our microscope, we see economic growth being dominated by a relatively few highly innovative firms, most of which have started small and grew by creating a whole new way of making or doing something. We will call them "high-innovation firms," and the sectors that house large concentrations of them "high-innovation sectors." High tech is but one small part of high innovation in America.

Our microscope will be directed at other countries as well as the United States, in particular at Canada, Sweden, and, through someone else's microscope, at the United Kingdom. We find striking differences in the behavior of corporations in these few countries, most of which is traceable not to superficial differences in legal structures but to far more profound differences in cultures, in the attitudes and beliefs that inhabitants of each nation bring to the workplace each day.

Culture does not change rapidly. Charles de Gaulle once remarked that nations such as France, Germany, and Russia have pretty much the same drives and interests as they did two centuries ago, and there is something to this. It is our conclusion, in Chapter 4, that changes in the economic anatomy of these countries will not come quickly.

* Quoted in Kishor Parekh, *USA: The Brains of the World* (Miami/South Florida Magazine, June 1986), p.75.

4

Most of the new firms that are taking the place of the older ones prefer different kinds of locations and work forces, present different needs for capital, transportation, government services, education and recreation, and energy. Chapters 5 and 6 will look carefully at the spatial implications of the innovation revolution. We will look 10 years down the road to learn what places will boom and what places will not do so well. We will also discover that any locale's future lies in its own hands to a much greater degree than at any time in the past. We will explore the kinds of human-initiated (rather than God-given) action that might make a difference.

The electronics engineer who drops into the local pizza parlor for a quick snack and the baker who provides it are both Americans living in the waning years of the 20th century, but in terms of outlook and work, they are centuries apart. In a year or so that baker could lose his job to a machine; however, if he knows what is happening and the options that exist, he could wind up better off than before. The engineer will become even more prized as a worker than ever—assuming he plays his cards right. Or he could go down with the technological ship if he makes the wrong choices.

The victims of economic turbulence will be discussed in some detail in Chapter 7. These are the people who work for an increasingly unstable and ailing set of corporations. Make no mistake about it, they will be hurt, financially and psychologically. Yet by looking down the road a few years they might be able to perceive opportunities for better, more satisfying, and more highly remunerated work. This, too, will be discussed, analyzed, and specific recommendations offered in concrete dollars-and-cents terms. For those soon-to-be-unemployed workers who are flexible and who, most important, possess the requisite knowledge and the willingness to use it, the future could be far brighter than the past or present.

Those who are unaware of the situation and rigid about change will suffer the most, usually to the degree of their ignorance and rigidity. To succeed means getting accustomed to the idea of multiple jobs and careers and a willingness to move and shift. For people ready to adapt, this book could be very valuable. Before coming to any conclusions, however, we must look carefully through our economic microscope and understand how those millions of firms create and destroy millions of jobs each year and function as the engine of the modern American economy. This is the subject of our first chapter.

CHAPTER 1

The Invisible Hand

Fly over any large American city on a clear day during the morning rush hours, and you will see lines of autos moving at varying speeds, as corpuscles might in the veins and arteries of the human body. Everything seems arranged to achieve utmost harmony, with adjustments made for detours and stalled vehicles. From a mile up, the traffic appears orchestrated as though by some master plan.

Of course, this is only an illusion. As all who have made such commutes realize, each driver is out for himself, attempting to maximize ease, minimize tension, and get to a destination as rapidly and safely as possible. This is the reason for the unspoken cooperation near stalled vehicles; the drivers know some mutual aid is required on such occasions. Should you switch from one lane to another? Try an alternate route to avoid possible jams? Is it worth taking the toll road rather than the freeway at certain times of the day or days of the week?

Drivers engage in this kind of calculus automatically and in almost subconscious fashion, and out of it comes the picture of seeming harmony. It is of a piece with Adam Smith's famous "invisible hand" that orders the marketplace without being directly perceived.

What does all of this have to do with the real economy? The answer is that, from what I have observed, most economists seem to believe the nation's corporations and their work forces function like that rush-hour traffic, when viewed from on high. They see the economy in terms of gross national product, unemployment rates, tons of steel, cars produced, and the like. They concentrate upon behemoths like General Motors, IBM, and Exxon—and the Dow

Jones Industrial Average—to determine where the economy is headed, ignoring their hundreds of thousands of supplier firms, most with fewer than a dozen workers. They speak of how government spending will impact on the macro economy, ignoring the fact that a majority of American workers are employed by concerns where what the government does affects them only indirectly. In essence, most economists believe that there is such a thing as a whole economy, when there are really only individual units working with others to maximize advantages.

This is to suggest that such economists are dealing with abstractions (perhaps with an illusion) and speak of forests without fully understanding that what we have is collections of trees. Similarly, the morning traffic looks harmonious, when in fact each driver in every car is an individual agent, sometimes cooperating with others but usually not.

THE BUSINESS ENTERPRISE

So there is no such thing as an American economy, at least not in the way the term is usually employed. Rather, there are about 7 million companies, close to 90 percent of which employ fewer than 20 workers. Taken together these small companies create more jobs than the giants comprising the *Fortune 500,* grow more rapidly, run greater chances of failure, and show more adaptibility.

This is an important concept requiring some elucidation, because the facts run contrary to the conventional widsom.

Start with the idea that the function of an economy is to produce desired goods and services. Firms that succeed in tapping customers' wellsprings receive orders, which down the road translate into a call for additional workers. But we begin with the cravings for goods and services, either by consumers, other companies, or government, and not the need to create jobs. Successful gratification of the former results in expansion of the latter.

This is not to say that at some times, for some economies, job creation does not become a paramount political and sound need. Such was the case during the Great Depression; while under the Works Progress Administration a number of famous "boondoggles" existed, leaf-raking jobs created to salvage personal esteem, provide a living for destitute workers, and prime the pump of the national economy. But this was an anomaly, certainly not in the interest of economic efficiency most of the time. We know that the U.S.S.R. has very little unemployment, and for good reason: the economy is amazingly inefficient.

Progress has always caused the loss of jobs. It used to take two men upward of ten hours to dig a grave; now a machine does it in half an hour. A snowstorm in New York or Chicago used to mean that thousands of men with shovels would be hired to clear the streets; now the task is done better by a fraction of the number formerly employed. Of course, new jobs are created, too, and these are usually ones requiring greater skills than those displaced.

Accordingly, in the universe of small businesses, struggling entrepreneur-managers are always seeking ways to economize, and if replacing a worker with a machine will turn the trick, it will be done. Those workers who cost more than they produce cannot be tolerated; they will go, their slots taken by more efficient individuals or machines. Even economist John Kenneth Galbraith, who in most of his writings suggests that competition is absent in much of American industry, that the American and Soviet industries are coming to resemble one another more all the time (a doctrine known as "convergence"), and that they are increasingly bureaucratized and less receptive to consumer need, was obliged to recognize that his general view does not apply to small business. In *The New Industrial State* Galbraith wrote:

> It will be urged, of course, that the industrial system is not the entire economy. Apart from the world of General Motors, Standard Oil, Ford, General Electric, U.S. Steel, Texaco, Gulf, Western Electric, and Du Pont is that of the independent retailer, the farmer, the shoe repairman, the bookmaker, narcotics peddler, pizza merchant, and that of the car and dog laundry. Here prices are not controlled. Here the consumer is sovereign. Here pecuniary motivation is unimpaired. Here technology is simple and there is no research and development to make it otherwise. Here there are no government contracts; independence from the state is a reality. None of these entrepreneurs patrol the precincts of the Massachusetts Institute of Technology in search of talent. The existence of all of this I concede.*

Galbraith concludes that "this part of the economic system is not insignificant." Yet this is akin to talking about the non–New England sector of the American economy. The rest of the country exists to be sure, and indeed is the larger portion of the nation, but

* John Kenneth Galbraith, *The New Industrial State* (Boston: Houghton Mifflin, 1967), p. 187.

Galbraith implies the reverse. Galbraith and others who think that big business is the American economy don't seem to realize fully that the bubbly, yeasty, creative segment is the small businesses segment. Moreover, most American workers can be found in their employ:

DISTRIBUTION OF ESTABLISHMENTS AND EMPLOYEES BY
ENTERPRISE SIZE

ENTERPRISE SIZE (NUMBER OF EMPLOYEES)	PERCENT OF ESTABLISHMENTS	PERCENT OF EMPLOYEES
0–19	83.4	25.2
20–99	9.9	19.8
100–499	3.2	16.7
500–4,999	1.9	18.3
5,000 or more	1.5	19.8
	100.0	100.0

The small operations here run the gamut from a corner candy store in Seattle, Washington, to a high-tech startup in Austin, Tex. Some locales have more of them than others. In recent years, Austin has had one of the highest rates of significant startups per capita in the United States. Just behind Austin are Dallas, El Paso, and Phoenix—followed by San Antonio, Houston, Orlando, and Atlanta.

From the conclusion of the 1982 recession to the end of 1985 some 8 million jobs were created. As might have been expected, California ranked first in absolute numbers, followed by Florida, New York, Georgia, New Jersey, Massachusetts, Texas, North Carolina, Virginia, and Ohio. An odd mix, but most of these locales come as no great surprise. There are states in the Sun Belt and the Northeast with great think tanks. If we categorize the states into regions we come to a startling discovery:

JOB CREATION IN THE AMERICAN
ECONOMY, 1982–1985

AREA	JOBS CREATED
Northeast-Midwest	3,046,000
South	2,911,000
West and Plains	2,178,000
	8,135,000

Hardly a Sun Belt sweep.

These numbers represent an attempt to illustrate that the highly complex mechanism we call the economy continually moves and changes, just like those lines of cars wending their way to or away from the city. From afar it appears relatively sluggish and peaceful. It has its ups and downs, measured in terms of growing 1 instead of 3 percent a year, hardly the stuff of which high drama is made.

What happens when you look more closely? What do you see when you put this amorphous abstraction under the economic microscope, and look at individual units? You will see a mass of confusion, a chaotic, turbulent collection of individual companies, all of which are constantly undergoing change. Some are organized as single units with a single headquarters; others have many divisions, each with its own section chief. Some are being born, others are dying; some are growing rapidly, while others are shrinking. In recent years there have also been large-scale reorganizations through mergers and acquisitions. But the net change is small, primarily because the micro changes tend to offset each other. There is some balancing principle—a "conservation of corporate energy"—involved. Startups are offset by closings, expansions are offset by contractions, and moves in the aggregate usually net to zero.

To employ another analogy, think of the economy as a thundercloud. It looks placid from afar, towering some 60,000 to 70,000 feet into the sky, a large, beautiful, fluffy mass of moisture. Viewed from within, however, one sees only turbulence. Moisture is sucked up from the surface of the earth, and some of it rises rapidly, only to be offset by cooler air dropping from the top. The key word to describe what goes on is "balance." The cloud looks more or less the same from one minute to the next from the outside because the moisture drawn in is balanced by the rain falling out, and the wind moving up is offset by the wind moving down.

Much the same flow exists in the economy. A large number of new firms appear each year and are sucked into the economic system, as is the moisture in a thunderhead. Some of them grow rapidly. They often do so at the expense of others that experience offsetting declines, and a large number of them go out of business every year.

The remarkable thing, I'll say again, is the balance that is maintained. The number of firms of different size and the number of jobs fluctuate by only 1 or 2 percent a year, yet the individual firms

10

are bouncing around like droplets in the interior of that turbulent cloud.

I have tried to make these movements both graphic and quantitative in Figure 1–1. Here the universe of firms is divided into five segments, starting from the smallest ones (0–19 employees) and going on to the giants (5,000+), and shows job gains and losses from 1981 to 1985. The numbers within each category stand for jobs gained or lost from the others. In the 20–99 grouping, for

FIGURE 1–1. Flows Caused by Enterprises Expanding or Contracting

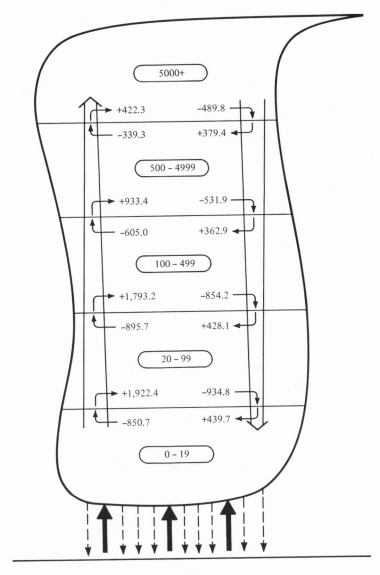

example, starting with a 1981 base of 12,127,400, there were 1,922,400 jobs gained through the expansion of smaller enterprises that grew and brought their establishments with them and 428,100 gained from firms that contracted in size. Some 895,700 workers were employed by firms that grew out of the category, while 934,800 were in firms that contracted to the point where they had fewer than 20 employees.

Of course this is only part of the picture. What of those firms that grew or contracted within the 20–99 range? These are accounted for in Figure 1–2, which takes account of all movement: within categories, across categories, and newly formed and recently closed establishments as well. We see, for example, that the net change for internal growth in this group was 413,000 jobs.

From 1981 to 1985 the 20–99 category had added 1,109,800 jobs, but the other components had altered drastically. Newly formed establishments had accounted for 2,976,800 jobs. 2,350,500 were added by firms moving up or down into the group, while 1,830,500 were subtracted to account for firms moving out of the group. Establishments going out of business resulted in a further diminution of 2,800,000 jobs, while 413,000 were created by firms remaining in the category.

Thus, almost half the pool turned over. Yet, when it was all done, the group—as a group—was about the same size as it had been in 1981.

Size of pool in 1981	12,127,400
Gains	5,740,300
Losses	4,630,500
Size of the pool in 1985	13,237,200

Moreover, the distribution of jobs in the business universe also remained virtually the same:

	SHARE OF JOBS in 1981 (%)	SHARE OF JOBS in 1985 (%)
1–19	25.3	25.2
20–99	19.2	19.8
100–499	17.1	16.7
500–4,999	18.3	18.3
5,000+	20.1	19.8
	100.0	100.0

FIGURE 1–2. Complete Flows in the Economic Thundercloud

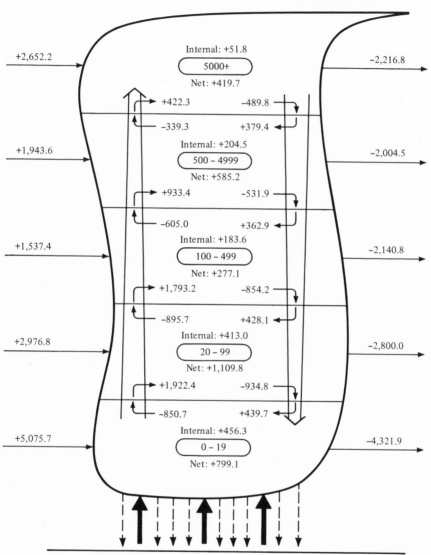

By now you can see that those economists who claim that American business is coming to be dominated by the giant corporations are off the mark. Put aside the fact that in this four-year span the 5,000+ company category actually declined in its share of workers. Consider, instead, that the companies comprising that group changed, as did the others. To the macroeconomist looking at snapshots of the economy in 1981 and 1985, not much had happened. To one looking at the economy from the inside and taking

13

account of the components, there obviously had been tremendous changes.

Take a quick glance at Figure 1–3 for insights on where job creation has occurred in recent years. Looking first at expansions and contractions of existing companies, you will note that most of the net expansion among single-unit companies comes from the smaller ones. Of course there are job losses as well, but the net change for these comparatively diminutive companies is far more than that for the giants, which actually lost jobs from 1981 through 1985. The same holds for multidivisional or multi-unit corporations. Taken altogether, companies with 1–19 employees accounted for 82 percent of the job expansion and concerns with over 5,000 employees lost 13.5 percent net. Clearly, on balance

FIGURE 1–3. JOBS CREATED BY ESTABLISHMENTS EXPANDING AND CONTRACTING IN FIRMS OF DIFFERENT SIZES, 1981–1985

ENTERPRISE SIZE	JOBS GAINED THROUGH EXPANSION	JOBS LOST THROUGH CONTRACTION	NET CHANGE	PERCENT OF NET
SINGLE UNIT COMPANIES				
1–19	2,240.6	704.2	1,536.3	91.2
20–99	1,195.2	923.7	271.5	16.1
100–499	453.5	590.9	−137.3	−8.2
500–4999	255.4	218.3	37.1	2.2
5000+	13.4	36.4	−23.0	−1.4
	4,158.0	2,473.5	1,684.5	100.0
MULTI-UNIT COMPANIES				
1–19	359.6	86.3	273.3	52.2
20–99	672.0	340.0	332.0	63.4
100–499	810.6	639.5	171.1	32.7
500–4999	844.3	822.4	21.8	4.2
5000+	980.4	1,255.1	−274.7	−52.5
	3,667.0	3,143.3	523.7	100.0
ALL COMPANIES				
1–19	2,600.2	790.5	1,809.7	82.0
20–99	1,867.2	1,263.7	603.5	27.3
100–499	1,264.2	1,230.4	33.8	1.5
500–4999	1,099.6	1,040.7	58.9	2.7
5000+	993.8	1,291.5	−297.7	−13.8
	7,824.9	5,616.7	2,208.2	100.0

small firms demonstrate a greater propensity to expand than do large ones.

Single-unit startups tend predominantly to be small (see Figure 1–4); one simply doesn't create a new concern with over 5,000 workers the first day, and few appeared from 1981 to 1985. On the other hand, larger, complex firms tend to start up new units in almost all enterprise categories, which is where jobs are created in giant enterprises. That is to say major corporations generally create jobs through the formation of new business units, as when IBM established its PC (personal computer) operations at Entry Systems. This is another way of going into a startup. Mom and Pop Deli opens a second store managed by the owners' daughter; Nissan opens an American branch in Tennessee, staffs it with Japanese managers, and goes out and hires an American work force, thus

FIGURE 1–4. JOBS CREATED BY THE STARTUP AND CLOSING OF ESTABLISHMENTS, 1981–1985

ENTERPRISE SIZE	JOBS CREATED BY STARTUPS	JOBS LOST THROUGH CLOSING	NET CHANGE	PERCENT OF NET
SINGLE-UNIT COMPANIES				
1–19	4,502.6	3,846.2	656.4	296.9
20–99	1,969.7	1,822.1	147.6	66.8
100–499	385.2	762.4	−377.1	−170.6
500–4999	89.0	307.9	−218.9	−99.0
5000+	13.1	0	13.1	5.9
	6,959.6	6,738.6	221.0	100.0
MULTI-UNIT COMPANIES				
1–19	573.1	475.7	97.4	20.3
20–99	1,007.2	977.9	29.2	6.1
100–499	1,152.2	1,378.4	−226.3	−47.1
500–4999	1,854.6	1,696.6	158.0	32.9
5000+	2,639.1	2,216.8	422.3	87.9
	7,226.1	6,745.4	480.6	100.0
ALL COMPANIES				
1–19	5,075.7	4,321.9	753.8	107.4
20–99	2,976.8	2,800.0	176.8	25.2
100–499	1,537.4	2,140.8	−603.4	−86.0
500–4999	1,943.6	2,000.5	−61.0	−8.7
5000+	2,652.2	2,216.8	435.4	62.1
	14,185.6	13,484.0	701.6	100.0

creating new jobs. But large firms also sell divisions or close them down, resulting in job losses.

Both kinds of events are reflected in Figures 1–3 and 1–4 in the segment entitled "Multi-Unit Companies," where we see that the smallest firms created 573,100 jobs in new units while losing 475,700, for a net gain of 97,400, while the 5,000+ firms added 2,639,100 jobs and lost 2,216,800, for a net gain of 422,300. So here, too, small businesses hold their own. *For both single and multi-unit concerns, there was a job creation of 753,800 for the 1–19 and a gain of only 435,400 for the 5,000+ firms.*

Indeed, pulling it all together (Figure 1–5) we can see that very small firms have created about 88 percent of all net new jobs in the period being considered. Contrary to some popular opinion, smaller firms are more than capable of offsetting their higher failure rates by their ability to organize and then grow.

FIGURE 1–5. NET JOB CREATION BY SIZE OF ENTERPRISE 1981–1985

ENTERPRISE SIZE	NET OF EXPANSIONS- CONTRACTIONS	NET OF STARTS- CLOSINGS	OVERALL NET JOB CREATION	PERCENT OF NET
SINGLE-UNIT COMPANIES				
1–19	1,536.3	656.4	2,192.7	151.1
20–99	271.5	147.6	419.0	22.0
100–499	−137.3	−377.1	−514.5	−27.0
500–4999	37.1	−218.9	−181.8	−9.5
5000+	−23.0	13.1	−9.9	−.5
	1,684.5	221.0	1,905.5	100.0
MULTI-UNIT COMPANIES				
1–19	273.3	97.4	307.7	36.9
20–99	332.0	29.2	361.3	36.0
100–499	171.1	−226.3	−55.1	−5.5
500–4999	21.8	158.0	179.8	17.9
5000+	−274.7	422.3	147.7	14.7
	523.7	480.6	1,004.3	100.0
ALL COMPANIES				
1–19	1,809.7	753.8	2,563.4	88.1
20–99	603.5	176.8	780.3	26.8
100–499	33.8	−603.4	−569.6	−19.6
500–4999	58.9	−61.0	−2.0	−.1
5000+	−297.7	435.4	137.7	4.7
	2,208.2	701.6	2,909.8	100.0

THE WORKER'S DILEMMA

Well and good, you may think. So the action in America is in the smaller firms, which is where one might expect dynamism and growth. And, of course, things work the other way around as well. When General Motors cut its work force from 853,000 to 741,000 from 1979 to 1981, it sent shudders through many communities and a few states. But this is on the same order of magnitude as if Mom and Pop, with a total of eight workers, let one of them go. Likewise, the addition of 100,000 workers by a General Motors is like Mom and Pop taking on a single new clerk. Clearly small firms can rack up huge growth and decline percentages. An ocean liner may take a couple of hours and 50 miles to turn around 180 degrees; a 16-foot fishing boat can turn on a dime in a few seconds.

But the little boat also can be swamped, while the survival rate of ocean liners is pretty good. In this vein, new employees would be prudent to ponder the question of whether the place where they work or plan to work will be around in the next few years. The lucky soul who selects the right small firm could start out in Year 1 as a gopher, be a manager in Year 4, and a divisional vice president in Year 8. Or he/she could be pounding the pavements in Year 2. Some employees prefer the perceived security and stability of the giants, where movement up the ladder is slow but security is deemed a sufficient compensation, while others prefer the chance to grab the brass ring and are willing to risk falling on their faces should the grab fail. It is the difference between organization men working from nine to five and aggressive, ambitious people who are in the shop weekends and labor at low wages for a chance at a piece of the action.

Still, those who were employed by small firms that failed are hardly consoled by the fact that others in their size category are doing well. Such knowledge does little to reduce the hassle of finding a new job when an employer goes out of business or is forced to lay off a worker or two. So most workers think about a risk–reward calculus given an employment choice between an industry leader and a smaller entity. Prospective employees might ask themselves three questions:

1. What are the odds of the place where I work not existing next year?
2. How long can I expect my firm to stay in business beyond that?
3. What are the odds that I will be laid off?

FIGURE 1–6. ODDS OF AN ESTABLISHMENT CLOSING
AS A FUNCTION OF COMPANY SIZE, 1981–1985

SIZE OF COMPANY	PERCENT THAT CLOSE
0–19	7.2
20–99	6.1
100–499	6.7
500–4999	7.3
5000+	7.6

FIGURE 1–7. Survival Rate of Firms

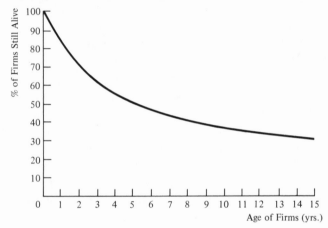

Figure 1–6 summarizes the chances of an establishment failing as a function of the size of the company to which it belongs. Smaller companies are actually less likely than larger ones to liquidate a facility in today's economy. Figure 1–7 presents graphically the picture for longevity. For every group of companies that open their doors, approximately half will last five years, 38 percent will be around after ten years, and 31 percent will survive 15 years.

For the employee, whether a job is lost through corporate failure or a layoff is far less important than whether he or she is drawing a paycheck. What is the relationship of the size of the firm to job security? One might think that just as there is safety in numbers, the larger the company, the more secure would be its employees, especially during hard times. After all, that ocean liner can pull through a storm that would sink many a small craft. Yet such is not the case in the world of work. Smaller firms may close down with greater frequency, but overall, they have offered just about as much job security thus far in the 1980s as have the larger ones:

18

SIZE OF COMPANY	PERCENT OF EMPLOYEES LAID OFF, 1981–1985
1–19	7.3
20–99	8.7
100–499	10.1
500–4999	7.8
5000+	8.9

The unreliability of larger firms collectively as job creators becomes even more evident when traced over longer periods. Correcting for the business cycle, I extended the behavior of the firms in my data bank over a 10-year period. Figure 1–8 summarizes the findings. One can see that smaller firms, as a group, are remarkably steady creators of jobs, while the larger ones, again as a group, performed quite unevenly. But here, too, the principle of conservation of corporate energy can be seen. Look at Figure 1–9, and you will see that while the small business share of net job creation varies from period to period (due largely to erratic large-business performance), the percentage of overall jobs in the economy remained remarkably consistent.

The "erraticness" of large-firm performance (and the corresponding small-firm share of job creation) over time extends also to space. Large firms may be doing quite well in some states and areas, and poorly in others—with a corresponding variation in the relative contribution of smaller companies. In the early 1980s, for example, large, technology-based firms fared much better than large firms in general. States with significant concentrations of such firms—like Massachusetts and Minnesota—created a much larger

FIGURE 1–8. NUMBER OF JOBS CREATED BY SIZE OF ENTERPRISE

YEAR	NO. JOBS CREATED IN ENTERPRISES WITH FEWER THAN 100 EMPLOYEES	NO. JOBS CREATED IN ENTERPRISES WITH 100 OR MORE EMPLOYEES
1	21,548	20,438
2	20,856	9,387
3	16,873	6,118
4	19,644	−8,622
5	18,076	3,377
6	18,873	329
7	21,233	31,117
8	22,549	8,458
9	25,311	16,354
10	23,939	21,132

FIGURE 1–9. SHARE OF NEW JOBS CREATED AND SHARE OF
OVERALL EMPLOYMENT EACH YEAR BY SIZE OF ENTERPRISE

YEAR	PERCENT OF JOBS CREATED BY ENTERPRISES WITH FEWER THAN 100 EMPLOYEES	PERCENT OF TOTAL JOBS HOUSED IN ENTERPRISES WITH FEWER THAN 100 EMPLOYEES
1	51%	41%
2	69	41
3	73	41
4	178	42
5	84	42
6	98	42
7	41	42
8	73	42
9	61	42
10	53	41
10-Year Average	78	41

share of their jobs in large firms than did the United States as a whole. States with big concentrations of automobile and/or resource-based (particularly oil) companies showed exactly the opposite pattern, with small firms frequently creating over 100 percent of all net new jobs. In short, the small-firm share of job creation varies a great deal. The time period and location will affect the outcome dramatically. It is only over several longer periods and for large aggregations that any general pattern emerges.

How long has this been going on? Are these the kinds of forces that enabled the United States to become the world's dominant economic power, or have they developed with the more recent perceived decline? Unfortunately we lack the kind of data for the pre-1969 period that would enable us to offer an informed answer to the first question, and we can only make an attempt to do so for the second. The evidence suggests that the dynamics within the system are increasing rather than declining. For example, as illustrated in Figure 1–10, the rate of new incorporations has been accelerating since 1950 and doing so faster than the increase in real gross national product (GNP).

As with all such things in the microworld, not all places are sharing equally in this emerging economy, once again measured in terms of job creation. Consider the overall picture presented in Figure 1–11 of growth and employment during the turbulent years from 1969 through 1976. GNP appears to have grown amazingly—until the figures are adjusted for inflation, when we see a period of

FIGURE 1–10.   Growth of New Incorporations and Real GNP Since 1950

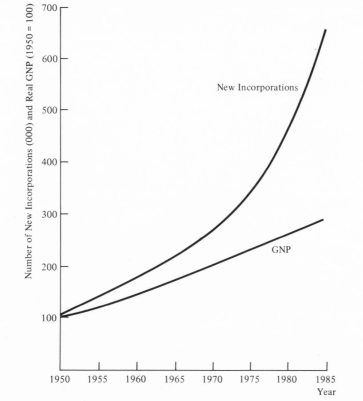

good growth sandwiched by down years. And the unemployment rose irregularly, a tendency that continues to this day.

Now look at Figure 1–12, which shows what happened to employment for 10 representative metropolitan areas during these years. It should come as no surprise that Houston did so well; the growth of that city in the energy-short 1970s has been well-publicized. Likewise the decline of textile-producing Greenville, N.C., was well-known to denizens of that city. To the macroeconomist, these years were ones of irregular growth and inflation. To workers in Houston and Greenville, there was nothing irregular about it.

Had you lived for a while in both cities you would have been struck by the differences. Leaving aside matters of regional customs, Houston was on the move, while the pace of life in Greenville was quite slow. The point is that the healthiest economies have more rather than less internal turbulence. They experience greater levels of startups, of growth—and often decline and failure as well—than do the more stagnant ones. Places like Dallas,

21

FIGURE 1–11. GROSS NATIONAL PRODUCT, REPORTED AND ADJUSTED, AND UNEMPLOYMENT, 1969–1976 *(Figures in billions of dollars)*

YEAR	GNP	PERCENT CHANGE FROM PREVIOUS YEAR	PERCENT CHANGE FROM PREVIOUS YEAR ADJUSTED FOR INFLATION	UNEMPLOYMENT RATE
1969	944.0	8.1	2.8	3.5
1970	992.7	5.2	−0.2	4.9
1971	1077.6	8.6	3.4	5.9
1972	1185.9	10.1	5.7	5.6
1973	1326.4	11.8	5.8	4.9
1974	1434.2	8.1	−0.6	5.6
1975	1549.2	8.0	−1.1	8.5
1976	1718.0	10.9	5.4	7.7

SOURCE: *Economic Report of the President, 1985*

Atlanta, Los Angeles, and Denver once were (and some still are) among our most internally turbulent places. There has been more "action" in them than in New Haven, Buffalo, and Cleveland.

Look again at Figure 1–12 and you will see that variations in aggregate job growth from place to place are much more a function of variations in replacement rates than in loss rates. You would not have known this by simply looking at the loss rates. Note that the metropolitan area with the highest loss rate was Charlotte, N.C., second to Houston in our sample, while Worcester, Mass., had the lowest loss rate but had fewer jobs on balance at the end of the period. Indeed, the loss rate is one of the poorer indicators of economic health.

By now you might have concluded that there exists some qual-

FIGURE 1–12. LOSS AND REPLACEMENT RATES FOR TEN METROPOLITAN AREAS, 1969–1976

AREA	LOSS RATE	REPLACEMENT RATE	NET CHANGE
Houston	35.7%	62.7%	27.0 %
Charlotte	40.4	48.0	7.5
Dayton	31.4	36.4	5.1
Rochester	29.3	33.7	4.5
Boston	33.7	37.4	3.8
Baltimore	32.9	36.5	3.5
Hartford	35.5	36.6	1.1
Worcester	25.1	24.6	− .5
New Haven	29.5	27.0	−2.6
Greenville	35.1	26.9	−8.4

NOTE: Losses are the sum of closings, contractions, and out-moves. Replacements are the sum of formations, expansions, and in-moves.

FIGURE 1-13. DETAILED SOURCES OF JOB CREATION AND LOSS FOR TEN METROPOLITAN AREAS, 1969–1976

AREA	STARTUPS	CLOSINGS	EXPANSION	CONTRACTION	IN-MOVES	OUT-MOVES	NET CHANGE
Houston	+40.2%	-25.0%	+14.4%	-6.3%	+8.1%	-4.4%	+27.0%
Charlotte	+32.8	-27.4	+8.1	-7.4	+7.1	-5.6	+7.5
Dayton	+24.9	-17.4	+8.4	-11.3	+3.1	-2.7	+5.1
Rochester	+17.3	-17.7	+11.5	-7.8	+4.9	-3.8	+4.5
Boston	+21.8	-20.2	+11.1	-10.0	+4.5	-3.5	+3.8
Baltimore	+23.8	-21.3	+8.2	-7.6	+4.5	-4.0	+3.5
Hartford	+22.5	-19.4	+9.1	-11.6	+5.0	-4.5	+1.1
Worcester	+13.3	-13.7	+9.1	-9.4	+2.2	-2.0	-.5
New Haven	+15.0	-17.9	+8.1	-7.2	+3.9	-4.4	-2.6
Greenville	+18.3	-25.6	+6.1	-5.4	+2.5	-4.1	-8.4

ity about rapidly growing areas which, if understood, could be applied as an elixir to less fortunate places. A corollary would be that there are certain occupations which, if entered, are more promising than others. To some extent this is so, and will be talked about later, but close study also reveals that some of the conventional wisdom about economic growth is false. For example, contrary to popular belief, the movement of firms across metropolitan areas is negligible. Companies move a great deal, but they tend to do so within very short distances—usually no more than a mile or so. The reason isn't difficult to fathom. Bigger moves, even within metropolitan areas, would disrupt companies' relationships with customers and with their commuting employees. In Figure 1–13 we note the relatively minor role that movement of firms in and out of areas plays—even for the more dynamic places.

Also, an analysis of all places reveals almost a tenfold spread in the odds that a young firm will start and reach 10 employees during a 4-year period and more than an eight-fold spread in the odds that a young firm will grow significantly. It appears the odds of a business contracting or failing are not particularly sensitive to where it is located, but that the characteristics of a place do significantly affect where businesses will start and grow.

What this means is that dynamic metropolitan areas are noted for attracting *startup* operations and not for luring outsiders from their old domiciles. Birth, not rebirth, is the hallmark of the most dynamic places in the country.

What seems like chaos from the perspective of someone inside a single firm is in fact order when the collection of firms is viewed as a whole. The ability of the economic cloud to sustain itself and grow depends upon the activity, not the inactivity, of its individual components. Healthy economies experience a great deal of action within their boundaries—the greater the action, the healthier the economy. Job creation is not a steady ramp, but a wild dance in which a constantly changing cast flits on and off the stage.

The volatility of the job creation process raises a number of issues. How can it be fostered? How does the individual worker achieve at least a modest sense of security in a chaotic world? Does it have to be this way? And if so, why?

Before trying to answer the questions, it would be prudent to understand in even greater detail the experience of the individual firm. We must strap ourselves into them for a while and understand what they experience, before we can understand the consequences of their behavior.

24

CHAPTER 2

The Nature of the Firm

There is a natural tendency to think of businesses as we might of ourselves, which is to say that they are born, go through a period of rapid growth, then level off and mature, and eventually die. This tendency to anthropomorphize business is understandable, perhaps, but is also a dangerous form of reductionism that can lead to false conclusions.

Some economic historians tell us whole industries experience a "life cycle" of sorts. In the beginning there is a host of new companies, most of them small, all of which challenge products manufactured by old, large concerns that have a stake in their entrenched, familiar technologies and markets. The new firms grow at varying speeds, but eventually most either fail or are taken over by other companies, leaving a handful of giants and perhaps a few smaller entities. Then, should a rival technology appear, all of these will suffer, perhaps die. Such was the pattern in railroads, steel, and automobiles, and now seems to be happening in various parts of the data processing industry. Or, at least, so it appears, when looking at the macroworld.

Apply this industry version of the life-cycle model to individual companies, and we would expect to find:

1. Younger firms are more likely to be growing.
2. Middle-aged firms are more likely to be stable.
3. Older firms are more likely to decline.
4. Very old firms are most likely to die.

25

There is some support for this view. A study we undertook for the period 1969–1976 disclosed the following:

Age of the Firm in 1969	Average Percentage Net Growth, 1969–1976
0–4	11.2
5–8	14.4
9–12	13.7
13+	4.5

As can be seen, the growth of companies under 4 years old is comparatively fast, but not as much so as those from 5 to 8 years old. After that the growth declines, and the rate for companies over 12 years old is less than a third of that for the 5-to-8 group.

Yet these data are somewhat deceiving. On the average, young companies are smaller than older ones, and the number of employees in small companies tends to grow faster than in larger ones, as we saw in the comparison of Mom and Pop operations and General Motors.

Take account of size (see Figure 2–1), and you get a different picture of what is happening. Among smaller firms (which represent most firms) older firms grow faster than younger ones. It is only among larger firms that there is any tendency to decline with age. Far more striking is the tendency to tail off with increased size. Each age group in Figure 2–1 reveals a marked tendency for its larger firms to grow far more slowly than its smaller ones.

Some of the variation is due to the kind of business involved. The biological analogy tends to fit somewhat better for manufac-

FIGURE 2–1. Net Employment Change, 1969–1976, for Establishments Existing in Both 1969 and 1976

	Net Employment Change, 1969–1976				
	Age in 1969				Total
Size in 1969	0–4	5–8	9–12	13+	
0–20	21.4%	29.8%	30.5%	26.7%	26.1%
21–50	7.5	9.2	7.9	3.2	5.4
51–100	2.5	1.0	−2.6	−5.1	−2.8
101–500	−1.3	−2.9	−8.9	−7.7	−6.1
Over 500	−2.7	−13.2	−3.1	−6.4	−6.2
All firms	11.2	14.4	13.7	4.5	8.0

turers than for others during this same 1969–76 period. For other kinds of business, older firms grow faster than younger ones:

NET EMPLOYMENT CHANGE, 1969–1976, FOR FIRMS BY AGE IN 1969

BUSINESS TYPE	AGE (IN YEARS)				*Total*
	0–4	*5–8*	*9–12*	*13+*	
Manufacturing	6.3%	10.6%	12.2%	2.6%	4.9%
Trade	9.9	13.8	19.2	14.1	13.5
Service	7.6	9.3	12.6	11.3	10.4

The biological analogy works best for manufacturing perhaps because of the need for constant technological innovation and the apparent inability of the older, large firms to keep pace. Or it might plausibly result from the difficulties larger firms have in changing with the times and markets, since the smaller ones do quite well. In fact, when you look at the manufacturing sector in greater detail (see Figure 2–2) you will see that the growth of companies is far more a factor of size than of age.

Go down all of the columns in Figure 2–2, from 1–4, 5–8, 9–12, and over 13, and you will witness the steady decline for net employment change in every one of the size groups. The same pattern holds for the trade and service sectors, though the relationship of size to growth or decline is not as neat. Indeed, while the aggregates show a perfect correlation for manufacturing and trade, you can see that in the service sector firms with over 500 workers turned in a showing second only to those with from 1–20, with the older, larger firms performing progressively better than the younger ones. We suspect this is due largely to the flexibility one finds in the service sector.

What about the odds of dying? Begin by examining Figure 2–3, which takes a universe of 4.5 million firms and divides it according to age. Note that older firms are just as likely as younger ones to destroy jobs by going out of business; age has little effect here. As we saw earlier, there is a marked increase in the propensity to decline with maturity, but that is offset by a similar *decrease* in the propensity of older firms to die, with the very old firms being the *least* likely to do so.

This much is to be expected; young, undercapitalized companies have ever been at deep risk, while older firms, having presumably dug themselves into a market niche and developed experience

FIGURE 2-2. NET EMPLOYMENT CHANGE FROM 1969–1976 BY INDUSTRY FOR ESTABLISHMENTS EXISTING IN BOTH 1969 AND 1976

| | MANUFACTURING NET EMPLOYMENT CHANGE, 1969–1976 | | | | |
| | *Age in 1969* | | | | *Total* |
SIZE IN 1969	0–4	5–8	9–12	13+	
0–20	31.4%	38.8%	43.4%	34.1%	35.0%
21–50	11.5	13.0	16.6	10.8	11.8
51–100	3.3	4.7	8.8	2.6	3.5
101–500	−4.1	1.8	−2.2	−1.8	−1.9
Over 500	−7.6	−17.1	−8.2	−7.6	−8.1
All firms	6.3	10.6	12.2	2.6	4.9

| | TRADE NET EMPLOYMENT CHANGE, 1969–1976 | | | | |
| | *Age in 1969* | | | | *Total* |
SIZE IN 1969	0–4	5–8	9–12	13+	
0–20	15.3%	22.6%	28.4%	25.8%	22.6%
21–50	0.6	1.4	6.1	5.3	3.9
51–100	−7.3	−9.2	6.1	−4.0	−5.5
101–500	−9.1	−15.4	−7.9	−7.5	−8.6
Over 500	−13.5	−11.4	0.	−7.9	−8.9
All firms	9.9	13.8	19.2	14.1	13.5

| | SERVICE NET EMPLOYMENT CHANGE, 1969–1976 | | | | |
| | *Age in 1969* | | | | *Total* |
SIZE IN 1969	0–4	5	9–12	13+	
0–20	17.6%	22.3%	25.7%	25.3%	22.8%
21–50	1.7	2.3	7.3	−2.9	0.1
51–100	−3.8	−4.9	−4.0	−2.8	−3.4
101–500	−3.5	−6.4	−1.4	0.7	−1.2
Over 500	−7.8	0.7	1.5	16.7	13.4
All firms	7.6	9.3	12.6	11.3	10.4

with customers and suppliers, will withstand buffeting that might smash a less experienced and established operation.

Companies do not develop like human beings. Young, small firms, unlike youngsters and trees, do not necessarily grow. And not all large, old firms decline. We need to discard anthropomorphic inclinations and obtain a more sophisticated model of the economy, based upon empirical evidence rather than imagery, to understand what has happened to American business in the last decade or so and what might be expected in the future.

FIGURE 2–3. RATE OF JOB LOSS DUE TO DEATHS OF EXISTING ESTABLISH-
MENTS BY SIZE, 1969–1976

SIZE IN 1969	PERCENT JOBS LOST DUE TO DEATHS, 1969–1976				
	Age in 1969				
	0–4	*5–8*	*9–12*	*13+*	*Total*
0–20	41.0%	47.2%	52.5%	51.5%	48.0%
21–50	35.7	37.5	39.0	31.8	34.1
51–100	34.4	38.4	38.0	29.0	32.0
101–500	33.1	42.7	38.0	26.5	30.2
Over 500	22.1	35.9	37.7	11.9	15.3
Total	36.4	42.9	44.9	31.9	35.4

So just how *do* firms behave? Do they merely grow and decline at random, in harmony with the business cycle or some other exogenous force? Is it a matter of good fortune, having the right product or service at the right time and in the right place? Or could it be that the talents of extraordinarily gifted entrepreneurs and managers make the differences between success and failure? One is tempted to take the easy way out and reply, "All of these, and perhaps others." Moreover, it might be the correct answer. But we can do better than that by looking at the evidence.

INCOME SUBSTITUTORS AND ENTERPRENEURS

In the first place, there has been nothing random about the successes of young firms that joined the *Fortune* 500 in rapid fashion—Control Data, Polaroid, Texas Instruments, and Xerox in their time come to mind here, and, in more recent years, Wang Laboratories, Apple Computer, and Compaq. What did these have that others did not? Or to put it in specific terms, why did Texas Instruments succeed and Transitron fail? What enabled Compaq and Apple to make the grade while Osborne and Kaypro foundered? Funding, leadership, and good fortune played their roles, but surely there is more to it than that. And so there is. Look at the universe of small firms, try to discern patterns, and some will spring forth.

You will conclude that most of the small firms fall into one of two groupings. The first, the larger by far, rapidly reaches its final size—usually quite small, one or two employees and not much more—and remains there. We call this group "income substitutors." Think about those you come across every day. The local pizza parlor is one such firm, and so is the corner video store, the doctor and dentist whose services you use, and even the franchiser of most Burger Kings. That executive who quit Procter & Gamble after 20 years to become a consultant is running a small business, as is the hotel executive who saves and borrows and opens a 10-unit motel. I could go on and on, but you get the idea, and understand why such people started small and will remain so. Their main purpose is to establish a substitute form of income that does not entail working for someone else.

We know of dozens of astute and versatile executives who left highly paid posts in order to achieve independence, to give orders to three or four employees rather than take them from a boss. Perhaps you do, too. As far as can be told from the data, the old American dream of owning and managing one's own business is stronger now than ever in our history. According to a 1986 poll conducted by D'Arcy Masius Benton & Bowles, when asked what "dream job" they would like to have for one year, 38 percent of men answered, "head of own business," far ahead of the runner-up, professional athlete (30 percent). American women are even more entrepreneurially inclined; fully 47 percent wanted to head their own business, with tour guide (30 percent) in second place.

Consider the case of Carolyn See, a divorcée who couldn't even drive a car until three years after getting a Ph.D. in English. According to her own account in *The New York Times,* of June 28, 1986, she once took as much as fifteen minutes to write a check. Unable to find a job and demoralized, she went to a personal financial expert to wail about an empty bank account and no typing skills. What kind of job could she hope for? The advice: "Don't worry about it. And think twice before you go back to work. Life's no fun on a salary. Go into business for yourself. Strike out on your own." The reason given was that "in this country, everyone hates an employee." Said the expert:

> Democracy and capitalism are built on striking out on your own. Sure, you have your millionaires on top, but from underneath them on down to the bottom, every law in the land favors the small businessman—in your case the small businesswoman. They can change the tax laws all they want, but the person in his own business will always have the advantage.*

The advisor offered all kinds of suggestions, from opening a bed-and-board in her home to starting a potted plant business. Ms.

* *The New York Times;* June 28, 1986, p. C2

30

See obviously made it, as her appearance in the *Times* showed, as a free-lance writer.

Others go off on their own without giving the matter much thought. For the doctor or dentist, private practice is the tradition. The founders of the other businesses appear to share a modest goal: to provide a source of income to themselves and their families that does not depend upon the whim of an employer. Or to find work when no other employment seems available. The laid-off automobile worker may become a handyman. He would love to go back to the assembly line, but if that seems improbable, he will try several things, perhaps as a temporary worker.

In sharp contrast with the income substitutors are the entrepreneurs. They know from the start that they are trying to build a significant corporation. So much has been written about entrepreneurs recently that the concept and their characteristics have become annealed in the consciousness of most adult Americans. To recapitulate some of them, income appears not to be their primary motivation. They are driven by a desire to create an innovative force in the corporate world. We think immediately of Steve Jobs and Apple Computer, An Wang and Wang Laboratories, and Mitch Kapor and Lotus Development, and of course there are hundreds of others. Tom Fatjo who founded Browning-Ferris Industries is an excellent example of the breed. He built what is today the world's largest waste collection organization and did it in two years. Fatjo, who had started numerous other companies with only slightly less startling results, is now creating a network of physical fitness centers. He certainly is not driven by a simple desire for an alternate source of income. The same kind of motivation he demonstrates has propelled others to nurture small companies into larger ones.

Yet not all entrepreneurs are as driven as Fatjo. Take the case of Ben Cohen and Jerry Greenfield, two unlikely entrepreneurs who are making a dent in the $2 billion a year superpremium ice cream market. Ben dropped out of Colgate after a year and a half; school was not for him. Jerry gave up on the idea of becoming a doctor when he failed to be accepted anywhere. They knocked around for a while and in 1977 found themselves in Vermont, where they decided to open some kind of small business.

Neither was especially interested in becoming wealthy, or had any vision of heading a giant enterprise. In fact all they wanted was some interesting, engaging work that would tide them over. This is to say, they were fairly typical income substitutors.

Initially, they thought of opening a bagel bakery but gave up on that when learning the price of equipment was too high. Instead, they opted for ice cream. Neither had much experience in the field, though Ben had sold ice cream from a truck years earlier. For $5, they took a correspondence course in ice cream making from Penn State and started out with a total capital of $12,000, half of it borrowed. Ben and Jerry opened an ice cream shop in Burlington and, bowing to the advice of an experienced friend, also offered crepes, soups, and lasagna in their restaurant—really a converted gas station, which provided the townspeople in Burlington with a few laughs.

As it turned out, the other foods were greeted with indifference, while the ice cream was a roaring success—but only in the summer, when the tourists were around and the hot weather prompted sales. Not so in winter. That was when Ben and Jerry decided to try to sell packaged ice cream in food stores.

Business was good; the partners prospered. Within nine years "Ben & Jerry" with sixteen "scoop shops," was a major factor in New York and New England markets. It was expanding to other parts of the country and had made a public stock offering. Ben and Jerry became rich but were uncomfortable with the idea—and with running a $10 million operation. Jerry dropped out for a while and then returned, but most importantly, they took on a manager, Fred Lager, who conducted day-to-day operations and kept costs (and the partners) under control. Ben and Jerry started out as typical income substitutors who became entrepreneurs in spite of themselves.

Most income substitutors pretty well know what they are after, as do the entrepreneurs. The American landscape is strewn with the corpses of entrepreneurial startups that have failed, some of them spectacularly, like a shooting star that burns itself out. Likewise, you doubtless are aware of income substitutors who silently departed the scene—the pizza shop that folded when Pizza Hut opened an outlet down the street, the video store that vanished as the area became saturated with competitors, the pet or beauty shop that for one reason or another couldn't hack it.

We know the successful (and some of the failing) entrepreneurial stories by reading of them in such publications as the *Wall Street Journal, Business Week, Forbes, Fortune,* and *Inc.* Renovations and "For Let" signs in the shop windows in downtowns and malls attest to the successes and failures of income substitutors.

32

Occasionally, however, an entrepreneur finds himself in the role of income substitutor—the dream of starting a chain of Mexican fast-food operations ends with only one or two units surviving. Entrepreneurs who find themselves treading water often will leave the scene. Likewise, an income substitutor who had modest aspirations can wake up one day to find himself a key player in a glamour industry, and become positively bewildered—like Ben and Jerry.

The computer industry is replete with tales of many kinds of mismatches. The saga of Gene Amdahl is perhaps the most famous instance. A brilliant scientist, Amdahl came to IBM in 1952 and so was there shortly after that firm decided to make its major push in computers. He was a key figure in the design of the 360 and 370 mainframe families. By 1970 he was working on the design of a supercomputer, which top management decided not to produce. Irate, Amdahl left IBM, intent on starting his own company to challenge Big Blue.

The wonder of it all wasn't that Amdahl quit, but that he remained so long at the job. He clearly was an entrepreneurial type, who chafed at working for others and had dreams of glory.

With help from Nixdorf Computer, Fujitsu, and some California venture capitalists, Amdahl founded the company that bore his name. In mid-1975 he introduced the 470 V/6, which was compatible with the giant IBM 370/168, ran faster, and cost 20 percent less. For 1976 Amdahl placed 35 systems worth $140 million, had revenues of $93 million, and earnings of $11.7 million.

Elated, Amdahl predicted that he would place one machine a week in 1977. What were his ambitions? To track IBM, and produce low-cost superior compatible machines that would enable him to garner a major share of the mainframe market, and for a while it really seemed possible. Then IBM counterattacked, coming out with new models at an accelerated rate while slashing lease and sales prices. Amdahl tried to keep pace, but by 1979 clearly was faltering. There were merger talks with Memorex and Storage Technology that fell through. Revenues continued to expand, but profits declined sharply. Then Fujitsu gained a larger stake in the company, and it appeared that Amdahl had lost control of the firm. He departed in 1979 to form another company, Trilogy, which failed in 1984. Gene Amdahl threw in the towel, but with a typical gesture: he wasn't through yet; other companies would be on the way. Most entrepreneurs are power junkies; they can't get enough of it, and can't quit.

Some—a very few—have managed to hold their competitive juices in check and even quit the game. Max Palevsky was one of these. A University of Chicago graduate who dreamed of becoming a college professor, Palevsky decided to give business a whirl and got an engineering post at Bendix. Palevsky soon found he enjoyed business and, like Amdahl, was frustrated by having to take orders from others. With a promise of independence, he left for a better job at Packard Bell, but this lasted only four years. In 1961 Palevsky raised capital and organized Scientific Data Systems, which was to design, manufacture, and market small to medium-sized scientific computers. The machines were advanced and attractively priced and soon found a market niche. Now Palevsky moved into larger machines, intending to go head-to-head against IBM in the scientific market, and once again he was successful. SDS went from one worker (Palevsky himself) in 1961 to more than 4,000 by 1969, by which time it was the eighth or ninth largest computer manufacturer in the country.

Many in the industry thought Palevsky was yearning for new empires to conquer, but such wasn't the case. Rather, he wanted to get out of business entirely. Two years earlier he had become interested in motion pictures, which he was finding more fascinating and glamorous than computer hardware. Then came involvement in the anti—Vietnam War movement and the Robert Kennedy presidential campaign. It appeared the Kennedy assassination crippled his spirit, but his desire to leave SDS had other reasons. Like many computer entrepreneurs, Palevsky felt more comfortable when SDS was a small operation, and he could have a hand in everything, from research to manufacturing to marketing. So he sold SDS to Xerox for $920 million. In less than six years that company ran the renamed Xerox Data Systems into the ground, and all but wrote it off.

Entrepreneurs like Amdahl resemble cars equipped with a five-speed transmission in which the first four don't work. They are fine for cruising along at 60 miles per hour, but conk out below 30 mph. Entrepreneurs are great when growth is the order of the day; they don't perform as well in stable environments. Few are astute or fortunate enough to leave the game at the right time, as did Palevsky.

To continue the analogy, income substitutors who find themselves in entrepreneurial situations have a first gear great for 10 mph. Finding themselves in the fast lane they burn themselves out trying to keep up.

34

Consider the sad case of Andrew Kay, who in 1953, armed with an MIT engineering degree, founded a company called Non-Linear Systems, which turned out a line of voltmeters and oscilloscopes. Non-Linear's products developed a good reputation. By the late 1970s Kay headed a firm with $3–$4 million in sales, housed in a small factory, which he had little trouble managing. It was very much a family affair. Kay's wife Mary was his secretary and sons David and Allen soon became vice presidents. Kay's daughter Janice married Michael Barret, whose construction firm handled most of Non-Linear's very limited needs. When Non-Linear fell into trouble in 1978–1981, Kay's father-in-law helped out with loans.

Because of these difficulties Kay decided to enter what then was a new field: "transportable" microcomputers. The leading manufacturer at the time was Osborne, and the market was so small and unpromising none of the big, established companies thought to turn out competing machines. So Kay took a stab at it. Cobbling together parts purchased from others, Non-Linear developed and then marketed a machine called the Kaypro II. It sold for under $2,500, and came with software worth almost as much if purchased separately. It was an enormous success; 42,000 of the homely grey machines, known as "Darth Vader's lunchbox," were sold that first year. Kaypro II so dominated the field that Osborne was forced out of business.

In whirlwind 1983, Non-Linear (soon to be renamed Kaypro) introduced the Kaypro 4 and then the Kaypro 10, slashed prices, and seemed on its way to great things. Revenues, which came to $3.9 million in fiscal 1981, rose to $5.5 million in 1982, rocketed to $75.5 million in 1983, and on to $120 million in 1984, Some industry analysts were talking about Kaypro becoming the next big player in the small end of the industry.

Of course there was competition, but Kaypro had legions of satisfied users and a good reputation for quality. What it lacked, however, was management. Andrew Kay had been very happy as a small manufacturer. He had produced the Kaypro II as just another item to be marketed like his oscilloscopes and probably wouldn't have entered that area had sales for his voltmeters held up. Now everything went awry.

From a handful of employees Kaypro went to over 500, and Kay and his family had trouble keeping things running smoothly. Inventories were "lost," Kay had troubles with suppliers, costs careened out of control. Lawsuits and troubles with the IRS followed. Management seemed petrified, afraid to move. Kaypro, which utilized the CP/M operating system on its machines, was hurt when IBM opted for MS-DOS, a different system, for its microcomputers, and Kay delayed making his new offerings IBM-compatible. To his credit, Kay realized he lacked the abilities and perhaps even the interest to run so large an enterprise. At bottom, he was an income substitutor who found himself running on the same track with entrepreneurs. Now he began the search for new management, perhaps wondering how he got into such a mess.

The Kaypro experience isn't all that unusual; reversals are the constant risk run by such enterprises. With all of this, however, it remains to be noted that entrepreneurial companies account for most of the job creation attributable to small business. To verify this we first must find some means of differentiating them from the majority of less ambitious concerns.

THE TRAVAILS OF GROWTH AND CORRECTION

Identifying firms that are entrepreneurial is not as difficult as may first appear. Start with the concept that simple measurements, such as growth rates or absolute levels of employment growth fail to make the distinction we're after since they are based by the size of the firm. Typically, small, entrepreneurial firms demonstrate phenomenal percentage rises in employment in their early stages, while there is a leveling off of the percentage rate later on. It is the reverse with the absolute levels of employment growth. They are small initially, larger afterwards.

In order to create an unbiased measure of growth we have created a Growth Index, which is computed as the absolute growth times the percent growth (expressed in decimal terms). For example, a firm that in one year increased its employment by 20 workers and by so doing doubled its work force would have a growth index of 20—that is, 20 additional employees times a 100 percent increase (expressed in decimal terms as 1.0). Likewise, a fast-growing firm later in its evolution that added 80 employees for a 25 percent increase would have a Growth Index of 20—that is, $80 \times .25 = 20$. A small firm interested primarily in income substitution would have a low Growth Index. A company with no additions would be at zero. Should the firm add a single worker for a 10 percent increase, it would come to .1—that is, $1 \times .10$. A declining firm that dismisses 15 employees for a 30 percent decline would have a negative Growth Index of 4.5—that is, $15 \times -.30 = -4.5$.

36

FIGURE 2–4. Plot of All Firms with a Growth Index of 20

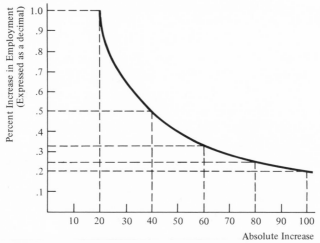

Figure 2–4 plots the curve for all firms that have a Growth Index of 20. The smaller the absolute increase, the larger the percent increase we demand in order to be comparable.

The relatively simple concept of the Growth Index allows us to compare firms of different sizes and maturities. We see immediately in Figure 2–5 that very few firms have high indices and that most firms are in the stable, income-substitution category mentioned earlier.

Finding cut-off points presented the usual difficulties. Somewhat arbitrarily we decided upon breakpoints of 5 and 20, knowing of course that firms with a rating of 19 might be deemed rapid growth by most subjective standards, while some with 21 might be having a spurt of growth but really be income substitutors. In any case, those firms with ratings of 21 or over account for only 18

FIGURE 2–5. PERCENT OF GROWING FIRMS AND PERCENT OF REPLACEMENT JOB CREATION BY GROWTH INDEX VALUE OF FIRM, 1981–1985

GROWTH INDEX RANGE	GROWING FIRMS	REPLACEMENT JOBS CREATED
0–5	65.6%	6.9%
6–20	16.3	6.7
21+	18.0	86.4
	100.0	100.0

37

percent of the business universe but provide 86 percent of all new jobs created. The entrepreneurial firms are thus the key to job creation. *Those economies that provide the proper environment for them to appear and grow flourish; those that fail to provide such an environment languish.*

This leads to the inevitable question: What *is* this environment? What *is* the evolutionary path of entrepreneurial companies? Do they form and then shoot right up into the Fortune 500 ranks? Hardly. It appears to be a tortuous route, indeed. The entrepreneurial firm is in a constant state of flux. Just when management thinks it has figured out how to grow forever, something unexpected comes along and the firm falls flat on its face. Typically management learns from these setbacks, however, and the firm comes back stronger than before. This process appears to continue throughout the life of the firm—a constant pulsation, growing and contracting, taking false paths, retreating, and trying again, up and down, down and up. The ups are progressively higher, however, and the downs do not seem more than a detour when viewed in retrospect.

This is not an unusual concept. If you think about it for a while, you will realize that the ability to meet new challenges through adaption is the key to growth in almost any area. Since change is the rule, change in meeting new opportunities is required. More than three decades ago British historian Arnold Toynbee, in his massive *Study of History,* wrote of civilizations thriving when they were challenged and found the means to respond. So it is with individual corporations in the American business universe.

Why is it like this? Must it be ever so? Why can't firms get smart and stay smart? The answer seems to lie partly in the context in which the firm functions—the national and international economy, the industry in which it is engaged. It also lies in the nature of the management. The process frequently goes in five stages, along these general lines:

1. The company gets new ideas and insights or receives new information. A new technology could be developed or licensed. A new market could develop. The point is that change arrives and is perceived. Management decides to act.
2. Production and/or marketing is revamped, or in the case of a service company, techniques and offerings are altered. If successful, rapid expansion will follow. If not, there would be retrenchment until the next idea or market comes along.

3. Assume the operation succeeds. The firm expands to the limit—the way Kay and Amdahl did in their time—and in fact overextends itself by going too far, akin to the thermostat heating a room above the temperature setting.
4. If fortunate, the company recognizes this soon enough, cuts back on production and employment, and tries to learn from the experience and alter procedures. This is a vital moment, where the risk of failure is particularly high.
5. Back to stage 2. When the next idea or market is generated, the entrepreneurial firm prepares to capitalize on opportunities.

In this kind of a business universe, companies that rise in one period can fall in the next and vice versa. Indeed, this is the case more often than not. Rarely does the economy undergo anything like the Great Depression in the 1930s, when just about everything was in decline, or like the boom in the late 1960s, which seemed to touch all industries. Most of the time, the economy moves in a most dissonant fashion. Economists can always find reasons to cheer or despair, depending how the mood strikes.

It is a truism that the world is constantly changing. New technologies surface and obsolete existing products. New cravings develop, old ones fade. Big shocks, such as the oil crisis, ripple through the economy and alter basic balances and relationships. Fluctuations in the performance of our trading partners strengthen and weaken our abilities to sell what we make abroad. Movements in interest and currency exchange rates alter buying and selling decisions. This is an increasingly important issue, because imports and exports have tripled as a percentage of our GNP since 1950, making us far more vulnerable to world conditions than used to be the case. Large corporations also follow a cycle of sorts. Periods of centralization and consolidations often are followed by ones during which diffusion of power becomes the norm. Companies will expand plant and equipment until they clearly have gone too far, and then will contract—occasionally to the point where they become too lean. In the clothing industry, changing fashions are a key factor. Women's skirts move up and down, men's ties get wider and then narrower, the hair of both sexes fluctuates between short and long.

Then there are the multitudinous fluctuations cyberneticist Norbert Wiener used to talk and write about, when activity reaches certain self-limiting boundaries, usually determined by prior experience, and reversals take place almost automatically. There are thermostats in all business enterprises that place entrepreneurs and income substitutors alike on guard once the limits are approached. The warning signal can follow forays into new markets in adverse circumstances or invasions of existing markets by competitors. The familiar "cold sweat syndrome" comes into play on such occasions.

Cycles are all about us—the day, week, month, and season, the switch from home heating to air conditioning, from hot meals to cold, from overcoats to short sleeves and summer dresses. All of these require adjustments, and while most can be anticipated, some creep up unawares, like a spring frost or a balmy day in December. It is found in the Bible: In Ecclesiastes, we read: "To everything there is a season, and a time to every purpose under the heaven."

The author of Ecclesiastes goes on to enumerate these times. Perhaps it would not be thought sacrilegious for business people to read the famous words in the light of their own operations:

A time to be born, and a time to die;
A time to plant, and a time to pluck up that which is planted;
A time to kill, and a time to heal;
A time to break down, and a time to build up;
A time to weep, and a time to laugh;
A time to mourn, and a time to dance;
A time to cast away stones, and a time to gather stones together;
A time to embrace, and a time to refrain from embracing;
A time to seek and a time to lose;
A time to keep and a time to cast away;
A time to rend and a time to sew;
A time to keep silent and a time to speak;
A time to love and a time to hate;
A time for war and a time for peace.

It may be significant that the litany begins with people being born and dying, meaning that individuals with a lifetime of desires and values are replaced by newcomers with blank slates.

Think of the company as a fish swimming upstream in a river (the economy) that can be treacherous. There are sharp bends, whirlpools, rapids, shallow spots, and at times storms above the surface. There are predators at all turns—and smaller fry upon which to feed. Along the banks are fishermen offering attractive lures. The wonder is not that some fish don't make it, but that so many do. The survivors have several things in common—intelligence, foresight, the willingness to take calculated risks, and determination, along with a little bit of luck.

40

Management psychology plays a major role in the microworld. When things are going well there is a tendency to assume: (1) that what you are doing is correct and will continue along the same lines; and (2) that almost anything you do will be right. As a result there is temptation to coast with what the manager is doing, or to seek ways of applying the "magic" to other products and services. The former path is taken by income substitutors because to do so is the path of least resistance and less trying; as Bert Lance once recommended, "If it ain't broke, don't fix it." And the latter path is followed by those entrepreneurs who feel they are on a roll and can conquer new markets simply by entering them. Either way, the odds of a setback are high. Both standing still and moving ahead have pitfalls.

For the entrepreneur, the individual seeking to move ahead, the setbacks that invariably occur constitute learning experiences. Something went wrong, and the challenge to discover what it was and do something about it is exciting. The entrepreneur responds by either cranking the innovative processes into high gear again, selling off the extraneous excursions, laying off people and retrenching, or all three. The good entrepreneurs get through the tough periods intact and come back stronger than ever but no less vulnerable to making all the same mistakes again, with some new ones thrown in to boot.

The business universe abounds with examples of the phenomenon we are describing. We came across a coin collector who took his company from three employees to well over 200 by specializing in rare gold coins. Now, coins have no intrinsic value, and the purchase of one by a dealer can turn out profitably only if someone else appears later on to buy it at a higher price. This dealer was on top of the market and prospered. He received awards for his achievements and started to feel that he could make no mistakes.

Diversification soon followed into other collectables, of which he knew little. Now this is a fickle market, in which tastes and prices are continually shifting, often in irrational fashion. Our coin expert soon learned that the collectors of other items were quite different from those he encountered in coins. A series of unwise moves followed; simply stated, he bought when he should have sold. So within a year or two he was back to three employees. We haven't kept track of him since then but suspect that by now he is on his way back, after having corrected for mistakes.

Several years ago a group of MIT students sold quality high-fidelity equipment at reasonable prices from their dormitory room.

As the whole industry boomed the students expanded their operations, opening their first retail outlet, which was called Tech Hi-Fi. The store was a success, prompting them to expand, and soon they had 70 stores throughout the Northeast.

The young tycoons thought the best route for expansion rested in opening new outlets, not by diversifying their product lines. This seemed to make sense, but soon it became clear that they zigged when they should have zagged. What they missed—or ignored, which was worse—was the videocassette. Yuppies switched their entertainment dollars from hi fi to VCRs, and Tech Hi Fi failed to catch that next wave. By the time the businessmen realized what had happened, it was too late to recoup. Tech Hi Fi went into Chapter 11 bankruptcy, and at last count was back to 15 stores.

This phenomenon is not limited to small firms. Reflect upon the might-have-beens for Radio Shack, which in the 1970s was a distributor of radio supplies and leather goods to hobbyists. Seeking diversification in mid-decade, Radio Shack took on lines of citizen band radios and for a while rode the crest of that boom. Then, in 1977, it opened a retail microcomputer operation in the basement of the Fort Worth headquarters and appeared about to get in on the ground floor of an even bigger market. Sales took off, and Radio Shack integrated backward by purchasing component companies and putting together its own machines. By the late 1970s the company seemed on its way to becoming the McDonald's of microcomputers, a force even mighty IBM would have trouble beating.

This might have happened were it not for a major blunder. Radio Shack was accustomed to dealing with knowledgeable hobbyists and later on with computer freaks, people who understood the equipment they were purchasing, needed little in the way of hand-holding, and spoke an arcane language all their own. Some of these became Radio Shack salesmen, who while working with their peers did quite well. But now customers who wanted computers for video games, educational purposes, or for small business and word processing started to come through the doors. Many of these insecure novices were confused by the brash young salesmen whose technical jargon seemed foreign, even threatening. Moreover, the very name "Radio Shack" turned off many would-be purchasers, who went instead to the "user friendly" Apples and, later on, to the familiar IBM. So Radio Shack declined, losing its opportunity to become a microcomputer giant.

Management was not fazed, however, and by late 1983 had come out with the Tandy line, IBM-compatibles that even looked like the IBMs. These now replaced the battleship grey hulks that were the original backbone of the Radio Shack offerings. The company probably will never get over its initial errors, but at least it has remained a player in the game.

There are yet more familiar tales of entrepreneurial firms that surged ahead, fell back, and then moved on once again. Polaroid, for example, went from a peak of 22,000 employees in 1978 to about 12,000–13,000 in 1985, due in part to competition from Eastman Kodak and in part to a stale product line. Now that a successful lawsuit has forced Kodak to leave the instant photography market and Polaroid has new product offerings, a bounce-back may take place. Computervision and Wang Laboratories have allowed their products to get behind those of their competitors and have experienced setbacks; they, too, are taking steps to rectify the situation, and will probably return to their former eminence.

Some will not. Software Arts dominated the small spreadsheet computer market a few years ago but could not keep up with the grueling rate of innovation. So it threw in the towel and was absorbed by the firm that because the pacesetter, Lotus Development. How long can Lotus keep it up? No one knows. In the world of entrepreneurship, danger and opportunity wait around each bend, and the trouble is, they wear the same face.

FLUCTUATIONS IN THE MACROWORLD

Fluctuations such as those we have described are the rule, not the exception. When we look at millions of entrepreneurial firms, we often discover that the rapidly growing ones are most likely to decline in the future and that declining ones are most likely to grow. We came to this conclusion after studying two initial spans, 1970–1972 and 1973–1974 and then a two-year period, 1975–1976. For the purposes of our study, we defined changes in the following terms:

Label	*Change*
BIG +	Over 50 Percent
SMALL +	1–49 Percent

NO CHANGE   0
SMALL –   –1 to –49 Percent
BIG –   Less than –50 Percent

Of course, conditions in these three periods were quite differ-ent. Here are the GNP and Consumer Price Index (CPI) figures for these periods:

Year	GNP (Billions)	Change in GNP %	CPI Increase %	Real Growth %
1970	992.2	5.1	5.9	–0.8
1971	1,077.6	8.6	4.3	+4.3
1972	1,185.9	10.0	3.3	+6.7
1973	1,326.4	11.8	6.2	+5.6
1974	1,434.2	8.1	11.0	–2.9
1975	1,549.2	8.0	9.1	–1.1
1976	1,718.0	10.9	5.8	+5.1

Source: *Economic Report of the President, 1985.*

As can be seen, from 1970 through 1972, after adjusting for inflation, the economy grew on the average of 3.4 percent a year while from 1973 to 1974 the growth was 1.4 percent. The periods, therefore, were not comparable insofar as the macroeconomy is concerned. And 1975–1976 saw moderate growth. This would seem to imply that all things being equal, most companies should have done worse in 1973–1974 than they did in 1970–1972. But in the microeconomy all things are rarely if ever equal. The big losers in 1970–1972 were quite likely to the big gainers in 1973–1974.

Figure 2–6 summarizes the experiences of one-and-a-half mil-lion firms in 1970–1972 and 1973–1974. Note that of the compa-nies that experienced big growth in 1970–1972, only 12.5 percent did as well in 1973–1974, while 19.8 percent of those that suffered major losses in the earlier period bounced back with large advances afterwards. Likewise, 10.8 percent of the big winners became big losers, while 5.6 percent of the big losers continued to perform poorly.

There is a rough but nice symmetry here. If trying to predict the major winners, you would be best served by looking among the firms that suffered most in the previous period. Does a time of major decline mean liquidation is in the wings? Not necessarily.

44

FIGURE 2–6. EMPLOYMENT CHANGE DURING THE 1973–1974 PERIOD AS A
FUNCTION OF THE ESTABLISHMENT'S 1970–1972 HISTORY

CHANGE 1970–1972	CHANGE, 1973–1975				Sample Size
	Big+	*Neutral*	*Big−*	*Death*	
Big+	12.5%	66.3%	10.8%	10.4%	478528
Small+	11.5	71.9	8.4	8.3	99123
No Change	11.4	69.2	6.1	13.4	735646
Small−	13.7	67.1	8.9	10.3	91493
Big−	19.8	62.1	5.6	12.5	151585
All Firms	12.7	67.7	7.8	11.9	1,556,375

Only 12.5 percent of the big losers of 1970–1972 died in 1973–
1974, not all that more than the 10.4 percent of the big winners.
Indeed, the category most likely to die turned out to be those with
no change in either period, indicating that they did not roll with
the business cycle and were in businesses where demand was
steady and relatively inelastic.

One might also suppose that there were more income substitutors in this category than any other. This is to suggest that nonentrepreneurial firms are the most likely to go out of business. The
message here might be that *the non–risk takers are among the most
likely candidates for liquidation.*

Now let's look at what happened to these categories of firms in
1975–1976. To do this, we have established a table to recapitulate
the experiences of 1970–1972 and 1973–1974. As can be seen,
companies that expanded importantly in *both* periods will be
referred to as EE+ +, while those that contracted importantly in

FIGURE 2–7. EMPLOYMENT CHANGE DURING THE 1975–1976 PERIOD AS A
FUNCTION OF THE 1970–1974 ESTABLISHMENT HISTORY

CHANGE 1970–74	EMPLOYMENT CHANGE, 1975–1976				Sample Size
	Big+	*Neutral*	*Big−*	*Death*	
EE/+ +	11.1%	68.1%	16.5%	4.3%	90944
EE/+	8.9	78.8	9.5	2.8	12421
EC/+ +	9.4	63.8	10.8	16.0	334491
EC/+ −	9.4	58.5	7.6	24.6	850825
EC/− −	17.9	56.2	4.9	21.0	51950
CC/−	11.4	69.4	11.6	7.6	15829
CC/− −	21.9	57.6	8.0	12.6	13461
All Firms	9.9	60.7	8.9	20.5	1,369,921

the same two periods will be designated CC− −. For the sake of simplicity—and becuase the net effects are quite similar—companies that expanded and then contracted and those with the reverse experience are grouped together; those with big changes are designated EC/+ + and with small ones, EC/+ −. These effects and the others are as follows:

Type of Change		Net Effect of Both Changes	Abbreviation
1970–1972	1973–1974		
expansion	expansion	big+	EE/+ +
expansion	expansion	small+	EE/+
expansion	contraction		
or		big+	EC/+ +
contraction	expansion		
contraction	expansion		
or		small chg.	EC/+ −
expansion	contraction		
expansion	contraction		
or		big−	EC/− −
contraction	expansion		
contraction	contraction	small−	CC/−
contraction	contraction	big−	CC/− −

Figure 2–7 shows what happened to each of these groups of firms in 1975–1976. Note that big gainers have more of a likelihood of being big losers (16.5 percent) and that big losers led the way in becoming big winners (21.9 percent). Which companies had the greatest risk of dying? Once again, the ones that showed small changes in previous periods (24.6 percent).

Remember, in considering all of this, that we are looking at close to 1.4 million firms, each of them thinking of itself as unique, each headed by a CEO out to maximize advantages. Recall the analogy of the traffic pattern at the opening of Chapter 1. What we are trying to do is to see if there are any patterns to be discerned, and we think we have found them.

Appendixes 2-1 through 2-3 summarize the "disaggregated" results when we break down these figures by size of company, age, and industry. The results present few surprises for those who have followed the path laid down, which is to say the growers of one period become the laggards during the next and the failures tend to be the more stable companies. Larger firms are less likely to die (although not by much) and are more likely to contract. This is especially true after hard times. Age seems to be comparatively inconsequential; nor does industry seem to matter much, though there are minor exceptions.

In sum, the "pulsation model" seems to offer the best explanation for how corporations respond to a changing economic and technological world. That there is a business cycle cannot be doubted; by one count there have been 43 recessions since 1970 and, of course, 43 recoveries. For the business firms and their leaders, these events have not been circular but rather akin to a roller coaster, which is to say they move along straight lines but also up and down, often sharply, with businesspeople knowing as they go up the incline that a falloff awaits around the bend.

To most of them—small companies in particular—survival may seem quite chancy. The message here is that those who take risks, who reach beyond their grasp, have reason to hope. Those who fall off the roller coaster on the way down more often than not are the ones who avoid risks. The more dynamic the firm, the greater the amplitude of the swings. The road to the top indeed is a rocky one, but the old saw about "better safe than sorry" simply is not borne out by the empirical evidence. Rather, those who feel that they are playing it the safest often end up being the sorriest.

THE URGE TO MERGE

Telling some entrepreneurs that their chances of survival are pretty good is akin to an infantry platoon leader assuring his men that they each have a 90 percent chance of survival. After going through several assaults who could blame some for wanting a transfer to a safer place? This is why many battle-scarred small business people seek the shelter of a larger operation, usually accomplished by a negotiated purchase. The conventional widsom (with which we have become quite familiar) holds that in times of trouble, small companies seek security through merger into larger ones.

Consider the obvious argument. By selling out to a larger entity the founders are able to cash in their chips—walk away from the business with a sizeable chunk of cash, stock in the new parent, or perhaps a combination of both. This kind of move can be quite appealing in buoyant markets, when Wall Street seems not only to be discounting the future but the hereafter as well. The trouble is that on such occasions the more aggressive entrepreneurs become quite giddy, convinced they not only can survive but triumph.

When things look bleak at the bottom of the cycle, small businesses may be desperate to sell out. If they do so then, the price probably will be a fraction of what it might have been a few years earlier. As Will Rogers once said about stocks, "Only buy those that are going up, and when they go as far as they can, sell." So it is with entrepreneurs hoping to cash in their chips.

Do the acquired firms *really* find shelter with the new parent? Look at it from the point of view of the acquirers. They made the purchase either to obtain a firm with bright prospects likely to grow rapidly or a bargain at a rock-bottom price that could be revived with prudent applications of capital and leadership. Assuming that the larger firm acquires a growth company, will the new addition be able to use the resources of the larger firm to avoid the setbacks that its independent counterparts are forced to undergo?

To answer these questions, we traced the history of a pool of 6,221 takeovers during the 1981–1985 period, and contrasted their experience with that of 2.6 million independent firms that were not acquired—adjusting the figures for previous growth history. That is, we compared what happened to growing, stable, and declining firms. The results are presented in Figure 2–8.

As might have been expected, the independents oscillated—that is, the big decliners of the first period grew in the second, while the big winners underwent declines. The winners suffered a 27.2 percent falloff, the losers enjoyed a 22.1 percent advance.

Did the acquired firms find the shelter they desired? No. If anything, the acquisitions seemed to have accelerated rather than dampened the swings for the companies that had grown significantly prior to the takeover.

The arguments in behalf of acquisition are familiar and even plausible. During hard times, the acquirer is able to obtain valuable companies with fine expertise and potential at low prices, while the acquired firm obtains a safe harbor during the storm. For this reason it would be illuminating to look at the experience during the 1975–1976 period. As has been seen, the growth in nominal GNP in 1975 was 8 percent, but since inflation ran at 9.1 percent, there really was a decline. Unemployment that year averaged 8.5 percent, compared to 5.6 percent in 1974 and 4.9 percent in 1973.

The recession was about to end, but we didn't know it at the

FIGURE 2–8. AVERAGE ANNUAL GROWTH OF U.S. ESTABLISHMENTS BY GROWTH RATE AND LEGAL STATUS 1981–1983 AND 1983–1985

| | INDEPENDENTS THROUGHOUT | | |
| | GROWTH RATE | | CHANGE IN GROWTH RATE |
PERCENT CHANGE 1969–1972	1981–1983	1983–1985	
15+	29.8%	2.6%	−27.2
10–15	6.1	1.5	−4.6
5–10	3.7	1.4	−2.3
0–5	1.5	.9	−.5
Decline	−17.3	4.8	+22.1
	ESTABLISHMENTS ACQUIRED DURING 1981–1983		
	GROWTH RATE		CHANGE IN GROWTH RATE
PERCENT CHANGE 1969–1972	1981–1983	1981–1983	
15+	30.4%	1.6%	−28.8%
10–15	5.9	1.8	−4.1
5–10	3.6	−1.0	−4.6
0–5	1.4	2.3	+ .9
Decline	−18.0	4.1	+22.0

time. So big and small companies were encouraged to hunker down and lay low so long as the storm was raging. This is to say there was an inclination to seek shelter, although shelter may not be an appropriate term for what was going on; perhaps "cleaning house" would be more descriptive. At such times, in almost all cases, more jobs were lost in firms gobbled up by larger operations than were lost by those that remained independent. This is quite understandable; the acquiring firm clearly wanted to "streamline operations" by "cutting back on deadwood." So the response was not so much to weather the storm as it was to shrink in the face of it.

This can be seen in Figure 2–9, which is based on a sample of 6,046 acquisitions during the 1969–1976 period. Note that in all categories but one there was more shrinkage in acquired firms than in the independents, and the totals came to 10.5 percent for the former against 8.3 percent for the latter.

It might be reasoned that this situation developed because the acquiring firms expected that through cutbacks they could keep their investments intact. After all, this would clearly be in the self-interest of management. Imagine a CEO, after making a commitment to a company, ripping it apart. The board might be excused for asking why, if this had to be done, had he wanted the company

FIGURE 2-9. PERCENT OF JOBS LOST THROUGH CONTRAC-
TION BY ACQUIRED AND NONACQUIRED FIRMS DURING
1974–1976

PERCENT CHANGE 1969–1974	PERCENT JOBS LOST BY INDEPENDENTS THROUGH CONTRACTION IN 1974–1976	PERCENT JOBS LOST BY FIRMS ACQUIRED DURING 1969–1976 IN 1974–1976
15+	8.2	11.2
10–15	8.2	12.4
5–10	7.1	6.2
0–5	6.2	6.6
Decline	9.1	9.8
Total	8.3	10.5

in the first place? There were many red faces at Xerox after Xerox Data was disbanded.

So one might conclude managements have a stake in keeping things humming at acquired firms—at least until most at head-quarters have forgotten the arguments given for the purchase and the honeymoon period has ended. Often, the acquisition is made after the board has heard arguments that this fine company only needed an infusion of funds and a bolstered management to make it hum along merrily, and this, too, would militate against shrink-age. Conversely, the independent nonacquired firm might be expected to make cutbacks, holding that these were needed to keep the company "lean and mean" and because there was no alterna-tive, since there was no parent with deep pockets to carry it through the period of adversity.

The evidence does not support this point of view. As Figure 2–10 illustrates, acquirers are two to three times more likely to liq-uidate jobs by closing down the acquired firm than are comparable independents left to weather the storm on their own. You might seek an explanation in the tendency of companies to consolidate operations by absorbing the acquired firm into one or another of the preexisting divisions, and, of course, there is some truth in this. But not enough to explain the wide divergence indicated by the numbers in Figure 2–10. Once again, it would appear that small independents outperform large, entrenched operations.

We have since collected similar information for the 1981–1985 period and found the same answer. What we observed about the 1970s wasn't a fluke. It holds true for the present.

So there seems to be little evidence supporting the notion that

FIGURE 2–10.   PERCENT OF JOBS LOST THROUGH DEATH BY ACQUIRED AND
NONACQUIRED FIRMS DURING 1974–1976

PERCENT CHANGE 1969–1974	PERCENT JOBS LOST THROUGH DEATH BY FIRMS REMAINING INDEPENDENT DURING 1969–1974 IN 1974–1976	PERCENT JOBS LOST THROUGH DEATH BY FIRMS ACQUIRED DURING 1969–1974 IN 1974–1976
15+	7.8	17.4
10–15	4.1	8.2
5–10	4.1	7.2
0–5	3.4	24.1
Decline	7.9	15.3
Total	7.4	15.9

larger operations shelter smaller ones during recessions by acquiring them. Believe this and you'll believe that Lewis Carroll's wal-
rus and carpenter really wanted nothing more than to take a stroll
with the overly trusting oysters. Quite the contrary, acquisitions
appear far more vulnerable to disaster as part of larger organizations than on their own. Moreover, there is next to no evidence
suggesting that acquired firms do a better job of generating employment (or staying alive) than do those that remain independent. If
anything, all the evidence tends to go the other way.

PUTTING IT ALL TOGETHER

Change, adjust, regroup, innovate, or stagnate and die—this
seems to be the rule. Has it ever been so? We really can't say for
certain, for our data only goes back to 1969. Since then, however,
it is quite clear that *dynamic firms pulsate quite sharply as they
grow and that aggregate growth has a foundation of massive, con-
tinual failure.*
Managers and workers naturally look upon all of this from different perspectives. The former must learn to stress anticipation
and adaptivity; a premium is placed upon the ability to sense how
the business environment is changing and then capitalize upon the
shifts. Coasting of any kind can be disastrous, if not fatal. Managers have to develop sharply honed antennas, constantly scanning
the landscape for changes and opportunities. After a while they
learn just how insidious success can be, tending to breed content-

ment and a readiness to think that the magic formula has been discovered. Conversely, failure is the playing field where future success may be born and nurtured. Failure is to be avoided if possible but not at the cost of avoiding risks, for to do so would be to stagnate, and this is the greatest danger any business faces. Continually stretching resources is the way to keep a firm strong and resilient.

Of course, failure is not so benign for workers. Corporate failure usually means a pink slip in the pay envelope and the need to start all over again. Increasingly, turbulence can mean more dismissals and a greater need to become skilled at "switching canoes," even switching careers. A great deal more will be said on this subject in Chapter 7. Suffice it to note here that job security, in the traditional sense of performing a function at a particular place of work over a long period, is less common today than it once was. The Department of Commerce has estimated that in the future, half the work force will have to be retrained, and of those who undergo the experience once, half again will face the problem a second time. Education, in the broadest sense of the term, has become one of the faster growing American industries. Gold watches will still be given to employees with long service to the firm, but there will be fewer presented in the future. Efforts of unions to create job security to the contrary notwithstanding, security for many will have to derive from their own strengths and abilities to adapt and not from the security found at the job.

Finally, those who assist in the economic development process—the so-called policy makers—must learn not to panic at the first sign of failure. All too many of them are obsessed with job retention, avoiding layoffs, and trying to keep struggling firms alive. This is not to suggest that policy makers adopt a rigid attitude on such matters, but rather that they eschew knee-jerk reactions in periods of distress and consider all of the evidence. This suggests that losses are as inevitable as the tides and that, in the long run, corporate setbacks are a natural, even healthy, part of building a stronger organization. The healthier economies demonstrate higher rather than lower loss rates.

In fact, what we have learned about individual firm behavior strongly reinforces the notion that *the aggregate, macro stability of an economy flows from its micro instability, the instability of the individual firm.* The learning process associated with company instability is crucial to long-term adaptivity and job creation.

Before delving into the detailed implications of all of this micro turbulence for workers and work sites, we need a better understanding and appreciation of the underlying forces causing it. We must pay heed to Jesus' complaint to God in the rock opera *Jesus Christ, Superstar:*

> You're far too hot on what and how;
> And not so hot on why.

Why are formation rates for businesses soaring? Why are successful firms obliged to live with volatility in order to survive? Will this need for instability go away in a few years? Or is it a basic condition with which we must learn to cope? These are the matters to which we will next turn our attention.

APPENDIXES

APPENDIX 2–1. EMPLOYMENT CHANGE DURING THE 1974–1976 PERIOD BY SIZE OF ESTABLISHMENT AS A FUNCTION OF THE 1969–1974 HISTORY

	SIZE: 0–20				
1969–1974 HISTORY	EMPLOYMENT CHANGE, 1974–1976				SAMPLE SIZE
	Big+	*Neutral*	*Big−*	*Death*	
EE/+ +	11.2%	68.1%	16.4%	4.3%	82,396
EE/+	10.2	77.7	9.3	2.8	6,902
EC/+ +	9.4	63.8	10.5	16.3	321,760
EC/+ −	9.6	56.9	6.8	26.7	731,908
EC/− −	17.9	56.0	3.3	22.8	38,138
CC/−	13.5	68.3	10.3	7.9	9,820
CC/− −	23.1	58.7	5.9	12.2	8,346
All firms	10.0	59.7	8.4	21.8	1,199,270
	SIZE: 21–50				
1969–1974 HISTORY	EMPLOYMENT CHANGE, 1974–1976				SAMPLE SIZE
	Big+	*Neutral*	*Big+*	*Death*	
EE/+ +	10.6%	68.6%	16.7%	4.1%	5,722
EE/+	7.6	80.1	9.5	2.8	3,073
EC/+ +	9.3	64.6	18.8	7.3	8,664
EC/+ −	8.4	68.3	11.7	11.7	72,513
EC/− −	18.3	56.2	8.7	16.8	8,342
CC/−	8.6	70.6	13.4	7.4	3,187
CC/− −	20.0	57.2	9.8	13.0	2,931
All firms	9.7	67.1	12.2	11.0	104,432

APPENDIX 2–1. *(continued)*

SIZE: 51–100

1969–1974 HISTORY	EMPLOYMENT CHANGE, 1974–1976				SAMPLE SIZE
	Big+	*Neutral*	*Big−*	*Death*	
EE/++	9.3%	68.6%	18.0%	4.0%	1,691
EE/+	7.3	81.4	9.2	2.1	1,186
EC/++	8.1	63.5	20.0	8.5	2,376
EC/+ −	7.9	67.8	12.7	11.5	23,651
EC/− −	18.1	56.4	10.0	15.5	3,093
CC/−	7.8	72.0	13.0	7.2	1,407
CC/− −	19.1	54.4	12.1	14.4	1,122
All firms	9.2	66.7	13.1	10.9	34,526

SIZE: 101–500

1969–1974 HISTORY	EMPLOYMENT CHANGE, 1974–1976				SAMPLE SIZE
	Big+	*Neutral*	*Big−*	*Death*	
EE/++	8.6%	70.4%	16.9%	4.1%	1,029
EE/+	6.0	79.1	11.4	3.4	1,059
EC/++	6.6	68.6	17.1	7.6	1,491
EC/+ −	6.9	68.3	12.2	12.6	19,045
EC/− −	16.4	58.7	9.8	15.1	2,095
CC/−	6.9	72.0	15.3	5.9	1,173
CC/− −	21.1	51.8	14.5	12.6	902
All firms	8.2	67.7	12.6	11.6	26,794

SIZE: 501+

1969–1974 HISTORY	EMPLOYMENT CHANGE, 1974–1976				SAMPLE SIZE
	Big+	*Neutral*	*Big−*	*Death*	
EE/++	5.7%	74.5%	18.9%	0.9%	106
EE/+	5.5	79.4	11.1	4.0	199
EC/++	6.5	73.9	14.1	5.5	199
EC/+ −	6.1	72.4	11.1	10.5	3,664
EC/− −	13.1	65.0	12.4	9.5	274
CC/−	3.8	74.9	14.6	6.7	239
CC/− −	14.6	59.9	14.6	10.8	157
All firms	6.6	72.1	11.7	9.6	4,838

EMPLOYMENT CHANGE DURING THE 1974–1976 PERIOD BY AGE OF ESTABLISHMENT AS A FUNCTION OF THE 1969–1974 HISTORY

	AGE: 0–4				
1969–1974 HISTORY	EMPLOYMENT CHANGE, 1976–1976				SAMPLE SIZE
	Big+	Neutral	Big−	Death	
EE/++	13.1%	64.7%	16.6%	5.7%	25,896
EE/+	11.3	73.9	10.6	4.2	1,829
EC/++	10.8	61.4	10.7	17.1	75,618
EC/+−	10.0	54.7	6.8	28.5	152,052
EC/−−	17.3	53.6	4.4	24.7	9,450
CC/−	12.4	67.0	10.1	10.4	2,389
CC/−−	22.1	56.1	6.8	15.0	2,245
All firms	10.9	57.8	8.8	22.5	269,479

	AGE: 5–9				
1969–1974 HISTORY	EMPLOYMENT CHANGE, 1974–1976				SAMPLE SIZE
	Big+	Neutral	Big−	Death	
EE/++	11.7%	67.4%	16.6%	4.3%	15,444
EE/+	10.6	76.1	10.7	2.7	1,596
EC/++	9.6	63.7	10.6	16.2	53,799
EC/+−	9.6	57.6	7.3	25.5	119,941
EC/−−	19.1	55.0	4.5	21.4	7,420
CC/−	12.2	68.3	10.9	8.6	1,994
CC/−−	22.3	56.4	7.7	13.6	1,854
All firms	10.3	60.1	8.8	20.8	202,048

	AGE: 9–12				
1969–1974 HISTORY	EMPLOYMENT CHANGE, 1974–1976				SAMPLE SIZE
	Big+	Neutral	Big−	Death	
EE/++	10.7%	68.9%	16.9%	3.5%	9,120
EE/+	10.3	77.9	10.2	1.5	1,102
EC/++	8.5	65.4	10.2	15.8	35,211
EC/+−	9.3	59.6	7.3	23.8	83,360
EC/−−	19.5	57.0	3.9	19.5	5,195
CC/−	13.8	67.2	11.3	7.8	1,440
CC/−−	20.9	57.5	8.4	13.2	1,336
All firms	9.8	61.8	8.7	19.8	136,764

	AGE: 13+				
1969–1974 HISTORY	EMPLOYMENT CHANGE, 1974–1976				SAMPLE SIZE
	Big+	Neutral	Big−	Death	
EE/++	9.1%	72.9%	15.2%	2.8%	31,233
EE/+	7.8	81.7	8.4	2.2	6,468
EC/++	7.5	66.7	9.9	15.9	136,080
EC/+−	8.4	62.6	7.6	21.4	379,272
EC/−−	17.0	59.3	5.2	18.5	22,610
CC/−	10.1	71.7	11.8	6.4	8,064
CC/−−	20.7	59.8	8.0	11.5	6,252
All firms	8.7	64.2	8.5	18.5	589,979

APPENDIX 2–3. EMPLOYMENT CHANGE DURING THE 1974–76 PERIOD BY INDUSTRY OF ESTABLISHMENT AS A FUNCTION OF THE 1969–74 HISTORY

MANUFACTURING					
1969–1974 HISTORY	EMPLOYMENT CHANGE, 1974–1976				SAMPLE SIZE
	Big+	Neutral	Big−	Death	
EE/++	13.6%	65.5%	16.2%	4.6%	16,665
EE/+	8.5	77.6	11.1	2.8	3,663
EC/++	11.6	62.8	14.0	11.6	32,638
EC/+−	9.7	63.0	10.0	17.2	129,347
EC/−−	18.9	54.5	6.8	19.9	8,846
CC/−	10.3	68.8	13.0	7.9	4,080
CC/−−	20.9	55.9	9.2	14.0	3,008
All firms	10.9	63.1	11.1	14.9	198,247

TRADE					
1969–1974 HISTORY	EMPLOYMENT CHANGE, 1974–1976				SAMPLE SIZE
	Big+	Neutral	Big−	Death	
EE/++	10.2%	71.2%	14.5%	4.0%	50,397
EE/+	9.2	80.4	7.7	2.7	6,489
EC/++	9.1	64.8	9.2	16.9	210,740
EC/+−	9.7	59.9	6.6	23.9	458,676
EC/−−	19.4	55.9	4.2	20.5	18,097
CC/−	12.2	70.5	9.1	8.2	7,481
CC/−−	23.4	57.5	6.6	12.5	5,137
All firms	9.9	62.2	7.8	20.1	757,017

SERVICE					
1969–1974 HISTORY	EMPLOYMENT CHANGE, 1974–1976				SAMPLE SIZE
	Big+	Neutral	Big−	Death	
EE/++	11.9%	68.5%	15.8%	3.8%	7,556
EE/+	9.5	78.2	10.2	2.2	729
EC/++	8.9	63.3	9.8	18.0	33,135
EC/+−	8.2	50.1	6.2	35.4	92,742
EC/−−	17.6	54.4	4.7	23.4	4,948
CC/−	10.7	71.5	12.2	5.5	1,592
CC/−−	21.7	60.4	8.6	9.3	1,318
All firms	9.1	54.8	7.6	28.5	142,020

CHAPTER 3

The Context

It has become a cliché to assert that we are living in times of great social and economic change. When was this not so? In the early 19th century, when the factory system was in its infancy? Or later, when the telegraph and the railroads sharply altered communication and transportation? During the second half of the century, which saw the rapid growth of transcontinentals, telephones, factory cities, and large-scale immigration, the settling of half a continent, and the disappearance of the American frontier? Might it have been the early 20th century, with electrification, the auto, wireless, motion pictures, radio, and airplanes? Or the mass culture and mass consumption after World War I, along with urbanization and then suburbanization, and America's emergence as a world power? How about after World War II with television, electronics, new developments in pharmaceutical drugs, and the exploration of space?

No one familiar with the history of invention and innovation can doubt (1) that change has been a hallmark of Western civilization for as long as it has existed; (2) that each generation was convinced that the changes were accelerating; and (3) that all were equally convinced life was simpler in the good old days.

They were probably right. One thesis of the book is that there is more change now than ever before but, having said this, that the 1980s will be the good old days to our great-grandchildren.

We ever have experienced times of rapid change; America is the very embodiment of the old Chinese wish, "May you live in interesting times."

But unlike anything the Chinese have experienced, we face phenomenal rapidity in the translation of change into products and services in the marketplace.* The pace has been quickening. The technology for broadcasting was available a generation before it was introduced. Television sets could have been in living rooms in the mid-1930s but didn't appear in any great numbers for 15 years. King Gillette had the idea for the safety razor in 1895—a viable product didn't appear until 1901. Edward Land started working on instant photography in 1943; the first Polaroid camera came out in 1947. Time was when it took four to five years before new automobiles were translated from the first sketches on drawing boards to glistening models in showrooms. Given modern technology, the lead time has been halved.

So the pace has quickened. Yet this too has ever been the case. The changes of the 1820s seemed very rapid to people at the time. Going from 20 miles per hour to 40 is as great a change in terms of magnitude as accelerating from 600 to 1,200.

Scores of scholars and publicists have noted that we are on the cusp where the industrial age is being transformed into the postindustrial. Just as America started to go from agriculture to manufacturing in the early 19th century, so we are about to make the transformation from manufacturing to services. This means an increasing number of workers will be involved in the generation and transmission of information and the revamping of old, familiar industries into new ones.

But one runs the risk of oversimplifying such matters, of painting the changes in hues that are too elemental, sacrificing reason for drama. The factory workers of the 19th century had to eat; agriculture didn't disappear, but instead, thanks to the machines turned out by McCormick, Deere, Case, and others, fewer farmers were able to grow much more grain, fruits, and meat products. Similarly, the computer programmer is an information worker who could not survive without manufacturers. What of the individuals who put together that computer, the miners who dug the coal and ore to make the steel, the oilmen who extracted the crude oil that went into making the plastic for parts, and the factory workers who fabricated and assembled the components? By any reasonable definition of the term, they are in the manufacturing

---

* Economists usually differentiate between products and services by noting the former can be inventoried, which is to say turned out for future use, while the latter must be used as produced. A concert is a service, while a recording of it is a product. Surgeons and porters are service workers, while skilled technicians and unskilled handworkers are in the manufacturing sector. As can be seen, the differences are subtle and have little to do with skills required.

sector. And how they work has undergone great changes in the past quarter of a century. Like the farmers, their numbers are bound to dwindle in the future—at least in relative terms.

The fact of the matter is that every economy needs agriculture, manufacturing, and services, all of which are interrelated directly or indirectly. It is the mix that changes, not the components. In advanced capitalist countries, the action will be in the service sector. In less advanced capitalist economies, look for manufacturing to grow. Meanwhile, the so-called third world or emerging countries will see rapid increases in agricultural output and beginnings in manufacturing. We are living at a time when India is becoming a food exporter, The Republic of Korea is on its way to being a major player in the world automobile industry, and the United States sees farm and factory labor decline while information and services increase. To buck the trend here is akin to King Canute trying to sweep back the tide.

Looking at the aggregate figures, one can easily conclude that the United States is well on its way into the postindustrial world. From 1966 through 1986, for example, we added 36 million jobs to the economy, representing a 56 percent increase in total employment—and with this had fewer manufacturing jobs in mid-1986 than we did in 1966. In Figure 3–1 are some of the macrostatistics, along with an informed projection.

The manufacturing sector has eroded even more than the figures indicate. For example, fewer workers who are thought of as "making things" are actually doing so. In 1970, 54 percent of manufacturing workers were engaged in fabrication of any and all kinds—the other 46 percent were support workers. By 1980, the 54 percent had fallen to 48 percent, meaning that less than half of the workers the Commerce Department categorizes as being in the nonagricultural and nonservice sectors are engaged in turning out products. We are now at the point where only 10 percent of all

FIGURE 3–1. THE NATION'S WORK FORCE, 1900–1995

YEAR	WHITE COLLAR	BLUE COLLAR	SERVICE	AGRICULTURE
1900	17.6%	35.8%	9.1%	37.6%
1940	31.1	40.0	11.7	17.4
1980	52.2	31.7	13.3	2.8
1995 (est.)	54.9	26.3	16.1	2.7

SOURCE: *Office of Technology Assessment, Bureau of Labor Statistics*

workers in the American economy actually are employed in factories making goods—the others do something else. So if you hear that 10 percent of American factory workers are unemployed, the number translates to only 1 percent of the work force.

All of this is part of the macroworld, and as you already have seen, the picture becomes quite different when subjected to microanalysis. To return to the analogy offered earlier, manufacturing has its own thundercloud, continually being transformed through massive innovation. The product mix is constantly being altered, as are the locations in which they are turned out and the processes employed. The *Fortune* 500 may employ fewer people now than they did in 1970, but they certainly aren't manufacturing or selling less. In fact sales have increased 27 percent in real terms (after adjusting for inflation). This indicates that more, not less, is being manufactured by the largest industrial companies but with fewer workers, a point to which we will return.

How did this happen? What is going on?

HALF A LIFE IN AMERICA

In recent years, the shift from manufacturing to services has been taken to mean the United States is losing highly paid jobs while adding low-paid ones to its employment rolls. In the 1984 presidential campaign, Walter Mondale talked of America becoming a country where hoards of workers serve hamburgers and sweep places out, while the highly skilled production jobs go overseas, presumably to Pacific rim countries. Or perhaps you prefer the pungent Lee Iacocca version: "Are we going to be a service power? The double-cheeseburger-hold-the-mayo kings of the world?"

Such talk is expected in electoral campaigns and from a public relations-minded auto magnate, but this was hyperbole of the worse kind. The minimum-wage high school student who works at McDonald's and Michael Jackson, who makes millions at the flick of a gloved hand, are both service workers—along with Dwight ("Dr. K") Gooden and Dr. Michael DeBakey. So are business executives, like Lee Iacocca, and presidential candidates. Looked at in this light, the rhetoric is vastly oversimplified to the point of being useless. A better way to organize thinking is needed if we are to make sense of the job shifts now taking place.

60

One might refine the definitions by dividing workers into those who produce goods and services in which the innovation rate is high and those in jobs where the innovation rate is low, which is another way of saying rapidly changing companies and more or less stable ones. Apply this definition, and you will find the economy rewards those who are continually improving their products and services while lowering costs of production, expanding markets, or—ideally—doing all three. These companies can be in manufacturing or even agriculture. Frank Perdue, who helped revolutionize the production and distribution of chickens, certainly is entrepreneurial, as are the scores of scientists who have made the "green revolution" possible, transforming stark visions of world starvation into a generalized glut. Whether in agriculture, manufacturing, or service, the company that tries to coast is penalized. To stand still in an economy that is moving ahead is really to lose ground.

Why do some industries demonstrate more "updraft" in the thundercloud than others? Or to put it differently, why are firms in some industries more vulnerable to erosion than others? To repeat an admonition you have read before, and will see again, it is dangerous to generalize about so diverse and yeasty a universe, but it would appear from our figures that a good deal of the explanation rests in what might be called the "half-life" of the product or service being offered. As you probably know, the half-life of a radioactive material is the time it takes for half of its radioactivity to decay. In the same sense, the half-life of a product or service is the time that passes before half of its value dissipates.

Most fad products—the pet rock and Rubik's Cube come to mind—have a very short half-life. They flash across the economic firmament, grow rapidly, become a mania, and then fizzle. There are exceptions, even among fads. The Cabbage Patch dolls appear in for a longer run but not so long as the Barbie doll. The Zippo cigarette lighter had an amazingly long half-life. After its initial design was in place, it sold for decades without a significant change, used by soldiers in World War II, the Korean Conflict, and even Vietnam. The same is true of a wide variety of products from light bulbs to passenger ships.

In contrast, many very accessible and familiar products have short half-lives. Among these are the daily newspaper, which for most readers becomes obsolete in a day; the best-selling novel may last for a few months on the charts. Most computer software has a half-life of about 18–24 months in today's marketplace. Personal computers are becoming obsolete very rapidly; a writer can begin a book on the latest model, and before he is finished, learn that it not only has been replaced by one and then another upgrade but that spare parts for the original model are no longer available. The same is true of much new medical technology and financial services.

As a nation—in the macroeconomy—we are doing quite well in products and services with short half-lives, and poorly with those having long half-lives. The reasons have been hammered home on television specials, business magazine articles, and best-selling books; namely, that other countries, led by Japan, have become very adept at copying and improving upon products that have long half-lives. They study the product, identify its salient features, improve it either by raising its value or lowering its costs, and then introduce it into the world market on a competitive basis.

Recall, if you are old enough, the situation in many consumer goods areas during the 1950s and early 1960s. Plenty of Swiss watches, French perfumes, English tweeds, and German cameras sold in the United States. They were offered as distinctive products, quite different and, in many cases, superior to their domestic counterparts. Americans who purchased them understood the premium price was being paid for something American industry either wouldn't or couldn't make and sell.

The Japanese product invasion was another story. Japanese companies would purchase models of television sets, let's say, tear them apart to see how they worked, purchase licenses and patent rights, and then set about manufacturing a better (not different) model for sale at a lower cost. Where the Volkswagen Beetle and the Mercedes Benz were different from American models, the early Toyotas and Datsuns were really small, well-constructed, inexpensive models that looked and even drove like their American counterparts—only better, at least in the opinion of purchasers. The Japanese—and Koreans, Taiwanese, and others—have done the same with many other products which like autos have relatively long half-lives.

Now consider the situation for products with far shorter half-lives. These are more easily protected, because by the time the copy is ready, the public has moved on to newer versions. It is one thing to put out copies of Rubik's Cube, which can be done in a matter of weeks since the product is so simple. Cobbling together personal computers is another matter entirely. By the time the copies arrive the state of the art has moved on. In effect, industries with products that have short half-lives present the imitators with moving targets not easily hit. In 1986, for example, the Korean-manufactured Leading Edge Model D was not only compatible with and in some respects superior to the IBM PC but sold at a much lower price. By then, however, the PC was an aged model by industry standards, and IBM had started to move on to other versions. Indeed, by the summer of 1986 IBM's "old" PC was priced quite competitively against the Asian copies.

So the growth segments of the economy are those whose products and services have relatively short half-lives; the stagnant and declining ones feature products with longer ones. Anyway you look at it, innovation remains the basic theme. Short product half-lives and high innovation rates are, of course, simply different ways of saying the same thing. Both depend upon creativity, which is the hallmark of those small entrepreneurial companies we have been discussing.

In general, America has been blessed with an abundance of jittery, edgy, nervous characters who fairly ache to go off on their own. This isn't to say that the business schools are bulging with starry-eyed young men and women who will venture into the world and start their own firms, or that the high school student who works part-time in a computer store dreams of becoming another Steve Jobs. Most of the former want nothing more than to work for a large corporation and haul in the biggest salaries in the shortest amount of time, while the chances for that youngster becoming a tycoon are roughly the same as for his winning the sweepstakes.

Even so, we seem to grow more entrepreneurs than most other societies. Indeed, as Americans take the pilgrimage to Japan to learn the secrets of their manufacturing, the Japanese flood our schools and industrial parks searching for methods of transplanting our innovative, enterprising attitudes to their country. They are fully aware that with only 5 percent of the world's population Americans have accounted for 53 percent of all Nobel Prizes for science and for medicine since 1950. Western Europeans took another 39 percent, leaving only 8 percent for the rest of the world, including those nations who do so well in making better versions than Americans can of products with long half-lives.

All of us know what creativity means and implies, but measuring it poses a problem. How do we spot the beast, how can one distinguish between creator and the crackpot? In other words, is that wild-eyed Yuppie operating out of a storefront in a depressed neighborhood laboring over a perpetual motion machine to be taken seriously or dismissed out of hand? Then too, what forms does entrepreneurship take? To some, innovation conjures images of engineers and scientists inventing new gadgets or materials in laboratories; they think of computer chips, space vehicles, or new chemicals or drugs. But the innovator also can be a divorced former housewife peddling a gourmet tropical fish food, a salesman with a surefire apple corer, or a chemist about to crown years of toil with a patent on a pimple remover that he swears will sweep the teenage market. Are there differences between the CalTech engineer working on new microchips and the out-of-work Detroit assembly line mechanic who is certain he has stumbled upon a unique solvent that will clean all carburetors in a hurry? Of course, but we are hard put to say just what it is. As Supreme Court Justice Potter Stewart once said of pornography, he is hard-pressed to define it but knows it when he sees it.

The indications are that all (or even most) creativity in the American economy is *not* found in the small high-technology sector. As we looked through our economic microscope, it became evident to us that innovation is much more broadly dispersed and, certainly, is not limited to the design and fabrication of electronic gadgets and new biochemical compounds.

INNOVATION

Let's start out by agreeing that innovation and advanced technology do go together, and there is plenty of the former in low-technology operations. Then go on to agree that the individual who takes a familiar product or service and updates it to meet current needs is as much an innovator as the one who creates something that appears entirely new. And these, too, can be in low tech—even no tech—as often or even more often than high tech. Mrs. Fields and Famous Amos simply put out superb chocolate chip cookies and not electronic gizmos.

The business magazines are filled with tales of glamorous technology-based firms. Who doesn't know about Silicon Valley? But how many know of the revolution in steelmaking and marketing pioneered by Nucor and Florida Steel, who given a level playing field could undercut the Japanese producers in many product areas even in Asian markets? The answer is obvious: We want to know about microchips, and this generation of Americans is bored by steel making. Yet far more jobs are being created in no and low tech than in high.

What most people don't realize is that the high-technology segment of the economy is very small; according to the Bureau of Labor Statistics, it represents only 2.8 percent of all jobs. Peter Drucker† has estimated that as few as one new job out of every eight created in the American economy in the past 20 years can be classified as belonging to the high-technology segment. He notes that only a quarter of the fastest-growing companies as identified by *Inc.* magazine can be categorized as such. The others weren't founded on any novel invention spawned in glistening laboratories but rather through the shuffling of familiar products into new forms or the meeting of a felt need with some relatively simple product or service. Ray Kroc didn't invent the hamburger, after all, but only did it up in a new way. And he was as innovative in his way as was Edward Land, the father of instant photography.

Innovation, then, can take one of two forms: the creation of something novel, or the reshuffling of existing components to present the familiar in a new form. Moreover, the new or reshuffled product or service either can fill a new demand or replace an existing one by performing the task better or less expensively. The artificial heart is a good example of a new product with a new function, while the health maintenance organization is a new way to perform familiar services. Minnetonka Corporation's soft soap in a pump dispenser is a new product that partially replaced an old one, while supermarket checkout machines are a superior form of a familiar product that replaced a less efficient device. Figure 3–2 offers examples of the four different kinds of innovation.

The boundaries here are somewhat fuzzy. Some might argue that every invention is produced or at least suggested by what went before and that there can be no truly "new" devices or services. Our aim is not to produce the ultimate definition of innovation, however, but to illustrate its diversity and to point out that one form of innovation is not inherently superior to another. Rear-

---

† Peter Drucker, *Innovation and Entrepreneurship: Practice and Principles* (New York: Harper & Row, 1985), pp. 7–8.

FIGURE 3–2   AN INNOVATION TYPOLOGY WITH EXAMPLES

Nature of Innovation

		Creation of New Device or Procedure	Rearrange or Assemble Existing Device or Procedures
Accomplishment	Create New Function	Television Windsurfing Hula Hoop/Pet Rock Artifical Heart Telephone Visicalc Video Cassette Recorder Polaroid Camera	Money-Market Fund Fast-Food Chains Credit Card Chemotherapy CAT Scanner Individualized Group Ins. Health Maintenance Org. Telephone Answering Device

	Replace Existing Function More Efficiently Or Conveniently	Aluminum 2 x 4
		Computer
		Robot
		Soft Soap
		Automatic Translation
		Most Artificial
		   Intelligence
		Jet Airplane
		Satellite
		   Communications
		Synthetic Fibers
		Cuisinart
		Semiconductors
		Most Drugs
			Garbage Treatment
			Lotus 1-2-3
			MCI
			Federal Express
			   Zap Mail
			Health Care
			Cable TV
			Automated Checkout
			   Machines
			Beauty Care
			Real Estate
			   Development

ranging existing technology into new systems is just as creative as the invention of a new device. Similarly, doing something we now do better (e.g., the jet passenger plane and the computer) is as important an innovation as one that creates an entirely new function. Furthermore, scientists and engineers do not have a corner on creativity. People who filled a need by devising new methods of delivering health care have made just as great a contribution to our lives—and have created even more jobs—than those who labor on the cutting edge of high technology.

Yet they do share a common attribute. All require leaps of imagination, the ability to see things afresh that is the mark of the entrepreneur. There are more examples of this today than at any time in American history. Indeed, there are so many that we have become a trifle jaded and don't recognize change when it hits us on the head.

Think of one of the most familiar and mundane parts of the everyday lives of Americans—the mail.

Put yourself back in the late 1960s, when like the weather, everyone complained about the mail but no one did anything about it. For good reason. How could any private company hope to compete with the Postal Service, which not only was a federal agency but one mandated by the Constitution itself? Sure, there were some private firms that delivered small packages overnight— Flying Tiger and Emery Air Freight, to name the larger ones—and, of course, United Parcel. But even these were often unreliable.

In 1964 Fred Smith, then a junior at Yale, wrote a term paper suggesting the possibility of a delivery service for high priority, time-sensitive packages, for which a skeptical professor awarded him a grade of "C." Seven years later, after having raised almost $50 million, Smith incorporated his company, which was and is known as Federal Express. There were to be three basic services: guaranteed overnight delivery, a lower rate for second-day delivery, and a "Courier Pak," which was an envelope that would be transported for $5.

Operations began on April 17, 1973, with services to 22 cities. From the first, it was obvious Smith faced enormous problems, not the least of which being that few potential customers knew anything about the company. Large sums went into advertising, but after a while, word of mouth produced equally good results. Business customers soon learned that Smith was as good as his word, and Federal's rapid growth prodded the other private companies to greater efforts, while attracting newcomers to the field. By the early 1980s, the Post Office itself was obliged to offer special express services rivaling those of Federal. By then, however, Federal was grossing well over half a billion dollars a year and was deemed a viable alternative to the government operation—for parcels, that is.

Next Smith eyed the lucrative market for business letters, entering it in 1984 with Zap Mail. Taking advantage of electronic transmission, he guaranteed delivery in two hours. "The revolution in telecommunications will have enormous implications in the way Federal Express does business and we need to be aggressive in this area," he said.‡ Simply to start the program required an investment of $100 million, which Federal had little trouble raising, since by then it had $1.5 billion in revenues and was one of America's fastest growing companies.

While the success of the Zap Mail venture is far from assured, one can assume that like so many other entrepreneurs, Smith will regroup when and if the firm falters. "I think it's unfortunate that to some degree the word 'entrepreneur' has taken on the connota-

‡ Quoted in Robert Sobel and David Sicilia, *The Entrepreneur: An American Adventure* (Boston: Houghton Mifflin, 1986), p. 48.

tion of a gambler," he said in discussing Zap Mail. Supporting the point made here earlier, he added, "Many times action is not the most risky path. The most risky path is inaction."

Fred Smith is a prime example of a reshuffler who is engaged in wedding an old concept (the mail) to a new technology (sophisticated telecommunications). One might imagine he has gone just about as far as one might given the nature of this technology, but another entrepreneur, Gerard O'Neill, has taken the concept one step further. The founder of a minuscule firm, Geostar, O'Neill hopes one day to do no less than provide everyone on Earth who wants one with a "transceiver," a telephone-like device capable of sending and receiving signals to and from a space satellite. Anyone on the planet wanting to "call" anyone else would only have to know that person's number to give him or her a ring. The possibilities are endless. Doctors could monitor patients through transceiver hookups, truckers and taxi drivers could be routed and summoned by use of them, the police could be alerted to break-ins by special transceivers. Individuals stuck in elevators could send out a general signal for help, as could mugging victims. O'Neill claims he can do this for an initial charge of around $450 per unit and annual fees running from $30 to $40.

One can't really say whether O'Neill is akin to the aforementioned developer of a perpetual motion machine or a latter-day Alexander Graham Bell. If successful, Geostar could challenge AT&T, MCI, the U.S. Mail, Federal Express, Motorola, and much of Japan Inc. Failure of course would mean his company might vanish with little or no trace. What is clear, however, is that like Fred Smith, Gerard O'Neill is an innovator attempting to perform an old service in a new and improved fashion. And in a more efficient fashion. This too is a goal of innovation.

MEASURING INNOVATION

Once we accept this broader definition of innovation we can move on to other things, such as how to recognize it in action. In our research we experimented with several measurements that would enable us to screen out companies demonstrating innovation by putting the universe through our computers. First, we thought that innovative segments of the economy would make themselves known through a measurement we used earlier: turbulence, lots of comings and goings, ups and downs. But that proved unsatisfactory, primarily because it isolated as innovative many segments of the economy (e.g., retail trade and construction contracting) where turbulence is a way of life and has little or nothing to do with innovation.

We then speculated that innovation would manifest itself as "efficiency"—that is, an ability to produce a product more cheaply than competitors. Corporations that can either increase value with no substantial increase in cost (jet planes vs. propeller models) or maintain value while reducing cost (the transistor vs. the tube-powered radio comes to mind) or, in the best of worlds, increase value while reducing costs (hand calculators) are innovating and should be able to outperform those that are not. As a measure of efficiency, we used the company's ability to increase revenues relative to employment—simply stated, productivity. However, this didn't work out as well as we had originally expected. The big problem here was that the computer picked out many capital-intensive firms, such as utilities, and many wholesalers, whose dollar volume of sales can expand enormously with little increase in employment.

We finally realized the best way to spot innovation would be by studying what it enables firms to do—that is, to grow. The innovative firm—whatever the nature of its innovation—is able to outperform other firms in its field and by so doing, expand. It may be a marketing innovation (Domino Pizza), a technological innovation (digital thermometers), or systems innovation (Federal Express). Whatever its nature, the innovation creates growth opportunities upon which the entrepreneur capitalizes.

Henceforth we will call these firms "high-innovation" or "innovation-based" firms. This description refers to how the firm behaves, not to the product or service it produces. Some high-innovation firms make innovative products—computers, electronics, drugs. Some make traditional products in more innovative ways—steel, clothing, textiles. Most make no product at all, but produce, instead, an innovative service which, in most cases, capitalizes in one way or another on the availability of new technology—parcel delivery, health care, computer software.

Industries that contain large numbers of growing, aggressive, innovation-based companies we will refer to as "high-innovation sectors" of the economy. Some of these sectors produce advanced technology—the so-called high-tech sectors. Most do not. Most produce innovative services. Virtually all sectors, however, contain significant numbers of high-innovation firms. Innovation is found everywhere in America today—just more in some sectors (and places) than in others.

THE HIGH-INNOVATION SECTORS

In Chapter 2 we developed and then applied the Growth Index. You will recall that this is the product of the percentage and absolute growth of the firm and permits us to compare large and small firms on a common basis when analyzing their growth performance. By utilizing the index we can discover which industries have the largest number of firms with a very high rating (say, above 100). These are the industries, we have found, that are experiencing high rates of innovation. Putting all the data through the screen, we discover that there are seven broad categories into which highly innovative industries fall:

1. High-Technology Makers
2. Information-Age Group
3. "Trend Buckers"
4. Leisure-Time Group
5. Energy Group
6. Baby Boom/Yuppie/Women-in-the-Labor-Force Group
7. Aging Group.

Explanation is required regarding these categories. Some are fairly straightforward, others more complicated.

The High-Technology Makers is a pretty clear-cut category. The task of identifying its members has been simplified by the Bureau of Labor Statistics, which defines high-tech industries as those concerned with:

Computers
Communication equipment
Electronic components
Drugs
Radio and television-receiving equipment
Aircraft
Measuring and controlling devices
Medical instruments.

70

The Information-Age Group category is more complex. It includes all those firms that in one way or another participate in the growth of the office-related processing and distribution of information. Members of the group range from manufacturers of data-processing mainframes and software to the maintenance crews that keep things humming in the office buildings that house the information activities even to the airlines that move around the group's highly trained personnel to their endless series of face-to-face meetings. Companies in the group are concerned with:

Nonresidential buildings
Office furniture
Electric distribution equipment
Electric lighting and wiring equipment
Airlines for business travel
Noncertified air carriers
Service to buildings
Computer and data-processing services
Investment offices
Noncommercial research organizations.

Trend Buckers is a yet more nebulous and far more intriguing category, for its members have a most challenging task. These are innovators operating in industries that are declining, "contrarians" who see opportunites while others are leaving the ship. Nucor and Florida Steel are prime examples. Trend buckers are especially prevalent in:

Steel and steel products
Motorcycles and bicycles
Weaving and knitting mills
Textiles
Paper mills
Leather tanning
Nonferrous rolling and drawing mills.

Leisure time is one of the prime beneficiaries of technology. Greater productivity and robotization of functions formerly performed by human beings may mean higher unemployment—but also shorter work weeks and more time for a variety of nonwork-related activities. Travel, entertainment, sports, and so forth are bound to grow in the future as a result of these changes in the economy. The leisure-time beneficiaries include:

Airlines
Ship and boat building
Toys and sporting goods
Intercity highway transport
Charter services
Commercial sporting teams
Local water transportation.

The oil shocks of the 1970s spawned the Energy Group. While crude prices plummeted in 1986, they may well rise again by the end of the decade. The grave distress caused in Texas, Louisiana, and Oklahoma by the drop in the price of crude oil is probably temporary. The good times will return for these states (and bad ones for much of the rest of the nation) once this temporary lull has ended. There have been and soon will be once again many rapidly growing companies in the following areas:

Coal mining
Petroleum discovery and refining
Railroads
Natural gas production and distribution
Combination utility services
Oil- and gas-field services.

There is an old saying to the effect that "demography is destiny." We know that certain alterations will be taking place in the American population in the future, and can predict with some degree of assurance which industries will benefit.

The group of companies catering to Baby-Boomers, Yuppies, and Women in the Labor Force includes firms that have taken advantage of these demographic and social changes. The relationship becomes clear once you think about it. All of these firms are involved in providing goods and services in a fast, convenient fashion to people who are wrapped up in their work and/or have little time for traditional tasks, such as cooking meals from scratch or cleaning house. The fast-food organizations, home-cleaning companies, and office temporaries clearly sprang up to meet these needs. Be warned, however, that there are complications in all of these markets. The birth rate is rising, and this will alter the lives of many that fall into the three groups making up this category. Today's yuppie is tomorrow's parent, who will frequent fast-food operations rather than chic little French restaurants in order to save money for a vacation at Disneyworld, not a ski holiday in the Rockies. The cramped one-bedroom Manhattan condo may be sold in order to raise funds for the down payment on a suburban house.

Aging is the other major demographic force in the 1980s and clearly will become more of one in the 1990s and the early 21st century. Already it is spawning a host of opportunities for innovation, some related to health care but most to the needs of older people who remain vigorous and—in the aggregate—are comparatively well-off. There are signs of great activity in the segment of the economy catering to the desires and needs of this segment of the population. The American Association of Retired People is one of the nation's major special interest groups. Elderhostel, a Boston-based nonprofit organization that organizes vacation seminars for the over-60 group, is growing at a rate of 50 percent a year with no end in sight. As can be imagined, the Aging Group dovetails and in parts overlaps with some of the others mentioned and to be discussed.

It doesn't take too much imagination to isolate those industries and companies that makeup the Baby Boomer–Yuppie–Women-in-the-Labor-Force Group. Among these are:

Producers of preserved (dried and frozen) meats, fruits, and vegetables
Restaurant and fast-food chains
Home entertainment
Toys and games
Real estate
Resort and travel
Household appliances
Carpets
Colleges and universities
Women's business clothing

Motor vehicles
Prefabricated buildings and mobile homes
Footwear
Handbags
Pottery
Glassware
Department stores and video shopping
Individual and family services
Residential care
Medical and health insurance.

The industries that will benefit most from developments in the other demographic group, the elderly, are:

Life and health insurance
Nursing and personal care facilities
Education
Hospitals
Recreation
Travel
Health and allied services.

These seven groups simply describe the most important high-innovation and growth segments of the economy, but there are many others. Some are innovative almost by their nature—clothing is one example. Others thrive as suppliers to one or more of the groups. Some that come to mind are crushed stone and gravel, plastics and synthetic fibers, paving and roofing materials, fabricated rubber products, plumbing and heating equipment, fire, marine, and casualty insurance.

It is important to reiterate that innovative *firms* can be found in virtually every industry, though obviously some industries have a greater concentration than others. Figure 3–3 provides a sense of the relative magnitude involved in job replacement. Note that in the subgroup Expanding Firms, entrepreneurial operations in the innovative sectors account for 2.7 percent of the companies but 20.8 percent of replacement jobs; entrepreneurial firms in the non-

FIGURE 3–3. CREATION OF REPLACEMENT JOBS BY DEGREE OF INNOVATION OF BOTH FIRM AND SECTOR, 1981–1985

	FOR EXPANDING FIRMS					
	PERCENT OF FIRMS			PERCENT OF REPLACEMENT JOBS		
Firm Type	*Innovative Sector*	*Other*	*Total*	*Innovative Sector*	*Other*	*Total*
Entrepreneurial	2.7	15.4	18.0	20.8	65.6	86.4
Non-Entrepreneurial	5.9	76.0	81.9	1.7	11.9	13.6
Total	8.6	91.4	100.0	22.5	77.5	100.0
	FOR NEW FIRMS					
	PERCENT OF FIRMS			PERCENT OF REPLACEMENT JOBS		
Firm Type	*Innovative Sector*	*Other*	*Total*	*Innovative Sector*	*Other*	*Total*
Entrepreneurial	.3	1.4	1.7	3.1	14.0	17.1
Non-Entrepreneurial	8.7	89.6	98.3	9.9	73.0	82.9
Total	9.0	91.0	100.0	13.0	87.0	100.0

innovative sector are 15.4 percent of the universe while providing 65.6 percent of the jobs. Together they provide 86.4 percent of the replacement jobs, and the breakdown offers convincing evidence that innovative firms, no matter the industry, are the engines for job generation.

The nonentrepreneurial firms in innovative industries come to 5.9 percent of the total, but add only 1.7 percent of the jobs. So it would appear that there is no "neighborhood effect" at work in the rapidly growing industries—the sluggish firms there are not invigorated by the competition or the atmosphere of rapid change and growth. Indeed, entrepreneurial firms in the more mundane sectors of the economy create more expansion jobs than similar ones in the innovative sectors. Entrepreneurship and innovation are *not* concentrated primarily in the sexy, high-innovation, high-tech sectors of the economy. They are everywhere.

The new-firm picture is less extreme but conveys more or less the same message—namely, entrepreneurial births are few in number but account for almost 20 percent of all job creation attributable to births.

Recall the distinction made in Chapter 2 between income substitutors and entrepreneurs. In thinking about the figures for new firms consider that the microeconomy depends a good deal upon the ability of new shops to replace old ones, new restaurants to take the place of those leaving the business, and a new owner coming in to take over a gasoline station that was shuttered. A beautician with a following in one salon often leaves to open one of his or her own; an auto mechanic may work for a garage for a few years to get the hang of the business and then relocate to another city or state, where instead of looking for a job, he opens his own small repair operation.

Sit back and think about those numbers, and the people behind them. The act of starting a new business, be it income substitutor or entrepreneurial, requires a great deal of courage, even if the goal is to remain small, if it is only to survive. Our communities would be in great trouble if the desire for independence represented by these literally millions of attempts to start firms were somehow discouraged and made less attractive. Having said this, we must add that the income substitutors generally serve their own interests by making life more comfortable for their customers, while the entrepreneurial startups often can result in customers altering their ways of life, developing new tastes and habits by using different products and services.

THE ENTREPRENEURIAL IMPERATIVE

Why has there been a surge of entrepreneurship and growth in smaller businesses? First off, the allure of new products and services can be well-nigh irresistible and the costs of entry low. Recall how you might have felt when hearing about or actually seeing and perhaps eating your first portion of frozen tofu? Or buying a bag of hamburgers and fries at your first McDonald's or Burger King? Or viewing your first home-shopping show on television? Go back to the days of your grandparents or great-grandparents and imagine how they might have felt when seeing their first automobile. That frozen tofu stand, hamburger outlet, and shopping show couldn't have cost too much to open, you might have reflected. And the product and service certainly were attractive.

Desperation is another contributing factor. Seeking a job at another firm may not be a viable option if large companies, as a group, are laying off many skilled people. The options for a laid-off person may be to remain unemployed, to leave the area, or to start his or her own business.

Given the low barriers for many small businesses, the start-your-own option may be the most attractive. We thus observe surges of new business formation under depressed circumstances—during recessions in general, like the 1981–1982 period, and hard times in cities hit by some sort of economic shock—like the Boeing layoffs in Seattle, the defense/aerospace layoffs in Boston in the mid-1970s, the NCR layoffs in Dayton, Ohio, the auto layoffs in Detroit, and most recently, the oil-based cutbacks in Houston.

There are hundreds of such stories—every day of the year. We know of a salad chef who was fired when his operation cut back on personnel and wound up catering parties in a posh suburb. Then there was the actress who, unable to find work, became an agent. The Ph.D. in English literature who, after failing to achieve tenure, opened a tutoring service is another example. The out-of-work Louisiana oilfield laborer who went north to open a Cajun restaurant is fairly typical. Go to any area in which there have been widespread layoffs and you will find workers thinking about going it alone.

Indeed, the phenomenon has become so widespread as to inspire a pilot for a television series. Entitled *Hearts of Steel,* the show features four steelworkers who lost their jobs and Annie, the owner of a saloon they used to frequent. Since she has lost all of her customers, Annie intends to convert the bar into a yuppie restaurant, catering to employees of a microchip factory that had recently opened nearby. The five pool their savings—one of the workers goes so far as to sell his prized Corvette when additional money is needed. The saloon is remodeled and a chef hired. How did the venture turn out? It is difficult to say, because the series never made it off the ground.

Still, in television, art often imitates life. *Hearts of Steel* may never make it to network television, but it does reflect a phenomenon taking place in many parts of the nation. And while it was a situation comedy, not a tract for economic analysis, note that in the process of making the change, the five partners had to hire construction workers to remodel the saloon and then that chef. Restructuring the economy in such a fashion not only keeps people off the welfare rolls but also stimulates the economy.

A third factor is the increasing tendency of larger firms to sub-contract to smaller ones. As world markets tighten and become more volatile, big firms seek fewer full-time employees and rely instead upon flexible, cost-effective subcontractors to perform the kinds of tasks that used to be done in-house. We already have noted the willingness of the *Fortune* 500 companies to lay off almost 3 million workers so far in this decade as a vehicle for *increasing* sales.

Chrysler's use of 17,000 subcontractors was well publicized in the push for bailout legislation in 1979 and played a crucial role in obtaining the needed political support. Before he was finished, CEO Lee Iacocca had laid off fully 30 percent of his work force. Some of their jobs were eliminated as the company cut back. Others were replaced by machines or simply more efficient use of labor. But the biggest factor was the use of additional subcontractors. Chrysler and other companies boast they are turning out more product with fewer workers; this does not mean the labor content of the goods is sharply lower but rather that subcontractors account for a larger share than before. And many of these subcontractors are small firms, startups that are managed either by entrepreneurs or income substitutors, some of whom were laid-off workers in the same or a related industry.

Of course, for each of these new companies there will be scores of workers desperately seeking jobs, hoping that some firm in the area can use their skills and knowledge, relocating elsewhere if the call comes, and in the meantime, collecting unemployment checks and watching their savings dwindle. This pretty well describes most workers. They are bystanders. According to Peter Drucker,[#] "Bystanders have no history of their own. They are on stage but are not part of the action. They are not even audience. The fortunes of the play and every actor in it depends on the audience whereas the reaction of the bystander has no effect except on himself."

Most bystanders lack the interest or inclination to take the plunge, noting the high failure rate of new enterprises and that the most cited reason is shortage of capital. This certainly is true, but the situation may have been overstated.

Funds are available to support a large number of startups, though of course they are not evenly distributed by industry and region. The sums of money required to support our entrepre-

[#] Peter Drucker, *Adventures of a Bystander* (New York: Harper Colophon, 1980), p. 1.

78

neurial habits are not insignificant. Assume that each of the approximately 800,000 annual startups of corporations and partnerships need, on the average, $25,000 to open the doors—that comes to around $20 billion in net new capital. Now, add another $25,000 per business in expansion capital for approximately 300,000 rapidly growing new businesses, or $7.5 billion. So we are talking about a total of some $28 billion in net new venture capital per year.

In its *best* years, the formal venture capital industry raised $2 billion for new and ongoing firms. Banks and other financial institutions (pension funds, government agencies, insurance companies, etc.) provide at most another $4 billion. This leaves the "informal" capital network with the task of providing $22 billion each year. Some comes from the sale of equity and debt on the capital markets, but this is almost insignificant for the kinds of small companies to which we are referring.

We have found that the bulk of the $22 billion comes from personal savings, friends, relatives, or local informal venture capital groups formed by doctors or lawyers or business people. The raising of venture capital depends crucially upon the ability of private individuals to accumulate discretionary wealth.

Unlike many European countries, whose tax systems discourage the amassing of private wealth, the American system not only permits but encourages it, which is to say that the other fellow's tax shelter is your method of financing entrepreneurship. It remains so even with the reforms of the recent tax code overhaul. This may not seem so when viewing the macroworld—the low rate of personal savings for Americans is too well known to explore. In the microworld, however, there are millions of professionals and skilled workers who have accumulated six-figure assets. They simply haven't been counted in the statistics put out by the government due to the method of tabulation that is used.

For example, the sharp advance in the price of housing during the past decade has brought much pain and dislocation, but it has also increased indirectly the pool of investment capital. That this has not been fully realized is due to the way government categorizes spending and saving. Consider a family that puts away $50,000 in a bank. This, of course, is deemed to be savings. If the family withdraws the sum to purchase a $200,000 house with a $150,000 mortgage, the government says it has "dissaved," or consumed, the money. And if, after five years, the house goes up in value to $350,000 and the family borrows $20,000 for improvements, the statistics would show it was in debt.

Now consider that the family refinances the house to obtain $25,000 to support one of the children in a new business venture. That is how the needed funds are often obtained. Such private wealth, not tabulated in official accountings, is frequently the fuel for new enterprises.

If the private wealth is dried up or in some other way discouraged through adverse changes in the tax code or restrictive regulations, we would see a sharp decline in the formation of new businesses, both income substitutors and entrepreneurial enterprises. The money is there now, however, and many ingenious would-be business men and women are finding it.

Finally, the technology to support new businesses—especially entrepreneurial high-tech startups—is available and relatively inexpensive. Powerful computers can be purchased nowadays at relatively low cost. Telecommunications, too, is quite cheap. Specialized technology in the form of microchips, specialty metals and compounds, and sophisticated machinery for the office and factory are all available on lease. This surge in the availability of technology at low cost has been a major contributing factor to the host of small businesses capitalizing upon it.

Likewise, income substitutors may be able to get going by purchasing or leasing used equipment at low cost. The rapid rate of change means that a machine or other equipment that had been replaced by a superior model, but is still quite serviceable, can be had for prices often only slightly higher than their scrap value. And the high rate of failure has some beneficial fallout, in that the equipment goes back on the market at low cost. Typewriters and filing cabinets at the failed travel agency enable the new office temporaries operation to open at low cost. The closure of a pizza parlor in one part of town enables another, which purchased its oven, tables, and chairs at knockdown prices, to open in a different neighborhood.

To repeat, all this is not for everyone. Excitement and promises of satisfaction and rewards, and the yearning to be a player, not a bystander, are the lures extended by new, innovative enterprises. These elements are lacking or minimized in older, established, well-entrenched industries. David Liederman of David's Cookies knew he hadn't a chance of bucking the big players in packaged cookies, and what business person in his right mind would attempt to take on Coca-Cola or IBM in their own backyards?

Henry Kaiser, the world-famous engineer and ship builder, was one such individual. In the closing days of World War II Kaiser planned to create a car company to challenge the likes of General Motors, Ford, and Chrysler. Amid great fanfare he purchased the giant Willow Run complex from Ford, set up a steel company to provide raw materials, and announced the formation of Kaiser-Frazer Corporation and his intention to produce advanced cars such as the nation had never before seen. For a while Kaiser seemed to have won his gamble as auto buyers flocked to his show-rooms at a time when the demand for cars far exceeded the supply. But then the Big Three counterattacked, and by the early 1950s Kaiser-Frazer was in trouble. In 1954 Kaiser called a press confer-ence and told a group of veteran auto industry reporters that he had to suspend operations, having lost $110 million. "We were prepared to throw one hundred million dollars into the pool," he said ruefully, "but we were not prepared to see it sink without a ripple." To this, one reporter quipped, "In this game that kind of money will buy you one white chip."

IMPLICATIONS FOR EXPORTS

By now you have seen just how important small entrepre-neurial businesses are for the growth of the national economy. We also have noted that many of the new enterprises are in the service sector, the fastest-growing part of the economy today and for the foreseeable future. Were this all there was to it, we might be justi-fied in concluding that they are the engines for our well-being as a nation.

Having said this, other questions remain to be answered that involve our international stance. For example, many service jobs appear insulated from foreign competition. The high school teacher does not have to fear a mass desertion of students to an inexpensive, better-made Japanese model. The alternative to the office-cleaning service is another in the same town, not one based in Taiwan. Generally speaking, the American manufacturer of computer software should have no pressing reason to monitor the Koreans to see what they are generating. By the same token, American service workers cannot easily enter the export market. This is much the conventional wisdom, the conclusion being that we are, as a nation, losing jobs in industries that might export and replacing them with those in the purely domestic area.

Those who believe this to be a dangerous situation often raise several questions—among them, can we remain a great nation without a vigorous export trade? Or to put it another way, can we survive comfortably simply by taking in each other's wash and ignoring the greater world outside? And what about our security? How can we maintain a strong defense if we let our basic industries erode? How will automation affect job creation in the future? Might not word processors, expert systems, and fifth-generation computers do for the service sector what the combine did for agriculture and the robot is now doing for manufacturing? These are pressing matters, which we will deal with one at a time.

Let's begin with what we noted earlier, namely that the service sector contains a full range of activities from those requiring little in the way of skills and training to others that demand an abundance of both. Some involve services that haven't changed in technology for centuries; others are updated and altered at a dizzying pace. Also, consider a challenge to the conventional wisdom that service jobs tend to be local and national, since services cannot be inventoried and shipped as are manufactured products.

One of the more fascinating studies of this sector was undertaken by Professor Paul Reynolds of the University of Minnesota. Reynolds tracked down each firm started in Minnesota between 1979 and 1982 to determine what they did, how fast they grew, who they hired, and related matters. One of his more interesting findings was that liberally defined, fewer than 5 percent of the firms could be categorized as high tech—this in a state that thinks of itself as the home for sophisticated, future-oriented businesses requiring workers with high educational achievements. Even that figure may be too high. If we used the definition employed in this chapter, the number would drop to only 1 percent.

Consistent with our own findings, Reynolds discovered that a relatively few firms (around 10 percent) created the bulk of the new jobs and that these job-creating firms were in all parts of the economy. He then learned that of those firms that sold outside of Minnesota, the largest category was producer services and not manufacturing. Also, the growing new firms tended to hire people with above-average skills, the producer and distributive services having the most favorable mix.

In short, Minnesota's new service firms hire the best-educated people and sell the most outside of the state. They are hardly taking in each other's wash.

The phenomenon is not peculiar to Minnesota. Nationally, since around 1975, we have been offsetting a growing merchandise deficit with a service surplus (see Figure 3–4). We now sell 20 percent of the world's services, for example, and are its leading purveyor of services—from banking to insurance to advertising to consulting. It wouldn't be going too far to say that we have become successful at selling our wits at a time when our muscles offer little competitive advantage. We compete best in those forms of economic endeavor that require large inputs of brainpower and creativity, that have short product half-lives.

The idea that the service sector has become a major exporter and earner of foreign currencies may strain credulity, since it flies in the face of so much rhetoric one hears nowadays. The notion requires us to learn to recognize and accept the fact that American

FIGURE 3–4.   U.S. Balance of Payments Trade in Goods and Services

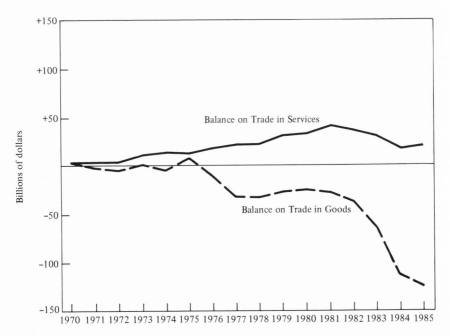

SOURCE: U.S. Dept of Commerce, Bureau of Economic Analysis, "Survey of Current Business."

brainpower is an important commodity on the world scene. We must come to appreciate the fact that among the largest exporters from New Haven, Conn. are Yale University—and the Knights of Columbus. Yale's research-generated expertise is in great demand on all continents, in both developed and developing countries, and probably doesn't come as much of a surprise. But the K of C? What on earth might that organization export? The answer is that the Knights, from its 23-story world headquarters on Church Street, operates one of the largest group insurance companies in the world, offering its service to each K of C chapter on the face of the globe.

This is a far cry from the days when New Haven sold firearms, carriages, and tobacco, a time some locals look back at with fondness as a period of vigor and growth. Do they really have a point? For those inclined to nostalgia, perhaps, but hardly anyone else. Is the processing of insurance claims inferior work to picking tobacco or making rifles? Professor Reynolds clearly would answer no. He observes that new firms in the producer services offer more of the better, high-skill kinds of jobs than do the old manufacturing and agricultural sectors.

Better new jobs are coming to dominate many local economies. A study of the Seattle metropolitan area,[1] for example, found: "In 1984 the number of jobs resulting from these exported services was larger than the number of export-tied manufacturing jobs in the central Puget Sound region. It would seem that the growth of our regional economy is being fueled more by the export of services than by goods."

Is this a bad thing? No, it's just different. We must come to understand and accept the differences and appreciate their implications for our position in interregional and world trade. We have to get used to the fact that workers who turn out goods are being replaced by workers who deal with services, that to struggle to preserve the former at the expense of the latter is akin to favoring the countryside over the factory in the early 19th century and will serve us poorly as an economy in an increasingly competitive world environment.

For what is happening in Seattle is happening throughout the developed world. Even in the sluggish economy of the United Kingdom, services are growing and manufacturing is on the decline. That country's Occupations Study Group (OSG) released

[1] Beyers, Alvine, and Johnson, *The Service Economy: Export of Services in the Central Puget Sound Region* (Seattle: Central Puget Sound Economic Development District, 1985), p. vi.

a report on June 16, 1986, forecasting a net loss of 125,000 jobs in the next four years. According to the OSG, manufacturing and agriculture will lose 665,000 jobs—while there will be an increase of 540,000 jobs in service industries, especially distribution, finance, and business information.

Our farming sector has been losing jobs for generations as productivity increases, and the same is now happening in manufacturing. We can even see it in such old industries as steel and railroads. Generally speaking, the American steel industry is in decline. The companies produced 117 million tons in 1975; ten years later the figure came to 92 million tons, a falloff of 27 percent. But in that same period, steel industry employment fell to 700,000 from 1.4 million, or by half. The railroads present a yet more striking example of job losses. In 1982 the Union Pacific had 52,000 workers, and at the end of 1985, 37,600, a reduction accomplished through early retirements and with the cooperation of the unions. Union Pacific's goal is to be down to 30,000 by 1989. And all the while the railroad has been handling a larger volume of traffic.

Productivity is rising as a result of the application of brainpower to old but reviving businesses. Jobs are lost in one area, while more of them are created in others. Companies in trouble—with declining revenues—slashed employment to the bone, as in the 1980s high productivity became a shibboleth in the face of the

FIGURE 3-5. REVENUES AND EMPLOYMENT CHANGES FOR SELECTED FIRMS WITH DECLINING REVENUES, 1981–1985 *(Figures in millions of dollars)*

	REVENUES		ANNUAL PERCENTAGE CHANGE IN EMPLOYMENT
COMPANY	*1981*	*1985*	(1981–1985)
American Can	4,836	2,855	−14
Armco	6,906	3,733	−12
Caterpillar	9,154	6,725	−9
Celanese	3,752	3,046	−10
Colgate-Palmolive	5,216	4,524	−3
Deere	5,447	4,061	−9
Dow Chemical	11,873	11,537	−5
Exxon	114,989	86,673	−5
Firestone	4,361	3,836	−6
Halliburton	8,508	4,779	−12
Hughes Tool	1,759	1,261	−10
Mobil	68,500	55,960	−5
Polaroid	1,420	1,295	−6

SOURCE: *Business Week,* June 23, 1986, pp. 136–54; *Moody's Handbook of Common Stocks,* Summer 1986.

FIGURE 3-6. REVENUES AND EMPLOYMENT CHANGES FOR SELECTED FIRMS WITH INCREASING REVENUES, 1981–1985 *(Figures in millions of dollars)*

| | REVENUES | | ANNUAL CHANGE IN EMPLOYMENT |
COMPANY	*1981*	*1985*	*(1981–1985)*
Boeing	9,788	13,636	−2
Borden	4,415	4,716	−2
Control Data	3,101	3,680	−6
Corning Glass	1,598	1,690	−6
Du Pont	22,810	29,483	−4
Ford	38,247	52,774	−3
GTE	11,026	15,732	−2
Goodyear	9,153	9,586	−1
Johnson & Johnson	5,399	6,421	−1
Lilly (Eli)	2,773	3,271	−1
NCR	3,433	4,317	−1
Pfizer	3,250	4,125	−2
RCA	8,005	8,972	−6
Texas Instruments	4,206	4,924	−1
Westinghouse	9,367	10,700	−5
Weyerhaeuser	4,501	5,206	−5

SOURCE: *Business Week,* June 23, 1986, pp. 136–54; *Moody's Handbook of Common Stocks,* Summer 1986.

Japanese, Korean, and other challenges. Indeed, many firms with increased revenues cut their employment. In Figure 3–5 can be seen the percentage of employment decline for representative large companies (all with revenues of over $1 billion). Note that the annual declines in employment are for each year of five.

Cutbacks in the face of declining revenues are understandable, but many large firms are doing so as their revenues increase, as may be seen in Figure 3–6. Some represent special cases, but there are enough of them to indicate that even here the drive to extract the last bit of productivity out of each worker is succeeding.

Now remember that in the face of the drive for productivity, the American economy has created over 9 million new jobs in the 1980s so far—more are coming. We are winning the economic war on the jobs front, though you wouldn't think this was so from reading the dire warnings on the front pages.

TRADE WARS

In his seminal *The Rise of the Trading State,* Richard Rosecrance notes that there are two kinds of conflict, economic and political-military. Some might argue that the United States is fighting an economic war against the Japanese and other rapidly developing economies and a military-political one against the U.S.S.R. The Japanese aren't in a political-military contest with us, and no struggle exists on the economic level between Washington and Moscow. In effect, the United States is fighting on two fronts—our adversaries each on one.

For people like Rosecrance, world trade is a metaphor for world war. They view our trade contests as the true battleground for the next generation. The winners will be the great powers of the 21st century, if not territorially then economically. All well and good, but at the same time the United States must stand prepared to meet the challenge of a *real* war. How can we maintain a strong defense without strong basic industries?

This is a difficult question to answer without much greater knowledge of our defense posture than most civilians possess. However, a superficial look at recent skirmishes and the general nature of our defense buildup would suggest that the next major war—should one come—would be fought quite differently than World War II. It is much more likely to be a contest of brainpower than massive quantities of steel and TNT. We do not need thousands of aircraft to destroy our enemies and protect ourselves; we can do it with sophisticated missiles and defense shields in space and on the ground. Very little will depend upon our abilities to produce huge quantities of boots and K-rations. During World War II America became the arsenal of democracy, the muscle for which were defense plants and installations throughout the nation. We are still the arsenal of democracy, but its sinews are now to be found in research laboratories. Rosie the Riveter has been replaced by Professor Rose Riveter, Ph.D. in astrophysics, working on a government grant at MIT, Stanford, or some other research-oriented institution.

Of course, this is a vast generalization that can't be pushed too far. Clearly those missiles and defense shields are created of metal and contain explosives; we can't simply think ourselves into military security. And we do need significant quantities of strategic materials—special chemicals, rare metals, and the like. But nothing in our present transformation prohibits stockpiling such material. And if worse comes to worst, we are still one of the world's largest suppliers of conventional military gear. So it is not that we do or should do less defense production but rather that it has not grown as rapidly as other parts of the economy. Perhaps we are less capable today of refighting World War II than we were in 1941, but what of it? There is no chance of 1941 returning. Likewise, our economy is less capable today of fighting the trade battles of the 1920s, 1930s, 1940s, and even the 1950s, which were almost completely based upon commodities and agricultural goods. But this is not as great a problem as might appear, since our economy, like our military, has been altered to meet the demands of the new technologies and markets.

The old cliché that the generals are always refighting the conflicts of the past is true not only for the military battlefield but for the economic one as well.

WILL INTELLIGENCE REPLACE INTELLIGENCE?

Perhaps the greatest—and most subtle—threat to job creation comes not from competitors in the world market but from our own internal technological development. We are now working on a series of machines that have the capability of "thinking" in limited but perhaps significant ways. This is not a new development. The thermostat, a 19th century invention, was a thinking machine; you told it when to turn the heat on or off and it then proceeded to do so. Early tabulating machines were programmed in the same way, almost like a dog trained to fetch a bone on command. Now there are many "paperwork automators"—computer software to perform accounting tasks, arrange spreadsheets and meet payrolls; process large amounts of bank transactions, insurance claims, and stock sales.

The next generation, the so-called expert systems, is just beginning to emerge. These go beyond simply automating existing manual functions; in some specialized fields, systems can actually make some of the decisions usually associated with human thought. An expert system in Pittsburgh does internal medical diagnosis in a way to rival human physicians. A California-based system analyzes certain chemical compounds as well as can most chemists. Expert systems have become quite good at playing chess; there is a standing prize for the first chess system that becomes a world grand master, an event that probably will occur in the early 1990s. There is a system about to be introduced that can generate business letters with no intermediaries involved. Already novels have been written by computer. They aren't especially good and, as might have been expected, run according to formulas, but they are novels.

This first generation of expert systems is emerging from a new high-innovation industry most commonly known as artificial intelligence. Today's devices and software doubtless will seem extremely primitive by the early 21st century, but they are a beginning. All the efforts going into the fifth-generation computer, and the ones that will follow inexorably, are aimed at creating increasingly generalized intelligence—that is, the ability to understand the spoken word, to see the surrounding world clearly, and, most important, to be able to learn and generalize about specific problems and come up with conclusions.

Machines with these abilities clearly will alter the need for labor in the economy. Initially they will affect the more mundane jobs; the immediate threat is to clerical workers. As they become more powerful, they will reach higher and higher up the corporate ladder. We already hear rumblings about threats to middle management whose primary function—assembling and interpreting information for upper management—is being assumed by database management systems and spreadsheets.

The path of such innovation seems fairly well blazed. In 1986, for example, we were involved in a study of several large Connecticut-based insurance firms. This group had been a major source of employment growth in the 1960s and 1970s, drawing in clerical help sometimes from beyond the state and prompting the founding of nearby community colleges to train the local population to meet its needs. Today, however, the industry is projecting stable or declining employment for the next 15 years. We read of layoffs in the brokerage industry and among large accounting firms for the same reason. They are, we have been told, "rationalizing" their operations. This may be another way of saying they are replacing human workers with electronic ones. In 1984, for the first time, the number of women performing clerical tasks in all companies actually declined in absolute terms, while the number going into data processing and computer programming increased by 24.3 percent.

Simply stated, we can accomplish more in the services area with machines than with human beings and do it faster and with more accuracy. And this is just the beginning. The artificial intelligence industry is barely off the ground. For a while there may be a net gain in jobs, but as we develop additional machines, job losses will appear. We then will face a genuine labor surplus. In the 19th and 20th centuries, we replaced many physical operations with machines; in the early 21st century, machines will replace more and more of our minds. In effect, we are running out of parts of the body to replace. The challenge to create meaningful work, as we think of it, will be enormous and tax our imagination—and perhaps those of some of the machines we create for the tasks.

Fortunately, the challenge will emerge over several decades, giving us time to adjust. There are several options which, if taken, will mitigate the stresses of change—shorter work weeks, earlier retirement, job-sharing, and probably a redefinition of work itself. We will place more emphasis on people helping people (health care); on leisure time (travel, lodging, recreation); on eating and drinking (restaurants and bars); and on basic social services (religion, teaching, counseling, day care, household services). As will be seen later, health care and eating and drinking places already have become the fastest-growing source of employment in the country. Tourism, if we could ever measure it accurately, is projected to become one of our largest industries by the turn of the century.

If we feel threatened by taking in each other's wash today, that threat will seem much greater 30 years from now. But during that time we will adjust, change, mold, refashion, relearn, and reformulate more than ever before.

The greatest threat to our economic future comes not from our competitors in world markets or potential battlefields but from within. The challenge of the future will be to create new services—and products too—to meet the needs of future customers. This challenge will not go away. Rather, it will intensify. Brainpower, always an area in which Americans have performed well, will become increasingly important. So we should ask ourselves why this was and is so. Are we going through something no one else is experiencing, or are we part of a global change over which we have little influence? These are significant issues, because the answers will say a great deal about our competitive position in world markets in the years ahead. If we are special, we may do quite well exporting what we are particularly good at. If we are not, then our years of comparative advantage may be limited. It is to these issues that we now turn.

CHAPTER 4

Are We Special?

America is a nation of immigrants, but this does not mean we are a cross section of Europe and Africa—and, increasingly, Latin America and the Orient. Rather, this country has always attracted malcontents, who chafed at feudal restrictions in the 18th century and the lack of economic and religious freedom and opportunity in their old countries in the 19th and 20th centuries. Wariness regarding governmental restrictions on these freedoms and opportunities could be seen in colonial unwillingness to follow British imperial policy, which led to the Revolution. In the Constitution are enumerated the powers of government, the understanding being that none others could be assumed. When asked to support a bill of rights, George Washington appeared puzzled, for he had assumed that all rights not specifically enumerated as being granted to the government remained with the people.

To this was wedded a pragmatic streak historian Frederick Jackson Turner attributed to the frontier experience, where theory was thrown to the winds and practicality was all that counted. Such astute European observers as Hector St. John de Crèvecoeur and Alexis de Tocqueville noted the American impatience with abstractions and delight in problem solving. "If it ain't broke, don't fix it," strikes a responsive chord; as does, "If it is broke, find some way to fix it." Americans seem to feel the shortest distance between two points is a straight line, and that all else is embellishment.

Many Americans tend to believe that government has become a pervasive influence in their lives and that measures should be taken to reverse the trend. The signs are all around, from the deregulation campaign to President Reagan's popularity to fears the computer will hopelessly destroy our privacy. Yet the American

91

economy is far freer than that of any in the developed world. Restrictions to enterprise are relatively few, and such has been the case throughout American history.

It is this generalized dislike of authority coupled with pragmatism and informed materialism that provided the fertile seedbed for entrepreneurial enterprise throughout American history. This isn't to say there weren't other threads in the design, some of them contradicting the dominant values and on occasion rising to cancel them out. As has often been observed, we are the youngest nation in the Western world—with its oldest written constitution. We are wary regarding alterations in the social and economic fabric but ever willing to experiment within its bounds.

It is because of this that, on the whole, America is adjusting better to the postindustrial dispensation than any other nation. Perhaps this is one of the reasons why from 1974 to 1984 the American economy created 18 million jobs on balance, an increase of around 20 percent, while in the same period the Common Market nations actually lost 3 million jobs. It's not that Europe can afford to lose jobs due to a stable population; Europe had its baby-boomers, too, and they flooded the job market in the same decade. Rather, its labor force was expanding when the job base was shrinking. Four million more Europeans entered the labor force than left it in this period.

During 1986, the American unemployment rate hovered over 7 percent, which as many Administration critics observed was historically high for a nonrecessionary period. Critics note that from 1965 through 1969, unemployment averaged 3.8 percent with inflation at 3.4 percent, while in the 1981–1985 period unemployment averaged 8.3 percent and inflation, 7.8 percent. The nature of American unemployment will be discussed later, but here it might be noted that it makes as little sense to compare unemployment rates over time as it does to compare cars, airplanes, or any other product that is changing. The labor force today is quite different from what it had been a generation ago. More than half of adult American females work today; in 1967 the figure was under 40 percent, and in 1947 below 30 percent. The rise of two-income families means that the loss of a job by one is a problem, but not the disaster it had been when the father worked and "the woman's place was in the home"—while husbands boasted, "No wife of *mine* is going to work!"

92

The European Malaise

Even if one concedes the American unemployment rate to be a problem, what might one conclude from the European rates—in the double digits in Belgium (13 percent), France (10 percent), the Netherlands (15 percent), Italy (13 percent), Spain (19 percent), and the United Kingdom (13 percent)? The German Federal Republic's rate is slightly under 10 percent, while Canada's a fraction over that figure. Sweden's unemployment rate of 2.3 percent is in line with that welfare state's historical experience. Of the major industrial countries only Japan, with under 3 percent, has a rate Americans might envy. But there are pressures in Japan—cultural, economic, and demographic—absent in the United States which enable that country to post such a low figure.

Much has been heard in recent years about the high unemployment rate among American youth, blacks especially, prompting critics to claim that we are raising a generation of undertrained young people who will not be able to find positions, owing in part, at least, to the loss of manufacturing jobs. Sure enough, 13 percent of the American labor force under the age of 25 was jobless in mid-1986, against 11.3 percent in 1979. No one can derive pleasure from the figures, but those who present them and let it go at that are not presenting the entire picture. The fact of the matter is that youth unemployment is a worldwide phenomenon, due to the combination of baby-boomers and technological transformations, and that the United States actually is doing *better* than most countries in providing jobs for young people. For example, in the United Kingdom youth unemployment jumped from 10.6 percent in 1979 to 21.7 percent in 1986. The figures for West Germany are 3.4 percent to 9.5 percent, and France went from 13.9 percent to 25.1 percent. Spain, currently heralded as one of the more rapidly growing countries in the European Common Market, had a youth unemployment rate of 22.3 percent in 1979; by 1986 it had gone to 44.1 percent.

One is reminded of the senior American military officer who in Congressional testimony painted a stark picture of American preparedness but then was obliged to concede that he wouldn't want to trade our defense capabilities with those of any country on earth. Likewise, with all of its problems, the American economy is performing better than those of most other countries.

Unemployment rates between countries are as difficult to compare as are those within a nation over time. Still, measured unemployment in Europe has climbed from 4 percent in 1974 to over 12 percent 10 years later. Those who claim this is not a major problem point out that many Europeans are supported by extensive social welfare programs (welfare, unemployment benefits, disability insurance, etc.) that are not duplicated to the same degree in the United States. Taking account of such matters, estimates of the effective "U.S. equivalent" unemployment rate in the Netherlands is about 25 percent, in Belgium approximately 30 percent, in the United Kingdom 17 percent, and so forth down the line. The subsidies required to support this level of unemployment are massive.

How might one explain this disparity between Western Europe and the United States? How does so large a job shortfall arise? Can it be the microeconomies of Europe function differently from those in the United States? One out of every four Dutch workers does not have a job, and while there has been some minor improvement, most have little prospects of obtaining one in the near future. This was where the United States was during the worst years of the Great Depression of the 1930s. Yet there is no sense of urgency in the Dutch society, such as what an equivalent macro rate would cause in the United States. Why is this so?

In our search for answers to these questions we conversed with several scholars who were engaged in the same probing. Professor Colin Gallagher of the University of Newcastle-on-Tyne was one of them. We developed other figures working in tandem with a Swedish consulting company, Consultus, and the Swedish Statistical Bureau. The Canadian government was most helpful in doing the same for that country. Armed with this input, we were able to come up with some intriguing comparisons of the four countries.

One of the more striking findings was that there are not great disparities between the economies in the matter of share of people working for different-sized firms. If anything, the American and Swedish large corporations account for a greater share of the labor force than do their British and Canadian counterparts. However, if we look at the portion of workers in firms with over 100 employees, we find a close similarity, ranging from 58.2 percent for Sweden to 50.9 percent for Canada. The statistics are presented in Figure 4-1.

The flows with these different systems are quite different. For one thing, the rates of change due to company startups and closure

FIGURE 4–1. DISTRIBUTION OF EMPLOYMENT BY ENTERPRISE
SIZE FOR THE UNITED STATES, CANADA, SWEDEN, AND THE
UNITED KINGDOM

SIZE OF FIRM	U.S. 1980	CANADA 1974	SWEDEN 1974	U.K. 1978
1–19	24.1%	26.7%	22.8%	21.2%
20–99	19.7	21.4	19.0	14.1
100–499	16.5	19.7	18.7	26.6
500+	39.7	31.2	39.5	28.0
	100	100	100	100

(Figure 4–2) vary sharply. The United States experiences far greater turbulence than the others. Of particular interest is the higher closure rate; despite all the talk about "corporate socialism" that was heard in the wake of the Chrysler bailout, the United States tolerates a much higher degree of failure than any other system we have studied in detail. Of course, it also produces a much higher rate of job creation. As has been noted, failure and job creation are not necessarily opposites but can be complementary parts of the same puzzle. The old adage 'Nothing ventured, nothing gained" appears quite appropriate in these economic systems.

The differences among the nations under review become more evident when we examine job creation by the size of the firm. When looking at these figures, bear in mind that the share of job creation by size of firm can fluctuate greatly from one period to another. Figure 4–3 indicates that for the United States the share attributable to the 1–19 group fluctuated from between 51 percent (in 1977–1981) and 88 percent (in 1981–1985). Unfortunately, statistics do not exist for the other countries' performance in different time periods, and we suspect they would show similar swings though not of the same magnitude. The data seem to indicate that Sweden relies almost entirely on larger enterprises for job creation,

FIGURE 4–2. RATES OF JOB CHANGE DUE TO STARTUP AND CLOSURE IN FOUR COUNTRIES

AVERAGE ANNUAL RATES	UNITED STATES (1981–1985)	CANADA (1974–1982)	SWEDEN (1974–1982)	UNITED KINGDOM (1971–1981)
Average Startup Rate	6.2%	5.0%	4.6%	2.4%
Average Closing Rate	6.0%	3.2%	2.4%	3.8%

FIGURE 4-3. NET EMPLOYMENT CHANGE BY SIZE OF ENTERPRISE FOR FOUR COUNTRIES

ENTERPRISE SIZE	UNITED STATES			CANADA 1974–82	SWEDEN 1974–82	UNITED KINGDOM 1971–81
	1969–76	1977–81	1981–85			
0–19	66%	51%	88%	55%	15%	+195%
20–99	16	18	27	9	−6	+84
100–499	5	10	−20	−3	−10	+3
500+	13	21	5	39	101	−183
	100	100	100	100	100	100

while the United Kingdom's net new jobs come almost exclusively from small firms, and Canada strikes a balance between the two.

Some of the variations can be attributed to the differing time periods studied (as the American figures illustrate so graphically). But we suspect that even more is due to the different national cultures and the forms of organization they engender. For example, in modern times Sweden has had tax policies that discourage small firms from organizing while at the same time benefiting the larger ones—there is far more industrial concentration in the private sector of socialist Sweden than in the capitalist United States. What seems clear is that the differences among economic systems are such that few "lessons" learned from one country's experiences can be applied without great modifications elsewhere. American companies attempting to apply Japanese production techniques are learning this to their frustration.

Much less data is available outside of Sweden, Canada, and the United Kingdom, but from occasional—often incomplete—studies, we may discern some patterns. A survey of German manufacturers with work forces of between 10 and 200 reveals that small firms in that country grew the fastest and that growth tailed off with size, the largest firms going negative. This same survey found the probability of growth between 1974 and 1980 was the greatest for the smallest firms and decreased with size, while the probability of contraction was lowest for small firms and rose with size.

Various French reports suggest much the same experience there as in Germany. A French researcher, Delattre, reported that between 1975 and 1983, small firms gained 50,000 jobs, medium-sized ones lost 150,000 jobs, and large firms lost 600,000, for a net loss of 700,000 jobs. Other French studies show more or less the same pattern. The Office of European Economic Cooperation, for example, reports that between 1974 and 1979, for a sample of 12,000 French firms with 20 or more employees in 1978, small firms (with 100 or fewer employees) grew by 2.5 percent, medium-sized firms (100–500) were stable, and large firms (over 500) fell by 1.2 percent.

It goes without saying that attempting to derive lessons from Iron Curtain countries would be futile, even if one considered government organizations as individual firms. In the first place, the data, if ever gathered and released, would be suspect, and in the second, categorization would have little similarity to Western countries. But most important, the social and economic systems are so different from those of the West as to make interpretation all but meaningless.

There is a report out of Poland, however, suggesting that entrepreneurship is alive in that country. Although the Poles do not appear to maintain files on histories of individual companies, they do note the emergence of smaller, private firms. Between 1981 and 1984, for example, employment in private small firms grew 135 percent while employment in smaller public firms fell by 4 percent.

It would be going too far to say that on the basis of this incomplete data we may conclude that the swing to smaller, more entrepreneurial activities exists in parts of Western Europe as well as the United States; the sketchy Polish statistics tell us very little about that country, not to say the rest of the Soviet bloc. Still, whatever evidence does exist points in that general direction.

CULTURAL CURRENTS

It has been said that economists use generalizations and macrostatistics as a drunk might a lamppost—more for support than illumination. We admit to being uncomfortable about making big generalizations about Europeans and Americans, yet it often is difficult to proceed without them. So consider the following, remembering all the while that the more sweeping the statement, the less precise the conclusions to be drawn from it.

The Europeans differ from the Americans in many respects, of course, but two interrelated variables in particular should be considered when comparing economies. Europeans tolerate much less turbulence and encourage much less entrepreneurship as a vehicle for replacing job losses. This does not mean that the Europeans, in the aggregate and on the whole, are less inventive or innovative than Americans. As noted earlier, Europeans have an inordinate share of Nobel Prizes awarded since World War II, while the United Kingdom, France, and Germany had good records in exporting technology. Some of the world's greatest research facilities are to be found in the three countries and elsewhere in Western Europe, and there are more computers per capita in Britain than in the United States. Why, then, don't they bring the fruits of their inventiveness to market more often?

There are some answers suggested by a superficial observation of the European economies, barriers that must frustrate would-be entrepreneurs. The tax structure of most European countries—Sweden's has already been mentioned—is very perverse, making it difficult to earn money on your own, and more to the point, keep it. Regulations there are much more onerous than in the United States, eliminating much of the flexibility that is bread and meat for entrepreneurs. Europeans face a host of rules governing their right to close down facilities, fire workers, relocate operations, reduce wages and benefits, and so forth. Venture capital is more difficult to locate. Finally, the great rebuilding surge that followed World War II has ended. The German "economic miracle," directed by Chancellor Konrad Adenauer and his finance minister, Ludwig Erhard, was based upon a freeing of regulations that unleashed that nation's entrepreneurial talents. The Germans "rebureaucratized" in the 1970s, and the miracle faded.

Underlying all of this is something far more important than taxes and regulation. The causes of both are entrenched attitudes and beliefs that are difficult for some Americans to understand, the implications of which tend to hold the Europeans back. There are deeply held attitudes toward entrepreneurship and failure that discourage Europeans from entering into entrepreneurial careers.

The Feudal Outlook

It may be difficult for Americans to fully accept the fact that entrepreneurship remains "low class" in Europe, though there are signs this is changing. Still, well-mannered and well-educated Europeans do not, as a rule, start and run small businesses. Very few graduates of Oxford or Cambridge would consider such a career path. Even most of those who attend the London School of Economics have government, academic, and big business ambitions, as do those who get through their continental counterparts of the English institutions.

This attitude was brought home to me by a conversation on an airplane flight with a British-born engineer. Over a rather drab dinner, I learned he was one of America's leading automation experts. When asked why he left the United Kingdom, he told me the story of his initial contact with his prospective in-laws in a London suburb. After the usual pleasantries, his fiancee's mother asked him what he did for a living. The engineer explained that he had been involved in starting two companies in the field of automation engineering—helping other firms to improve their efficiency. Imagine the reaction of most American mothers to such news. But the British lady looked a trifle distressed, exchanged embarrassed glances with her daughter, and muttered in a clearly disdainful sigh, "Oh dear!"

His career path clearly was unacceptable; she was hoping for a civil servant, a university don, a barrister, perhaps. The engineer then asked about his future father-in-law's occupation and was told proudly that he was a county surveyor, working in Her Majesty's Government. Now that is an entirely honorable post, but its American counterpart—a middle-level civil servant—certainly isn't deemed on par with a successful organizer and operator of two high-tech startups.

My acquaintance left Britain within a month of that conversation, wife in tow, and has not returned. He assured me a similar scene would have been played out in every West European nation.

The negative attitude toward business in general and entrepreneurship in particular is a vestigial remain of a feudalism that held Europe in its thrall until the 19th century and which still surfaces in economic and social activities. Herbert Hoover saw it as a young businessman in the late 19th century, when he was dazzled by London and British society in general but then noted that underneath it all was a dislike of what he deemed democratic egalitarianism. Others saw it before and later, to this day, and anecdotal evidence is easy to come by. Once, when in a London bus, I saw a middle-aged American women engaged in some kind of altercation with the ticket taker. "You are no gentleman!" she exclaimed, to which the puzzled busman murmured, "I never said I was." The Europeans are intrigued by American free-wheeling, just as Americans admire the pomp and ceremony of much they see in Europe. All of which is fine in things social and cultural. When it comes to business, however, the Americans' pragmatic approach is far more suitable than the hierarchical one so often present in Europe.

At the base of it all is the matter of equality, which means different things to Americans and Europeans. Building upon its feudal foundation of noblesse oblige, the Europeans have transformed the feudal contract, in which the serf pays allegiance and taxes to the noble in return for protection, into governmental guarantees that practically no one will go unfed, unhoused, and uncared for. It should have come as no surprise that the first comprehensive social insurance plan was engineered by German Chancellor Otto von Bismarck in the 1880s, no blazing reformer he, and that other European nations followed suit during the next half century and expanded the programs afterwards.

Likewise, some Americans complain that the federal government does not support the arts as do the Europeans. Of course it doesn't. Under feudal dispensations the monarch usually performs that role—composers like Mozart, Handel, Bach, and Beethoven were subsidized by generous aristocratic patrons. The absolute monarchs are gone, replaced by limited monarchs and republics, but the concept that the ruler supports the arts remains.

We have a different system: the marketplace. Tocqueville observed that America would never produce a great art but have a high *general* level of culture because of this. Yet jazz and rock made it without government subsidies, and the arts thrive in America as nowhere else on earth in our national marketplace.

These European programs must be funded, and the moneys derive from progressive taxes that hit hardest those with the highest income. Eighty-five percent brackets aren't all that uncommon, and in some countries they even go higher. In Sweden, for example, filmmaker Ingmar Bergman left the country because the taxes all but confiscated everything he made, and a female novelist later disclosed that the state had told her she had to pay more than 100 percent of her income. Sweden historically has had a low unemployment rate for two reasons: it is difficult for companies to fire workers, and the government provides assistance in finding new jobs for those who are laid off. Despite several highly innovative companies, Sweden is a laggard in the high-tech area.

Sweden's major products are steel, machinery, autos, ships, and lumber in its various forms. Most of these aren't doing well—at home, at least, for given the country's antibusiness climate, Swedes are encouraged to expand overseas. In the past decade, domestic manufacturing jobs fell from 1,000,000 to 800,000, while the number of workers employed by Swedish firms overseas rose from 200,000 to 400,000. On balance, Swedes lost 200,000 jobs that went to foreigners working for Swedish companies in their own countries. Indeed, it has got to the point where Swedish firms seeking highly qualified workers have had to conduct extensive recruitment overseas. Even here, however, they were frustrated by the country's archaic tax laws, which oblige guest workers to pay the onerous domestic levees once in the country for more than half a year. Saab-Scania hired several British aircraft designers who left one day short of six months for that reason.

As a result of tax policies and social welfare programs, extremes around the income and wealth mean are more uncommon in Europe than in the United States. It is seen in tax codes and on the streets. Europe has fewer wretched poor than America but fewer millionaires as a percentage of the population. Western Europe is the home for egalitarianism of this kind, which it goes without saying does have some appeal. It can be seen in little things that often illuminate a national character. For example, Swedes love the sea; in that country there is one boat for every three people. The careful observer of Swedish sailboats will note that all are about the same length—28 feet, give or take four feet. If asked, Swedes will explain the reason to curious foreigners. To own a larger boat would be "inappropriate," while to own a smaller one would be "unfair." A casual look at any American harbor will reveal a much greater disparity of boat sizes.

After listening to me speak of this at a convention, a labor leader sought me out with another tale regarding national differences. After a particularly hard negotiation a British union president turned to his management counterpart and, pointing to the Jaguar parked outside the office, said that he was working for the kind of society in which people like company presidents would drive Ford Cortinas. "When I heard this" said our labor leader, "I was struck with how different our attitudes are. Had the two men been Americans, the union leader would have gestured toward, say, a Cadillac, and say that he hoped for the day when workers would own cars like those of management."

The Meaning of Failure in Europe

It is difficult to accumulate wealth in a society wedded to the ideal of social and economic egalitarianism. This is hardly surprising, for that is the goal of egalitarianism, and from many standpoints it may seem fair and equitable. But there are prices to be paid: less private wealth means less private venture capital, which is overwhelmingly the major source for venture capital in the United States. The shortfall in private venture capital translates into a heavier reliance on institutional capital (e.g., banks, mutual funds, etc.). Institutional capital is notorious for its aversion to risk. One of the consequences of a social welfare system is conservative control of capital, hardly a situation to encourage entrepreneurship. In these societies there are few starry-eyed dreamers plunking down their life's savings to support someone else's vision of an enterprise. There are only steely-eyed bankers worrying about their fiduciary responsibilities and worse, the Tuesday afternoon loan committee meeting in which bad loans (and their makers) are criticized—and, perhaps, passed over when promotions come around. So we have the familiar colloquy: "What collateral do you have to offer, Mr. Jones," asks the loan office. To which, Jones replies, "If I had collateral, I wouldn't need a loan."

There are other reasons discouraging entrepreneurship in Europe: a major one is fear of failure. Failure is catastrophic. To fail there is to acquire a burden of shame and guilt that may be handed down to the next generation. You are branded as somehow inferior for having tried and failed. Social and economic ostracism is almost automatic. Having failed, you are very unlikely to ever receive future financial backing. In some European countries, there is a good chance your personal assets will be attached if your firm goes under.

Not so in America, where failure ever has been taken more lightly. In the 19th century, foreigners were amazed at how blithely American businessmen declared bankruptcy, moved on, opened a new enterprise, and then repeated the experience. This isn't to say that failure is admired or respected but that there is a generalized tendency to respect people who "give it their best shot," fail, and then try again. It has become part of the American mythology— the prizefighter who comes off the canvas to deliver a knockout blow has been a national icon from the days of Jimmy Cagney to Sylvester Stallone.

Remember Carolyn See? We met her earlier, the divorcée who

took the advice of a tax consultant and went off on her own. In her article,* she wrote of the dangers involved in so doing. "Of course the other side of striking out on your own is striking out, going for it three times with all you've got; missing, making a total fool of yourself, and slinking back to the dugout, where your teammates won't speak to you." She then goes on to write of the "tiny spark of altruism in the American patriarchy" that drives people like her on. What if all fails? She dreams of living in a big house on the beach, "bags of seashells, all for sale, and succulents in little pots, freelance editing by appointment, dump trucks for rent by the hour."

To paraphrase Shakespeare, in American business, to try and fail is deemed better than not to have tried at all.

It is thus not surprising to find that failure rates in Europe are substantially lower than in the United States. It also is not difficult to understand why so few entrepreneurs try to make it on their own. You get to keep relatively little if you organize a new venture and succeed, and if you fail, the stigma follows you for life. In contrast, a job with a large firm provides status, respect, position, generally pays well, and extends the lure of life-long security. In Sweden, with an industrial concentration far higher than the United States, young university graduates look to the giants for employment rather than considering starting out on their own. Entrepreneurial small companies are scarce there, where $4.3 billion L. M. Ericsson alone hires fully one-third of the nation's 1,500 graduating electrical and electronics engineers. In Holland, a similar situation prevails. It is no wonder that only 1.7 percent of the graduates of Dutch universities go to work for smaller businesses. The deck is stacked very strongly against entrepreneurs in both countries.

The high taxes and oppressive regulations and lack of venture capital in Europe are not a "mistake" that can easily be corrected by changing laws but rather the residue of centuries of history. They are symptoms of a deeply held (and thoroughly vested) set of beliefs about how the world ought to be that derives more from the historic experience of feudalism than the ideologies of socialism. Indeed, the yearning of socialists for governmental solutions to problems appeals to many Europeans for the very reason that they feel more comfortable with feudalism than freedom.

To change the conditions would be to strike at the heart of the social order. In particular, it would involve eliminating many of

* The *New York Times,* June 26, 1986, p. C2.

the social benefits upon which so many Europeans have become dependent and which they feel are an essential part of the humane treatment of people. For them to change their systems would be a revolutionary, not evolutionary, move. For them, it would be introducing social injustice so that a relatively few people could become wealthy.

All of this is reflected in labor costs, which have continued to rise. Social welfare was a fraction over 16 percent of Europe's total labor bill in 1968; now it is over 25 percent. Largely because of this and of union regulations that make efficiency difficult, Europe's labor costs have risen by almost 50 percent since 1970 (after adjusting for inflation) against only 10 percent for the United States. Forced to compete in a world market, this has placed a squeeze on profits, leaving little for research, development, and investment. And what surplus remained often was sent to the United States for investment. While Americans in recent years have been troubled that their country has become a net debtor for the first time since World War I, the Europeans realize that one reason for this is the flow of investment capital from their countries to the United States.

The squeeze on profits and high labor costs have encouraged companies to seek methods of laying off unskilled and semiskilled workers who would be difficult to fire. The way to go has been to replace workers with machines. As Europe's baby-boomers looked for jobs, they found that many they had been counting on were being performed by machines. On the one hand government raised minimum wages, while on the other, through investment tax credits, they encouraged this kind of worker replacement. The net result has been predictable: unemployment grows and entrepreneurship stagnates.

Can it change? The equity issues apart, there are far more voters who benefit from social welfare than there are potential entrepreneurs who might gain by ditching the system. The odds of things changing are not very good.

Only a crisis, precipitated by a lack of money to support the social welfare system or the crushing weight of unemployment are likely to lead to major alterations. The latter is a problem, and far more troublesome in the microeconomy than the macro numbers might indicate. True enough, Europe is suffering from much worse unemployment than the United States. But at the same time, all the West European countries are experiencing severe labor shortages, brought about by an educational system that makes the often-criticized American one seem a paragon of efficiency in meeting the needs of the economy. Go into the streets of Liverpool and Manchester and you will see knots of semiliterate young men and women, who are not only unemployed but unemployable. The British have a word for them—"The Yob Generation"—and their numbers are growing due to the breakdown of education in that country. Their counterparts can be found on the continent as well.

In the 19th century, while universal education was practiced in the United States and the public university system was growing here, Europe clung to rigid class education—classics for the nobility and gentry, practically nothing for everyone else. The result was economic rule by individuals who often were unqualified by intelligence, ability, and/or training, while large numbers of able but poor individuals were consigned to the economic scrapheap. In comparison, the admittedly flawed American system seemed a clear meritocracy. And this continued in the first half of the 20th century. Opportunities broadened in the United States, while in most European countries the struggle to reform didn't get very far. Changes began after World War II, but in some countries it may have been too late; in the rest, probably too little. "The problem of high unemployment in Europe is mostly a problem of education," said Professor Paul van Rompay at Belgium's Catholic University of Louvain, and he is echoed by counterparts elsewhere in Europe.

So even those entrepreneurial, high-tech firms that do exist alongside the industrial giants have trouble locating the skilled labor needed in an increasingly complex technological world. As Germany sent home many of its guest workers and politicians feared creeping unemployment, advertisements for highly trained machinists went unanswered. "We need hundreds of skilled workers for making machine tools, but we can't find a single man," said Thyssen Steel's Chairman Dieter Spethmann, while CEO Klaus Luft of Nixdorf Computer complained, "Our biggest constraint is getting people. It's not the potential of the market, it's not financing the growth. It's people." In 1986 the European Commission reported that "skilled workers, especially technicians and technologists, are in short supply" in one out of every five of the 8,000 companies it regularly polled, at a time when total unemployment remained extraordinarily high.

By then it appeared that some reduction in unemployment was being experienced, made possible by the adoption of harsh programs in the United Kingdom and on the continent. But some of this may be due to the maturing of the baby-boomers and the coming of a smaller cohort of young workers to the labor force. The average increase in the European labor force from 1980–1985 was 1 million; in the second half of the decade it will drop to an average of 692,000, and to 365,000 for the 1990–1995 period. Europe may be saved from higher macro unemployment by demography, but this won't change the micro picture. Indeed, it could get worse.

Thus entrepreneurship is unlikely to flourish in Europe in the near future. In our terms, the Europeans have opted for maximum micro stability—job security, firm security, income security—and are willing to collectively lower their standards of living if the resulting macro instability demands it.

POSSIBILITIES ELSEWHERE

We have compared job creation in Western Europe and the United States because the countries there represent a set of economies most like our own. True enough, in recent years Americans looking for economic miracles have made the trek to Japan, and now some are wending their ways to Korea as well. They will find the transplantation of Asian techniques to the United States presents many difficulties due to differences in culture. Nor can the reasons for American successes in job creation be adapted easily in economies so different from our own. We have discovered great differences between the United States and Europe in entrepreneurship; those between the United States and the developing countries are even greater. At the same time, however, there is some evidence that the United States shares some attributes with them.

Detailed micro data are much more difficult to come by for nations outside of Western Europe. We do have some statistics from the Japanese government (see Figure 4–4) that suggest an increasingly important role for small and medium-sized enterprises in that country—particularly in manufacturing during the 1970s—and dependence upon subcontractors has increased dramatically. Some students of the Japanese claim they have managed to achieve both job and income security with risk and innovation. Not really. From what we can gather from the Japanese statistics, their system is very much like ours—for good reason, since the Japanese deliberately followed the American pattern during the

FIGURE 4-4. EMPLOYMENT GROWTH IN JAPANESE ENTERPRISES OF VARIOUS SIZES FOR THREE DIFFERENT POINTS IN TIME

GROWTH IN LARGER ENTERPRISES DURING:			
	1959–1965	1965–1971	1971–1977
Construction	125	182	37
Manufacturing	1,754	908	−646
Trade and Banking, Insurance and Real Estate	255	1,063	478
Services	328	511	389
Total	2,462	2,664	258

GROWTH IN SMALL AND MEDIUM-SIZED ENTERPRISES DURING:			
	1959–1965	1965–1971	1971–1977
Construction	671	1,173	664
Manufacturing	1,338	848	334
Trade and Banking, Insurance and Real Estate	490	820	1,210
Services	397	624	670
Total	2,896	3,465	2,878

SHARE DUE TO SMALL- AND MEDIUM-SIZED ENTERPRISES DURING:			
	1959–1965	1965–1971	1971–1977
Construction	84.3	86.6	94.7
Manufacturing	43.3	48.3	100.0
Trade and Banking, Insurance and Real Estate	65.8	43.5	71.7
Services	54.8	55.0	63.3
Total	54.1	56.5	91.8

NOTE: Small- and medium-sized enterprises are defined as those with 300 or fewer workers in construction and manufacturing and 100 or fewer elsewhere. The unit of measure is thousands of employees.

post–World War II reconstruction period. Great wage disparities exist, and workers are far more responsible for their own social welfare than are their European counterparts. Most job growth there takes place in small firms that offer essentially no job security and minimal benefits.

The major difference between the United States and Japan is the source of our innovation. We develop most of our own ideas. The Japanese, historically, have imported them and licensed patents, after which they improve upon versions already on the market. The Japanese know this is a flaw and are working hard to change the pattern. We send our business people and engineers to Japan to learn the secrets of production, and they send theirs to the

United States to uncover the secrets of entrepreneurship. Each is convinced it is weak in the face of the tremendous challenge posed by the other.

Some fascinating statistics have emerged recently from the People's Republic of China. In its rural areas, China has started to rely more heavily upon private enterprises for its future development. The phenomenon, which started in the south and now is fanning out gradually to the rest of the country, could be one of the most important developments of the 20th century. Can it be that China is preparing to abandon communism or alter it in such a way as to transform it into a form of free enterprise? The answer could have monumental repercussions. There is a joke which has it that if Libya really went communist the country would run out of sand in five years, and another that the greatest threat to the United States would be China going capitalist, because given that country's entrepreneurial talents—the so-called overseas Chinese dominate Southeast Asian business—it would become the dominant economic power of the next century.

Things seem to have started, and the sons and daughters of those Americans who are now studying Japanese business may one day in the early 21st century explore the ins and outs of the Chinese miracle.

There certainly are signs of one. Xu Ji, a member of the board of directors of the China Enterprise Management Association, observed that since 1979 major advances have been made in rural free enterprise. The fact that he and other bureaucrats are talking it up is a strong indication that this is the direction China will take. According to the 1983 statistics, at the end of that year there were 1,346,000 rural enterprises employing 32,350,000 people. The gross output value of rural small business increased from $25.9 billion in 1979 to $60.7 billion in 1983, the equivalent of the total Chinese production in 1953 and a 1.3-fold increase over a period of five years. The average annual growth rate of rural small business was 18.6 percent. The proportion of rural small business in the total product of society increased from 7.6 percent in 1978 to 12.1 percent in 1983. Xu Ji went on to say that the time will soon be at hand for the focus to shift from rural free enterprise to its urban equivalent.

A few years ago the CEO of a major American hotel chain revealed that he had broken off negotiations with the Chinese regarding the opening of a new tourist hotel in Shanghai. When asked why, the American ticked off a list of what he deemed unreasonable demands, noting that the Chinese representative seemed to have only the barest idea of how business operated. "How can you talk a $100 million dollar deal with a person whose only possession is a bicycle?" he asked. Last year the company decided to go ahead with the project on terms acceptable to both sides. Something happened in between the two episodes. Only a straw in the wind, to be sure, but the stirrings on the mainland are unmistakable.

China still has to be classified as a "developing country," however. Most of the rest of that world offers fewer statistics, and generalizations are dangerous and difficult to make. In 1984, for example, a Dutch group interviewed over 4,000 leaders of small businesses in eleven different countries, five of them in the developing countries, six in the more developed ones. Figure 4–5 summarizes the answers to some of the more interesting questions:

1. Did you found the firm, did you buy it, or did you inherit it?
2. What led you to organize this firm at the time you did?

FIGURE 4–5. FACTORS AFFECTING ENTREPRENEURIAL ACTIVITY IN TEN NATIONS

NATION	PERCENT THAT INHERITED THEIR COMPANY	PERCENT THAT STARTED FIRM BECAUSE FIRED	PERCENT INVESTING IN OFFICE MACHINES AND COMPUTERS IN LAST 3 YEARS	PERCENT THAT WANT TO INCREASE EMPLOYMENT IN FUTURE
Kenya	4.4	3.5	10.3	90.0
Cameroon	2.2	2.0	9.2	81.9
Columbia	7.8	2.1	19.7	44.4
Brazil	5.7	2.3	36.0	79.8
Indonesia	12.1	1.8	2.8	89.7
Japan	19.2	3.8	13.9	55.0
USA	6.8	14.8	47.5	67.1
Canada	5.0	5.3	20.8	68.1
United Kingdom	11.6	12.5	26.6	70.6
W. Germany	21.6	11.0	48.0	46.6
Netherlands	10.5	14.8	26.4	45.2
Total	9.7	6.6	23.8	67.3
Averages:				
Third World Nations	6.4	2.3	15.6	77.1
United States	6.8	14.8	47.5	67.1
Other Developed Nations	18.4	9.5	27.1	57.1

3. Have you invested in electronic office machines and/or data-processing machines in the last three years?
4. Looking at employment in your firm, would you like your business to grow, stay about the same size, or is it already too large?

While the individual country samples are too small to make truly meaningful comparisons, some general patterns seem to exist. Such business people in the developing countries:

1. Are much less likely to inherit their own business, probably because there are so few to be passed on. For the most part, they have to start from scratch.
2. Are much less likely to start out of desperation and more likely to start for positive reasons. Lack of capital is perhaps a major reason for this.
3. Are less likely to be investing in technology than their developed counterparts, because labor there is so cheap as to enjoy a large comparative advantage over capital investments.
4. Are generally more likely to want their firms to grow. They see more opportunity in their economies than do their counterparts in the more crowded developed ones.

THE AMERICAN DIFFERENCE

The business people in developing countries share two attributes with their American counterparts: both rely little upon inheritance, and the former are even greater believers in their abilities to expand, but of course for different reasons.

American small business owners and managers are far more rough and tumble than those of any other nation and suffer failure better than them as well. We tend to be more advanced when it comes to the development and application of technology. We are the sophisticated cowboys of the world.

In general, one might think of nations in two dimensions: the degree of entrepreneurship and the extent to which entrepreneurship is based on self-generated innovation and technology or is based on imported technology. There are always exceptions and special cases, but Figure 4–6 offers a rough generalization of how some nations fall into this innovation–entrepreneurship rubric. We are unique because we are strong in both the creation of new ideas and the support (social as well as economic) we offer to those who wish to bring these ideas to market.

Does this mean we are "better" than the Europeans and Japa-

FIGURE 4–6. RELATIVE NATIONAL PROPENSITIES FOR NATIONS TO INNO-
VATE AND ENCOURAGE ENTREPRENEURSHIP.

		Source of Innovation	
		Imported	Self-Generated
Degree of Entrepreneurship	Low	China	Most of Europe
	High	Japan Italy South Korea Singapore Hong Kong	United States

nese? The answer calls for a value judgment. Our European allies look at our poverty—the ill-fed, ill-housed, the people without proper medical care—and say that in many basic respects we have failed. In their view, we are not using our wealth properly, and they have a point. Yet when Americans recognize a problem and set about to solve it, they often do so in innovative and ingenious ways. For example, rather than adopt universal medical care such as that utilized in Europe, we have patched together a combination of state and private programs—medical and hospital insurance, Medicare and Medicaid, and health maintenance organizations. The private sector today is doing more about health delivery programs than is government, working through once-small institutions that have become huge in the process. But the European critics continue to believe we have paid too high a price on the micro scale to achieve macro stability and growth. Americans might counter that without jobs and production, sooner or later there can be no macro stability.

The argument goes on indefinitely, with no resolution. It remains to be said that if job and income security are important, America may not be the ideal place to live. America offers most to those who crave opportunity and are willing to assume risks.

Where will our special role take us? Will the United States continue to be able to provide sufficient jobs to compensate for the turbulence and resulting micro insecurity the system implies? Or are we heading toward an impossible situation, in which we must run faster and faster simply to stand still only to have our own creations, manufactured by others, pull the rug out from under us? These are the questions we will address next.

CHAPTER 5

Where Does It Take Us?

A primary function of the kind of research we have been undertaking is to place the economy in time and space. If you were suffering from amnesia and lost, the first things you would want to know are your identity, where you are, and perhaps the date. Once these were known you might consider possible destinations, and only then would you start out. To head in one direction or another without such information would be obviously foolish.

No amount of research can tell you where you should head, however. That decision is based upon inclinations, interests, assets, and the like. So first comes knowledge.

For starters, ask yourself a big question: Is the United States stronger economically than most pessimists seem to assume? Our answer is an unqualified yes and is based upon evidence and analysis presented thus far with more to come. But how about questions of a different order: Should the United States stress manufacturing jobs over those in services, or vice versa? Should we worry more about preserving low-tech jobs than encouraging the high-tech segment? Should we aid the out-of-work assembly line workers in the Rust Belt or leave them to their own devices? The answers to such questions fall more in the realm of politics than economics. Often the economically sensible choice is rejected in place of the politically acceptable one. All we can do is offer the record and make suggestions, knowing that others, often from Washington, with agendas of their own will make the macro decisions.

At the local, micro level, though, economics more often than not takes precedence over politics. So if we are to respond in a useful way to the changes taking place on this level, we might start out by obtaining some idea of what the situation is and where existing trends are taking us, and then we will be in a position to pose questions and seek answers. Among the questions: How fast will the economy create jobs in the future? What kinds of jobs will they be? Which places will benefit the most from the ongoing dynamics of the American economic system, and which will come out losers?

Needless to say, we are not alone in being worried about the future; scores of groups are thinking about it. These include the U.S. Bureau of Labor Statistics, the National Planning Association, and several private firms that make projections for the economy as a whole and for specific industries and locations. While each of them has its own approach to estimating future job growth and shrinkage, all share one attribute: estimates are based upon historical trends in aggregate data. One way or another, all extrapolate trends, using snapshots of the state of the economy at different points in history. Is this the best way to go about making projections? Wouldn't it be better to start out with a study of the present internal dynamics of the situation? We think so, but almost all of the research groups opt for the extrapolation route, perhaps because they lack the means of measuring what we feel is really going on.

The difference in our approach is that we start out by assembling and then analyzing the micro empirical evidence. Then we go on to make generalizations and offer suggestions and recommendations. When presenting the material, however, it often is best to start out with those generalizations, which is what we will do here to give the reader an overview of the situation. After that, evidence to substantiate the generalizations will be presented. To return to the analogy we started with, we will tell you that we are headed for Los Angeles and then tell you why and how we plan to get there.

ELEMENTS OF GROWTH IN THE MICROWORLD

Begin with the observation that when the economy is advancing or declining steadily (as, for example, during most of the 1960s) extrapolating trends in aggregate data is well-nigh irresistible and often works out pretty well, mainly because the trends do not change. Problems arise during periods of transition when, almost by definition, the future will not be like the past. We appear to be in such a stage right now. Places that have boomed during the 1970s—like Houston, Texas, and Lafayette, La.—suddenly slowed down thanks to the bust in oil prices. Areas that seemed destined for slow or no growth—like much of eastern Massachusetts—took off abruptly. Areas that once exported workers now sent scouts to nearby states seeking them. As might have been expected, political leaders in Texas and Louisiana blamed the economy for the malaise, while their counterparts in Massachusetts and elsewhere in New England claimed credit for personal sagacity and cleverness in turning the economy around. In any case, the changes could not have been predicted by those economists whose most important tool is extrapolation. It is difficult to imagine a trend-based system using data generated through 1982 that would have predicted that Massachusetts would outgrow Texas in absolute terms from 1982 through the end of 1985.

It seemed time for a fresh approach based on the micro dynamics of company behavior. As we pondered our micro data, we noted that a good deal of the variation in aggregate growth can be traced to variations in the way individual firms responded in various locales. In particular, we noticed that:

1. Every locale in the United States loses about the same percentage of its company and job base each year due to firm layoffs and closings.
2. Virtually all the variation in growth was attributable to variations in the rates at which new firms started and grew to replace the fixed losses.
3. There was a great deal of variation in these formation and growth rates.
4. There were definite patterns to the variations.

Recall that severe economic setbacks often sow the seeds for recovery. We saw how the Boeing layoffs in Seattle during the early 1970s, the NCR layoffs in Dayton in the mid-1970s, and of course, the problems Detroit faced in the late 1970s and early 1980s were preludes to surges in small business formation and entrepreneurship. There is a moral to this: when all else fails and you can't get help from the outside, you are obliged to do the sensible thing.

We noted too that some places were far more dependent for their growth upon the branch facilities of corporations headquartered elsewhere than were others. As a consequence, the "branch-dominated" areas experienced greater fluctuations in employment. Denver is an example. In good times, large corporations expand their branch facilities in regional centers such as Denver. But when bad times descend, the same corporations pull in their horns, contract or eliminate branch operations, and consolidate their facilities closer to home. For this reason branch cities rise and fall more than the economy as a whole.

We noticed that some places did not seem to encourage entrepreneurship under any circumstances—there simply was no local tradition to draw upon. As innovation and new firm formation have come to power economic growth, these locales seem to gradually lose ground. The reasons are many and often complex—low educational levels; strong control of the local economy and politics by a few wealthy families or dominant companies with stakes in the status quo; a remote location with few opportunities for interaction with those who have new ideas; the lack of higher educational facilities resulting in ambitious young people leaving the area, often never to return; a poor climate; and so forth. Whatever the reasons, however, the consequence is persistent lethargy and an inability and unwillingness to participate in growth taking place elsewhere. The existence of these enclaves illustrates the point made at the beginning of the chapter; namely, that before making suggestions for change it is important to know the inclinations and interests of the society. No amount of research can tell you where you *should* be headed. The Amish in Pennsylvania, to cite the best known and most obvious example, have different goals than do Manhattan Yuppies.

A general pattern emerges: it is possible to anticipate future job growth in a locale by knowing the extent and nature of the "reseeding" process taking place in the present. If the response to a setback is an entrepreneurial surge, recovery is likely during the next five to seven years. If no surge takes place, recovery is unlikely. If an area is lethargic in starting and nurturing young businesses, its ability to replace the inexorable losses is low and its future as a generator of jobs bleak. If the place is seeding or reseeding mostly with branches of companies headquartered elsewhere, its future is likely to be volatile—rising and falling more sharply than the economy as a whole. Whatever the situation, the principle remains the same: the future can be observed in the present if you look in the right places with sufficient attention to detail.

115

ANTICIPATING THE FUTURE

Proceeding along the lines of this "bottoms up" approach, we find the keys to anticipating the future are:

1. Separating firms in any area into specific categories so that alterations from one period to the next will be predictable
2. Defining locales in enough detail so that differences between them will be captured.

The Bureau of Labor Statistics has established a series of labor market areas. The BLS areas are mostly metropolitan concentrations, which present only part of the total picture. In order to complete it, we have added the rural component, and between them we cover the entire country. The net result is 239 areas defined in terms of counties. These are listed in "Definitions of 239 Forecast Areas," pages 207–234.

Grouping firms that share a common set of behavior characteristics is a more complex matter. We have noticed that different groups of firms behave in different ways. One of the more obvious distinctions is between large and small companies, and they certainly behave differently—General Motors operates on a set of principles unlike those governing the neighborhood delicatessen. We also recognize that entrepreneurial firms (as a group) behave differently from income substitutors. McDonald's and Burger King are entrepreneurial, always on the prowl for new items to lure customers; not so the independent hamburger stands. But let McDonald's come up with a different kind of sandwich or snack that makes a hit, and within weeks or months the independents will have their version.

Our problem is selecting a set of dimensions that separates firms into groups that are (1) big enough so that the law of large numbers will work for us, (2) small enough so that micro processes can be capitalized upon, and (3) sophisticated enough so that proper distinctions between different kinds of firms can be made.

After a great deal of experimentation, we concluded that the best measures to distinguish firms from one another in terms of their job-creating abilities are (1) the size of the individual establishment, (2) the size of the enterprise to which the establishment belongs, (3) the age of the establishment, (4) ownership of the

116

establishment, and (5) the industry to which the establishment belongs. We then came up with the following breakdowns:

Size of Establishment
1. 0–4 employees
2. 5–19 employees
3. 20–99 employees
4. 100–499 employees
5. 500+ employees

Size of Enterprise
1. 0–99 employees
2. 100+ employees

Type of Establishment
1. Young, Single Unit or Headquarters
2. Old, Single Unit or Headquarters
3. Subsidiary or Branch of Multi-Unit, Regardless of Age

Industry of Establishment
1. Agriculture and Mining
2. Construction
3. Manufacturing Other Than High Tech
4. High Tech Manufacturing
5. Transportation, Communications, and Public Utilities
6. Wholesale Trade
7. Retailing (Except Eating and Drinking Places)
8. Eating and Drinking Places
9. Finance, Insurance, and Real Estate
10. Services Other Than Business and Professional
11. Business and Professional Services

This breakdown may appear unusual at first, but there is a purpose for each category. For example, we wanted to distinguish between high-tech manufacturers and others because they follow such different trajectories. We wanted to separate eating and drinking places from the rest of retailing because the former are major sources of employment growth in America, while the rest of retailing tends to be stable or declining. We have paid special attention to business and professional services because they provide much of the growth in service employment; they hire very different kinds of workers, and tend to have a high export content. A detailed description of exactly which industry codes are contained in each group is provided in Figure 5–1. It can be seen that 330 different combinations ($5 \times 2 \times 3 \times 11 = 330$) can be derived from these five categories.

These dimensions have been selected carefully so as to make some distinctions that might not be initially obvious. For example, by using age *and* size at the same time we have created a measure of growth. Firms that have become quite large at a relatively young age are often precocious. Chances are they are entrepreneurially directed, of the type discussed earlier. By placing them in an age–size grid, we can monitor their progress over time and separate them from more conventional firms that evolve less rapidly.

The distinction between enterprise and establishment size must be clearly maintained, since we do not want to confuse a small headquarters establishment of a large corporation with a small headquarters of a small corporation. Also, if at all possible, we want to make certain we keep track of whether that establishment is controlled locally or from somewhere else.

The Ground Rules

Our intention here is to estimate the comings and goings of each of the 330 cells, to discover as much as possible about each

FIGURE 5–1. DEFINITION OF INDUSTRY GROUPS IN TERMS OF 3-DIGIT SIC CODES

1	Agriculture/Mining	011–149
2	Construction	151–179
3	Manufacturing (except High Tech)	201–282, 284–356, 358, 359, 371, 373–375, 377–379, 391–399
4	High Tech Manufacturing	283, 357, 361–369, 372, 376, 381–387
5	Transportation/Public Utilities	401–497
6	Wholesale Trade	501–519
7	Retail Trade (except Eating & Drinking)	521–573, 591–599
8	Eating and Drinking Places	581
9	Financial, Insurance, Real Estate	601–679
10	Services (except Business & Professional)	701–729, 751–799, 821–869
11	Business & Professional Services	731–739, 801–811, 891–899

NOTE: The SIC (Standard Industrial Classification) codes have been developed by the U.S. government to describe industries in detail. Definitions of the codes may be found in U.S. Technical Committee on Industrial Classification, *Standard Industrial Classification Manual* (Washington, D.C., 1972).

one. We also want to see what the cells disclose about the nature of the American economy today and what might be expected in the near future.

So few corporations undertake physical moves for long distances that the ones that do may be ignored. Thus, we have to be concerned with four possibilities:

1. A new firm being started
2. An existing firm expanding
3. An existing firm contracting
4. An existing firm closing.

The chances for existing firms in each cell starting, expanding, contracting, and closing are fairly predictable over time and have been estimated from our micro data for each cell in each place. The universe of establishments in each cell is sufficiently large for the law of large numbers to work quite well.

Think about it and you will see that this approach has the virtues of simplicity and clarity: grow the corporate population in each cell in each place (just the way a demographer might grow a human population), capitalizing upon all of our knowledge about what kinds of firms are located in each place and how they tend to change (in microcosm) over time.

As a final step, we looked into occupations, attempting to discover some of the implications of the changes taking place for different categories of workers. Fortunately, the Bureau of Labor Statistics has also estimated how changes in technology are likely to alter the occupational mix for any particular kind of business. Utilizing this information, we can project future occupational mixes as well as jobs by type of business.

What do all of these numbers tell us? Figure 5–2 summarizes the views of the National Planning Association, the Bureau of

FIGURE 5–2. PREDICTED AGGREGATE ANNUAL JOB GROWTH RATES FROM DIFFERENT SOURCES

Our Forecast (1987–1997)	1.5%
BLS (1984–1995)	1.3%
NPA (1983–2000)	1.6%

Labor Statistics, and our group regarding the rate of job growth over the next 10 to 15 years. Naturally, each utilized a different methodology starting from different base points. Some estimates include the military and the self-employed, some do not, for example. Some forecast government employment, others ignore this segment. But generally speaking, the three of us are on the same wave length in predicting total growth.

Our disagreements arise more from assumptions regarding the job mix than any other factor (see Figure 5–3). We have already said that we are pessimistic about the growth potential of large firms. In the face of international competition, one major industrial firm after another has been obliged to lay off workers. The *Fortune* 500 collectively have laid off 2.8 million since 1980, and the percent of jobs in manufacturing has declined steadily since 1979 and is likely to continue doing so. To repeat, this is a time of transition and we do not believe the levels of manufacturing employment suggested by the Bureau of Labor Statistics and the National Planning Association are realistic. We also think that in the aggregate, retail trade (particularly eating and drinking places and tourism) and services will take up much of the slack.

The BLS takes its projections one step further to cover occupations. Figure 5–4 compares our occupational mix estimates with theirs. The main difference flows from their prediction of a growing manufacturing base that creates more operative jobs and fewer professional, technical, and service jobs than we anticipate.

In sum, while there are a few differences in how the three of us see the future mix of aggregate jobs and occupations over the next

FIGURE 5–3. PREDICTED MIX OF PRIVATE, NONAGRICULTURAL JOBS BY INDUSTRY BY VARIOUS SOURCES, 1995

INDUSTRY	OUR FORECAST	BLS	NPA
Mining	1.4	.9	1.1
Construction	4.7	4.8	6.7
Manufacturing	17.3	20.2	22.3
Transportation, Communications, and Public Utilities	5.1	6.4	6.8
Trade	27.7	25.5	27.8
Finance, Insurance, and Real Estate	8.1	6.5	9.2
Services	35.7	35.7	26.0

FIGURE 5-4. PREDICTED MIX OF NONAGRICULTURAL,
PRIVATE-SECTOR OCCUPATIONS BY VARIOUS SOURCES, 1995

OCCUPATION	OUR FORECAST	BLS FORECAST
Professional and Technical	18.3	18.6
Managers, Officials, and Proprietors	9.2	9.0
Salesworkers	8.6	8.5
Clerical	20.3	19.9
Crafts	10.7	11.4
Operatives	11.2	12.2
Service	17.8	16.4
Laborers	3.8	4.0

10 years or so, these are not significant. Where they exist, they flow from the methodologies utilized to make the estimate—projections based on past trends versus our attempt to anticipate the consequences of transition.

TRACKING THE CELLS

Looking below the national level (see Figure 5–5), it is apparent that the United States, as usual, will not grow in a homogeneous fashion. The South Atlantic States will develop about three times faster than those in the eastern North-Central region, for example, but we must keep in mind that the Northeast and Midwest start

FIGURE 5-5. PRIVATE SECTOR EMPLOYMENT CHANGE, 1987–1997

AREA	1987	1997	CHANGE	PERCENT CHANGE
United States	82,070,893	94,970,607	12,899,714	15.7
New England	5,461,566	6,536,328	1,074,763	19.7
Middle Atlantic	13,618,434	15,022,958	1,404,523	10.3
East Northcentral	14,467,367	15,543,150	1,075,783	7.4
West Northcentral	5,813,651	6,310,613	496,961	8.5
South Atlantic	13,951,086	17,551,589	3,600,503	25.8
East Southcentral	4,405,488	4,941,541	536,052	12.2
West Southcentral	7,976,294	9,149,594	1,173,300	14.7
Mountain	4,076,500	4,921,081	844,580	20.7
Pacific	12,300,505	14,993,754	2,693,249	21.9

out from a much bigger base. When we aggregate absolute employment change by broad region, we get:

REGION	EMPLOYMENT CHANGE	PERCENT OF TOTAL
North	4,052.0	31
South	5,309.9	41
West	3,537.8	28
	12,899.7	100

The South is the largest gainer, but the North outgrows the West. The North certainly isn't fading away into the sunset.

Figure 5–6 provides similar information for the states, where, as might have been expected, the spreads are much greater. California, Florida, Texas, New York, and Georgia stand out as major gainers in absolute terms. Texas is of particular interest in view of the problems relating to the Oil Patch. The state illustrates the phenomenon of regeneration following a setback. Our numbers suggest that one response to the petroleum problems there has been a surge of entrepreneurship which will lead to significant job growth in the years ahead. Don't write off Texas.

For the most part, however, people do not live and work in states; they do both in places. When someone asks me where I am from, I say Boston, not Massachusetts. I relate to the immediate area in which I live and work, and in which my friends can be found. I know that New Bedford, Springfield, Holyoke, and Fall River exist, and I have been to all on occasion—as I have New York, Seattle, New Orleans, and Denver. But I'm not from there. I'm from Boston.

Since people tend to seek work and shelter within the boundaries of an area, it is important to have some idea of the direction in which it is heading. Forecasting the growth of areas can be treacherous, mainly because events that are minor relative to the size of a state or region can be momentous to a town or small city. When oil drops to $10 a barrel, Houston suffers much more than most places like San Antonio and Dallas. A trade war in semiconductors can (and has) changed the business climate of Lafayette, La., which is known as Silicon Bayou. But Alexandria, in the center of the state, wasn't affected at all—that city's major employer is

FIGURE 5–6. PRIVATE SECTOR EMPLOYMENT CHANGE 1987–1997

STATE	1987	1997	CHANGE	PERCENT CHANGE
Alabama	1,155,895	1,316,898	161,003	13.9
Alaska	134,477	172,647	38,170	28.4
Arizona	1,099,949	1,507,241	407,292	37.0
Arkansas	639,551	688,483	48,932	7.7
California	9,585,246	11,670,175	2,084,929	21.8
Colorado	1,143,367	1,334,486	191,119	16.7
Connecticut	1,417,841	1,691,898	274,057	19.3
Delaware	244,351	307,733	63,381	25.9
District of Columbia	418,940	571,138	152,198	36.3
Florida	3,918,650	5,385,047	1,466,397	37.4
Georgia	2,174,514	2,794,763	620,249	28.5
Hawaii	338,662	421,862	83,200	24.6
Idaho	246,358	256,172	9,813	4.0
Illinois	4,109,050	4,304,135	195,085	4.7
Indiana	1,887,851	2,045,169	157,318	8.3
Iowa	847,273	847,696	422	.0
Kansas	767,020	816,890	49,870	6.5
Kentucky	1,001,177	1,084,698	83,521	8.3
Louisiana	1,126,160	1,227,681	101,521	9.0
Maine	381,473	452,683	71,210	18.7
Maryland	1,508,235	1,842,566	334,331	22.2
Massachusetts	2,670,231	3,167,900	497,669	18.6
Michigan	3,060,125	3,319,922	259,797	8.5
Minnesota	1,582,376	1,812,103	229,727	14.5
Mississippi	629,013	679,123	50,110	8.0
Missouri	1,767,082	1,927,856	160,773	9.1
Montana	195,498	204,075	8,577	4.4
Nebraska	500,656	526,209	25,554	5.1
Nevada	412,759	502,165	89,405	21.7
New Hampshire	417,431	548,878	131,447	31.5
New Jersey	2,808,004	3,098,133	290,129	10.3
New Mexico	366,400	415,748	49,349	13.5
New York	6,716,366	7,464,618	748,252	11.1
North Carolina	2,287,470	2,722,241	434,772	19.0
North Dakota	172,745	189,411	16,666	9.6
Ohio	3,780,287	4,101,524	321,238	8.5
Oklahoma	853,526	938,122	84,596	9.9
Oregon	848,075	1,019,046	170,971	20.2
Pennsylvania	4,094,064	4,460,206	366,142	8.9
Rhode Island	382,530	430,085	47,555	12.4
South Carolina	1,071,901	1,236,651	164,750	15.4
South Dakota	176,499	190,449	13,949	7.9
Tennessee	1,619,403	1,860,821	241,418	14.9
Texas	5,357,056	6,295,308	938,252	17.5
Utah	484,887	579,666	94,779	19.5
Vermont	192,060	244,884	52,824	27.5
Virginia	1,900,784	2,265,129	364,345	19.2
Washington	1,394,045	1,710,023	315,979	22.7
West Virginia	426,242	426,322	80	.0
Wisconsin	1,630,055	1,772,400	142,345	8.7
Wyoming	127,282	121,529	−5,754	−4.5

Procter & Gamble. A large cutback in Star Wars research could clobber Boston, but would not affect Litchfield or Williamstown.

When forecasting growth or decline in specific areas, we almost by definition have to ignore unforeseen events in the world economy or the federal funds allocation process that could prove us badly wrong. The best we can do is anticipate what would (and should) happen as a consequence of "normal" corporate activity in each place and put residents on alert to look diligently at events outside of their boundaries that could alter future developments.

Based upon the assumption that the "outside world" holds no surprises, we have estimated where each of the 239 areas under review will be heading over the next decade. This material can be found in Figure 5–7. Areas are ranked by a growth index which is identical to the one used to measure the growth of companies. We do not want to categorize areas simply by percentage growth (which favors small areas) or absolute growth (which favors large ones). The index combines the two (by cross-multiplying them, as we did in Chapters 2 and 3 for companies) to come up with a size-independent measure of employment growth.

Differences in employment growth are even more striking at the area level than they are for the states. As might be expected, all areas will not rise and fall in unison. Even contiguous ones will follow different trajectories—Atlanta at 40.5 percent, for example, as compared with Columbus, Ga. at 6.3 percent, or Seattle (30.8 percent) versus Eastern Washington (3.5 percent). Keep in mind, however, that these numbers must be constantly monitored to take account of a sudden squall or calm. In the autumn of 1986 it appeared that Silicon Bayou in Lafayette was feeling the pinch of the semiconductor glut more than any other similarly situated area and that this was compounded by the recession brought about in southern Louisiana by the decline in oil prices. But we also look for a bigger than normal bounceback once the storm clouds pass. Likewise, more may be going on in Columbus, Ga. than meets the eye, and the stirrings in that area might portend a faster than anticipated growth rate.

One has to be struck by the exceptional anticipated growth performances of some of the familiar Florida cities (Orlando, Tampa, and Miami), many western ones such as Phoenix, Denver, San Diego, Los Angeles, and Seattle, and such major Texas cities as Dallas, Austin, and San Antonio.

Places such as these with significant anticipated growth stand

FIGURE 5–7. RANKING OF AREAS BY GROWTH INDEX, 1987–1997

	FORECAST AREA	EMPLOYMENT (000's)			CHANGE, 1987–1997	PERCENT CHANGE, 1987–1997	GROWTH INDEX, 1987–1997
		1987	1992	1997			
1	Atlanta, GA	1,174.2	1,431.9	1,649.2	475.0	40.5	192,131.9
2	Los Angeles, CA	5,042.8	5,611.5	6,021.0	978.2	19.4	189,766.1
3	Phoenix, AZ	755.2	903.2	1,100.6	345.4	45.7	157,950.0
4	Washington, DC/MD/VA	1,414.3	1,638.0	1,867.4	453.1	32.0	145,144.9
5	Miami-Ft Ldrl-W Pm B, FL	1,381.4	1,585.6	1,811.9	430.5	31.2	134,172.9
6	Orlando, FL	402.1	506.8	619.2	217.1	54.0	117,200.3
7	Tampa-St Petersburg, FL	665.6	793.6	942.8	277.3	41.7	115,516.2
8	San Francisco, CA	2,376.0	2,635.4	2,893.6	517.6	21.8	112,768.9
9	San Diego, CA	695.8	833.0	973.3	277.5	39.9	110,654.3
10	Dallas-Ft Worth, TX	1,658.3	1,780.0	2,070.2	411.8	24.8	102,282.9
11	Seattle, WA	766.9	884.7	1,003.0	236.1	30.8	72,706.2
12	Boston, MA	1,768.5	1,962.7	2,114.2	345.7	19.5	67,583.7
13	New York, NY/NJ	6,756.0	7,184.4	7,417.9	661.9	9.8	64,847.7
14	San Antonio, TX	401.0	454.8	542.6	141.6	35.3	49,966.4
15	Jacksonvl-Gainsvl, FL	367.4	434.9	501.1	133.7	36.4	48,669.9
16	Austin, TX	268.9	308.2	382.9	114.0	42.4	48,310.0
17	Raleigh-Durham, NC	289.2	343.5	403.2	114.0	39.4	44,976.2
18	Sacramento, CA	355.6	416.8	474.4	118.8	33.4	39,703.9
19	Portland-Salem, OR	515.3	579.0	657.6	142.3	27.6	39,310.5
20	Denver-Boulder, CO	772.5	829.6	944.1	171.6	22.2	38,122.2
21	Minneapolis-St Paul, MN/WI	1,121.4	1,234.8	1,328.1	206.7	18.4	38,107.1
22	Philadelphia, PA/NJ	1,946.1	2,124.6	2,216.4	270.3	13.9	37,541.4
23	Rural South FL	226.2	271.8	313.5	87.3	38.6	33,662.8
24	Baltimore, MD	801.1	885.6	958.5	157.4	19.7	30,943.1
25	Northeastern Rural FL	136.4	167.0	196.6	60.2	44.1	26,551.0
26	Charlotte, NC	499.0	558.7	613.9	114.9	23.0	26,450.6

FIGURE 5-7. (*continued*)

	EMPLOYMENT (000's)			CHANGE, 1987–1997	PERCENT CHANGE, 1987–1997	GROWTH INDEX, 1987–1997
FORECAST AREA	1987	1992	1997			
27 Nrflk–Prtsmth–Va Bch, VA	400.0	445.4	495.1	95.1	23.8	22,633.6
28 Ft Myers, FL	90.6	112.3	135.8	45.2	49.9	22,530.6
29 Atlantic City, NJ	163.1	192.3	223.1	60.1	36.8	22,110.7
30 Nashville, TN	394.0	436.8	485.5	91.6	23.2	21,285.1
31 Brdgprt–Stmfrd–Nrwlk, CT	398.9	447.5	489.4	90.5	22.7	20,552.5
32 State of Hawaii	338.7	381.4	421.9	83.2	24.6	20,440.8
33 Eastern NC	689.7	756.0	808.4	118.6	17.2	20,399.1
34 Lakeland–Winter Havn, FL	112.9	135.5	160.3	47.4	41.9	19,865.7
35 Hartford, CT	592.1	664.6	696.9	104.7	17.7	18,517.7
36 Southeastern MA	164.9	191.7	219.4	54.5	33.0	17,996.3
37 Richmond, VA	333.2	373.1	408.3	75.1	22.5	16,939.4
38 Portsmth–Dovr–Rchstr, NH	107.7	127.9	149.6	41.9	38.9	16,308.2
39 Northwestern FL	91.9	112.5	130.4	38.6	42.0	16,183.2
40 Chicago, IL/IN	3,257.7	3,401.7	3,486.6	228.9	7.0	16,089.9
41 Columbus, OH	516.3	574.9	607.5	91.1	17.6	16,079.0
42 Detroit, MI	1,731.1	1,855.9	1,897.1	166.0	9.6	15,916.6
43 Fresno, CA	159.0	187.4	208.8	49.8	31.3	15,595.8
44 Portland, ME	185.7	212.9	238.2	52.5	28.2	14,818.8
45 Salt Lake City–Provo, UT	412.6	448.1	490.6	78.0	18.9	14,745.0
46 Memphis, TN/AR	347.3	387.8	418.8	71.6	20.6	14,744.6
47 State of Vermont	192.1	219.9	244.9	52.8	27.5	14,528.9
48 Manchester–Nashua, NH	163.8	186.8	211.9	48.1	29.4	14,131.0
49 Sarasota, FL	89.9	105.5	125.3	35.4	39.3	13,908.0
50 Las Vegas, NV	234.9	274.0	290.9	56.0	23.8	13,332.7
51 Daytona Beach, FL	93.6	110.5	128.3	34.6	37.0	12,787.3
52 Wilmington, DE/NJ/MD	210.5	243.9	260.6	50.1	23.8	11,915.2

53	Rural New Hampshire	146.0	166.2	187.4	41.4	28.4	11,761.8
54	Knoxville, TN	190.1	209.3	237.1	46.9	24.7	11,577.8
55	Tulsa, OK	271.9	291.6	327.0	55.1	20.3	11,176.5
56	State of Alaska	134.5	140.6	172.6	38.2	28.4	10,834.4
57	Indianapolis, IN	489.5	539.2	560.4	71.0	14.5	10,284.5
58	Cincinnati, OH/KY/IN	583.1	639.0	660.4	77.4	13.3	10,264.6
59	Kansas City, MO/KS	623.6	661.3	703.3	79.7	12.8	10,182.8
60	Eastern TX	422.0	448.1	485.6	63.6	15.1	9,586.5
61	Milwaukee–Racine, WI	680.7	730.4	760.1	79.4	11.7	9,253.9
62	Catskill–Southeastern NY	216.3	242.6	260.9	44.7	20.7	9,223.9
63	New Haven–Waterbury, CT	310.3	340.8	363.5	53.2	17.2	9,135.2
64	Tallahassee, FL	59.1	70.7	82.3	23.2	39.3	9,109.9
65	Stockton–Modesto, CA	189.1	214.2	230.0	40.9	21.6	8,860.3
66	Rural GA	533.2	582.4	601.3	68.1	12.8	8,699.3
67	Charleston, SC	122.8	138.3	155.1	32.3	26.3	8,511.4
68	Albany–Schnctdy–Troy, NY	281.3	307.5	329.5	48.2	17.1	8,264.3
69	Houston–Galveston, TX	1,324.5	1,270.6	1,428.8	104.3	7.9	8,212.5
70	Greenville–Spartnbrg, SC	300.2	332.3	349.5	49.3	16.4	8,099.2
71	St Louis, MO/IL	959.1	996.7	1,046.4	87.3	9.1	7,938.7
72	Greensboro–Wnstn-Slm, NC	411.8	440.4	469.0	57.2	13.9	7,934.4
73	Albuquerque, NM	174.4	195.1	211.0	36.6	21.0	7,682.4
74	Brownsville-McAllen, TX	116.9	127.2	146.1	29.2	25.0	7,284.1
75	Eastern Rural SC	293.8	318.8	339.1	45.4	15.4	7,002.9
76	Santa Crz–Sn Luis Ob, CA	107.4	120.9	134.1	26.8	24.9	6,682.0
77	Tucson, AZ	200.1	216.2	236.5	36.4	18.2	6,612.4
78	Western, WA	229.7	246.0	267.8	38.1	16.6	6,323.3
79	Reno, NV	115.0	130.2	141.8	26.7	23.2	6,216.6
80	Omaha, NE/IA	246.6	263.9	285.4	38.8	15.7	6,090.7
81	Louisville, KY/IN	360.6	390.1	407.4	46.7	13.0	6,058.6
82	State of Rhode Island	382.5	409.1	430.1	47.6	12.4	5,911.8
83	Birmingham, AL	374.6	395.1	420.5	45.9	12.2	5,618.1

FIGURE 5-7. (continued)

	FORECAST AREA	EMPLOYMENT (000's)			CHANGE, 1987–1997	PERCENT CHANGE, 1987–1997	GROWTH INDEX, 1987–1997
		1987	1992	1997			
84	New London–Norwich, CT	116.5	128.9	142.1	25.6	21.9	5,606.3
85	Lansing–Jackson, MI	182.3	199.7	214.0	31.8	17.4	5,534.3
86	Northern Rural AL	259.1	276.4	296.7	37.6	14.5	5,460.4
87	Toledo, OH	229.2	253.8	264.4	35.2	15.3	5,396.6
88	Jackson, MS	135.8	148.5	162.6	26.8	19.7	5,294.5
89	Dayton–Springfield, OH	341.6	370.7	383.8	42.2	12.4	5,222.7
90	Rochester, NY	389.3	406.9	432.7	43.4	11.1	4,830.8
91	Rural AZ	144.6	158.9	170.2	25.5	17.7	4,510.9
92	New Orleans, LA	410.1	411.0	452.9	42.8	10.4	4,461.8
93	Lancaster, PA	160.4	177.7	187.1	26.7	16.7	4,449.6
94	Syracuse, NY	240.5	261.1	272.6	32.1	13.4	4,293.0
95	Southern DE	66.6	76.4	83.5	16.9	25.3	4,266.0
96	Baton Rouge, LA	166.9	174.4	193.6	26.7	16.0	4,265.5
97	Adirondack Region, NY	142.5	156.6	167.0	24.5	17.2	4,196.0
98	Melbourne–Titusville, FL	115.7	120.7	137.6	21.9	19.0	4,159.4
99	Lexington, KY	129.1	142.0	152.3	23.1	17.9	4,146.7
100	Santa Barbara, CA	123.0	133.4	145.4	22.5	18.3	4,101.9
101	Northern Mtn Region, GA	145.8	160.5	170.2	24.4	16.7	4,083.0
102	Salinas–Seasd–Mntrey, CA	76.6	85.8	94.0	17.5	22.8	3,993.4
103	Worcester, MA	265.4	288.5	297.7	32.3	12.2	3,930.1
104	Rural UT	72.3	80.3	89.1	16.8	23.2	3,895.5
105	Huntsville, AL	85.8	95.6	104.1	18.3	21.3	3,883.9
106	Waco–Killeen–Temple, TX	119.6	126.6	141.1	21.5	18.0	3,870.8
107	Cleveland–Akron, OH	1,007.0	1055.2	1,069.1	62.1	6.2	3,824.5
108	Harrisburg, PA	222.5	241.8	251.6	29.1	13.1	3,802.6
109	New Bedford–Fall Rvr, MA	172.3	183.8	197.9	25.5	14.8	3,786.4

110	Binghampton–Elmira, NY	128.1	138.6	149.7	21.6	16.9	3,644.1
111	Eastern MD	87.5	97.1	105.3	17.8	20.4	3,624.9
112	Boise, ID	67.5	73.5	82.7	15.2	22.6	3,436.3
113	Macon, GA	80.5	89.1	96.9	16.4	20.4	3,343.7
114	Fort Wayne, IN	161.3	176.4	184.5	23.2	14.4	3,339.6
115	Augusta, GA/SC	110.5	120.3	129.6	19.1	17.2	3,285.5
116	S Bend–Bntn Hrbr, IN/MI	236.8	256.4	264.7	27.8	11.7	3,265.9
117	Tacoma, WA	118.7	127.5	138.4	19.7	16.6	3,264.9
118	Mountain Region, NC	429.5	455.9	466.6	37.1	8.6	3,201.9
119	Little Rock–Pine Blf, AR	199.3	210.2	224.4	25.1	12.6	3,165.9
120	Mobile, AL	131.8	140.3	152.0	20.2	15.3	3,104.2
121	Southwestern TX	58.9	62.9	72.4	13.5	22.8	3,071.2
122	Reading, PA	126.7	139.4	146.3	19.5	15.4	3,015.6
123	Southern Rural AL	204.1	216.9	228.8	24.7	12.1	2,987.8
124	Eugene, OR	76.6	85.0	91.8	15.1	19.7	2,983.4
125	Springfield, MA	221.4	240.1	246.9	25.5	11.5	2,932.3
126	Southern, Central WI	519.3	542.8	556.3	37.0	7.1	2,632.2
127	Pittsfield, MA	77.7	85.2	91.8	14.2	18.2	2,577.8
128	Oklahoma City, OK	302.6	298.0	330.3	27.8	9.2	2,546.1
129	Savannah, GA	82.9	91.8	97.0	14.1	17.1	2,410.0
130	Spokane, WA	111.5	118.5	127.8	16.3	14.6	2,371.1
131	Pensacola, FL	85.7	91.8	99.9	14.1	16.5	2,324.1
132	Corpus Christi, TX	98.3	99.7	113.0	14.7	15.0	2,199.1
133	Chattanooga, TN/GA	144.2	153.8	162.0	17.8	12.3	2,199.1
134	Southern MS	244.3	256.8	267.3	23.0	9.4	2,164.8
135	Montgomery, AL	92.2	100.0	106.3	14.0	15.2	2,139.1
136	Columbia, SC	143.6	149.2	160.9	17.3	12.0	2,084.0
137	Grand Rapids–Muskegn, MI	316.6	329.0	342.0	25.4	8.0	2,043.4
138	Western AR	201.8	216.0	221.5	19.7	9.8	1,929.5
139	Utica–Rome, NY	90.9	97.1	103.9	13.0	14.3	1,853.4
140	Des Moines, IA	176.8	191.8	194.7	17.9	10.1	1,808.0
141	Rural Maine	195.7	207.8	214.5	18.7	9.6	1,795.5

FIGURE 5-7. (*continued*)

	FORECAST AREA	EMPLOYMENT (000's)			CHANGE, 1987–1997	PERCENT CHANGE, 1987–1997	GROWTH INDEX, 1987–1997
		1987	1992	1997			
142	Western MT	95.4	101.3	108.2	12.8	13.4	1,711.6
143	Youngstown–Warren, OH	164.7	175.3	181.5	16.7	10.1	1,695.9
144	Allentown–Bthlhm, PA/NJ	233.2	243.8	252.8	19.6	8.4	1,644.8
145	Roanoke–Lynchburg, VA	167.2	177.0	183.6	16.4	9.8	1,610.4
146	State of North Dakota	172.7	179.8	189.4	16.7	9.6	1,608.0
147	Eastern Rural VA	277.4	293.6	297.2	19.8	7.1	1,413.1
148	Madison, WI	131.1	138.4	144.7	13.6	10.4	1,407.4
149	Western OR	179.6	186.8	195.5	15.8	8.8	1,398.4
150	Central Valley, CA	217.1	230.9	234.2	17.1	7.9	1,354.8
151	Colorado Spgs–Pueblo, CO	137.3	140.5	150.8	13.5	9.8	1,328.6
152	Northern Rural IN	584.5	602.7	612.2	27.7	4.7	1,308.3
153	Northern Rural MI	184.4	191.8	198.7	14.3	7.8	1,111.7
154	State of South Dakota	176.5	183.1	190.4	13.9	7.9	1,102.4
155	TN River Valley, TN	213.3	222.0	228.5	15.2	7.1	1,082.3
156	Lafayette, LA	66.3	65.2	74.7	8.4	12.7	1,073.7
157	Northwestern Rural SC	147.3	154.8	159.2	11.9	8.1	965.9
158	Northcentral TX	219.3	226.9	233.4	14.0	6.4	899.5
159	Battle Crk–Kalamazoo, MI	134.1	142.2	145.0	10.9	8.1	886.5
160	Bakersfield, CA	111.9	113.6	121.8	9.9	8.9	879.3
161	York, PA	145.2	151.3	156.1	11.0	7.6	827.9
162	Northern Rural MO	207.1	214.9	219.9	12.8	6.2	787.7
163	Mountain Region, VA	242.3	253.1	256.0	13.8	5.7	781.1
164	Evansville, IN/KY	142.5	147.5	153.0	10.5	7.3	766.9
165	Springfield, MO	89.0	93.9	97.2	8.2	9.3	763.9
166	Northern Rural MN	94.3	97.4	102.8	8.5	9.0	758.6
167	Johnstown–Altoona, PA	133.6	141.6	143.6	10.0	7.5	751.2

168	Canton, OH	136.9	143.0	146.9	10.0	7.3	735.0
169	Northern Rural LA	146.0	148.9	156.2	10.3	7.0	719.7
170	Rural NV	62.8	69.4	69.5	6.7	10.7	714.1
171	Pittsburgh, PA	775.5	784.5	798.4	22.9	2.9	673.7
172	Buffalo, NY	403.5	417.3	420.0	16.5	4.1	672.3
173	Southeast Rural KY	135.4	139.5	144.7	9.3	6.9	638.5
174	Wichita, KS	193.9	198.8	204.5	10.5	5.4	570.2
175	Finger Lakes Region, NY	217.7	226.9	228.6	10.9	5.0	545.3
176	Duluth, MN/WI	61.7	64.3	67.4	5.7	9.3	535.5
177	Northwest–East Rural CA	131.2	137.5	139.4	8.2	6.3	518.2
178	Western NM	123.4	128.6	131.2	7.9	6.4	500.4
179	Erie, PA	95.2	97.3	102.0	6.8	7.2	488.4
180	Topeka, KS	78.2	82.3	84.4	6.1	7.8	480.6
181	Shreveport, LA	109.5	107.1	116.6	7.0	6.4	449.9
182	Eastern KS	203.8	205.4	213.0	9.3	4.5	421.4
183	Lincoln, NE	75.9	77.9	81.5	5.6	7.4	414.5
184	Scrtn–Wlks–Br–Hzltn, PA	232.4	237.7	241.9	9.5	4.1	392.0
185	Northern Rural WI	90.1	93.7	96.0	5.9	6.6	388.8
186	Ft Smith–Fayettvl, AR/OK	98.8	103.2	104.9	6.1	6.2	374.2
187	Eastern NM	68.6	71.2	73.5	4.9	7.1	348.4
188	Southern Rural MO	239.9	246.1	248.9	9.0	3.8	340.1
189	El Paso, TX	141.4	144.9	148.2	6.8	4.8	329.5
190	Southern Rural MN	313.8	319.9	324.0	10.2	3.2	329.4
191	Charleston, WV	81.6	84.0	86.6	5.0	6.1	307.3
192	Appalachia–Rural East PA	238.0	241.4	246.3	8.3	3.5	291.4
193	Columbus, GA/AL	70.8	73.9	75.3	4.4	6.3	277.0
194	Lubbock, TX	72.2	73.3	76.5	4.3	6.0	260.3
195	Saginaw–Bay City, MI	128.5	132.0	134.1	5.7	4.4	248.5
196	Eastern WA	167.2	169.7	173.0	5.8	3.5	200.5
197	Southern LA	227.3	224.7	233.7	6.4	2.8	177.7
198	Green Bay–Appleton, WI	200.1	204.4	205.2	5.1	2.6	132.3
199	Beaumont–Port Arthur, TX	103.1	100.1	106.8	3.7	3.6	130.2

Figure 5–7. (continued)

	Employment (000's)			Change, 1987–1997	Percent Change, 1987–1997	Growth Index, 1987–1997
Forecast Area	1987	1992	1997			
200 Longvw–Marshll–Tyler, TX	107.9	104.4	111.6	3.7	3.5	129.8
201 Southern Rural IN	107.0	110.3	110.7	3.7	3.4	126.6
202 Western CO	126.5	127.7	130.3	3.8	3.0	115.4
203 Southern Rural MI	182.8	187.9	187.4	4.6	2.5	113.6
204 Springfield–Decatur, IL	106.6	105.8	108.9	2.3	2.1	49.2
205 Hntngtn–Ashlnd, WV/KY/OH	73.5	73.7	75.4	1.8	2.5	45.4
206 Eastern CO	107.1	109.2	109.3	2.2	2.0	44.6
207 Appalachian Mtn Area, WV	138.3	136.4	139.2	.8	.6	5.2
208 Northwestern IA	202.6	202.4	203.6	1.0	.5	4.9
209 Bloomingtn–Champaign, IL	97.5	97.8	98.1	.6	.6	3.7
210 Eastern OK	132.5	132.2	133.2	.7	.5	3.7
211 Western OK	142.8	142.3	143.5	.7	.5	3.6
212 Western Rural TN	248.6	256.4	249.4	.7	.3	2.0
213 Western MD	68.3	68.0	68.5	.2	.3	.7
214 Northern MS	249.0	253.5	249.3	.3	.1	.4
215 Rockford, IL	116.8	118.2	116.7	−.1	−.1	−.2
216 Dvnprt–Rck I–Moln, IL/IA	130.6	130.0	130.3	−.3	−.2	−.5
217 Jn C–Kgsprt–Brstl, TN/VA	132.6	134.3	132.4	−.3	−.2	−.5
218 Northwestern Rural OH	580.2	583.7	579.7	−.6	−.1	−.6
219 Western KS	85.1	85.5	84.4	−.8	−.9	−6.7
220 Cedar Rapids–IA City, IA	93.0	92.5	92.0	−1.0	−1.1	−10.9
221 North Panhandle TX	103.3	102.2	101.8	−1.5	−1.5	−22.0
222 Southeastern OH	292.4	291.8	289.8	−2.7	−.9	−24.9
223 Amarillo, TX	61.6	59.2	60.2	−1.4	−2.2	−30.5
224 Eastern OR	76.5	76.3	74.2	−2.3	−3.0	−70.6
225 Northwestern Rural KY	280.5	282.8	275.8	−4.7	−1.7	−79.3

226	Eastern Rural AR	133.0	132.1	129.7	-3.4	-2.5	-85.8
227	Peoria, IL	116.0	114.2	112.1	-4.0	-3.4	-135.3
228	Rural ID	178.9	178.1	173.4	-5.4	-3.0	-164.0
229	Eastern MT	100.1	97.8	95.9	-4.2	-4.2	-176.4
230	Flint, MI	148.3	143.4	143.0	-5.3	-3.5	-186.2
231	Rural Northwest, PA	261.3	255.2	254.0	-7.3	-2.8	-204.5
232	Southern Rural IL	68.8	65.5	64.6	-4.2	-6.1	-259.4
233	State of Wyoming	127.3	121.4	121.5	-5.8	-4.5	-260.1
234	Odessa, Midland, TX	79.7	72.2	74.1	-5.6	-7.0	-395.9
235	Northwestern WV	165.9	160.0	157.5	-8.3	-5.0	-419.4
236	Western NE	104.0	101.0	96.9	-7.0	-6.8	-475.6
237	Eastern NE	95.6	92.2	86.8	-8.8	-9.2	-804.9
238	Southeastern IA	293.0	279.9	272.2	-20.8	-7.1	-1,471.5
239	Northern, Central IL	339.0	312.3	299.3	-39.8	-11.7	-4,664.0

in sharp contrast to a collection of mostly smaller, rural areas spread throughout the United States that for one reason or another have not caught the imagination of people wanting to start and nurture growing companies. It isn't that Flint, Odessa, Peoria, and Eastern Montana are forever destined for slow or no growth, but we did find that right now—and for the next few years—they are sorely underpopulated by the kinds of companies that will help them keep pace with the leaders.

Can an area *will* itself to growth? Do individual people count; can they make a change? Is it carved in stone that San Diego will grow faster than the nation as a whole, or that Cleveland will not? We believe that within limits, the destinies of these places can be altered, for better or worse, if only those in charge understand the preconditions for growth. We turn, in the next chapter, to the new rules of the economic development game and the process by which almost any area can play that game better.

CHAPTER 6

The Changing Rules for Economic Development

As the structure of the economy changes, what it takes to prosper changes too. Such has been the case throughout American history. During the colonial period, seaports—doorways to Europe—were the economic focal points, with farmers funneling their crops into them. In the canal era, some of the action shifted to the interior, and later the once-bustling canal towns gave way to rapidly growing cities along the railroads—which bowed in turn when turnpike and air travel became more common. Cattle barons ruled at a time when the West was seen as a place to raise beef for easterners, and some of these vanished or changed their roles when oil and natural gas was discovered under the surface. The textile cities of Massachusetts became deserted when the industry shifted to the South and later to the Orient—only to be reborn as technological centers later on.

Adapt and grow or decay and die. But, above all, know the rules of the game at the time you are playing it.

WHY DO HIGH-INNOVATION STARTUPS LOCATE WHERE THEY DO?

Early on, we saw that net growth is the balance between flows. The expansion of existing operations, new startups, and firms moving into an area all contribute to higher employment, while the gains are offset by firms closing, laying off workers, or moving out.

In studying those firms that constitute the economic base for a locale, we discovered a curious fact. Most areas lose the same percentage of jobs from their base every year—about 7–8 percent. It doesn't seem to make much difference how fast or slow an area may be growing: its job losses are the same as they are in most other places. Two-thirds of all areas vary by less than 1 percent from this national average. Efforts aimed at retaining jobs that might otherwise be lost ("job retention" as it is usually called) are often quite futile—or, at the very least, no one has become good enough at it yet to have any significant effect on job-loss rates. In fact, if there is any variation, it is that healthy places like Phoenix, Atlanta, Orlando, and San Diego have slightly higher-than-average loss rates and unhealthy places lower rates.

Much is made of each firm that picks up and leaves. You are familiar with the drill. First come the rumors: a large employer is considering leaving because of union pressures, high utility rates, the local tax structure, and so forth. There are then denials followed by admissions that some exploratory efforts have been made. The local politicos and real estate interests panic. There are talks with union leaders, utilities, and others involved. Concessions are made, and in the end the company remains.

From all of this one naturally concludes (1) that firms relocating is a major problem, (2) that stopping firms from departing should be a high priority item, and (3) that getting the taxes and unions "squared away" should be a major concern of government.

True, some large corporations relocate, and when they do, it can have an important impact on both the old and new communities. Armonk, N.Y., boomed when International Business Machines arrived, and Union Carbide's shift to Danbury turned that sleepy part of western Connecticut into a hustling suburban enclave. When it seemed that Phillips Petroleum might leave Bartlesville, Okla., local solons predicted the city would become a ghost town within a year or so. But note this: IBM moved from New York to a suburb of that city, as did Union Carbide, while the Phillips situation was prompted by a threatened takeover, not the decision by management to relocate. Big moves are costly affairs, and the dislocations they engender rarely are worth it.

The fact of the matter is that however highly publicized they may be, relocated firms are insignificant from a job creation or loss standpoint. Many firms move each year, but the vast majority do so comparatively short distances, and virtually all—like IBM and Union Carbide—within the same metropolitan area. Most relocations out of New York, Philadelphia, and Washington (all of which are experiencing significant outmoves) are to nearby places—New Jersey, Connecticut, Virginia, or Maryland. The price of commercial real estate in Manhattan, for example, has soared, so firms there search for less expensive places for their back office and find it on Long Island. The result: outmoves from Manhattan and a building boom at Roosevelt Field, Long Island, where 3 million feet of office space was planned in 1984. But note: the firms will go a handful of miles to Long Island, not to Montana. Again, they can't move from their customers, work forces, or suppliers.

Think about the situation John Gutfreund, CEO of Salomon Brothers, faced in 1985. His operations at the tip of Manhattan at One New York Plaza had outgrown their offices, and a move was dictated. Where to? Columbus Circle just off Central Park in Manhattan. Earlier Salomon had moved from Wall Street to its present headquarters.

Might Gutfreund have considered a relocation to Miami? Denver? San Antonio? Of course not. No major investment bank could think of being anywhere but Manhattan. Likewise, the chances for Weyerhaeuser to move from Seattle–Tacoma or Procter & Gamble from Cincinnati are nil. And what holds for the giants seems to apply to small firms as well.

We can see, then, that losses from the job base are more or less the same throughout the country and moves into and out of metropolitan areas are insignificant. We are left with the conclusion, which the statistics support, *that virtually all of the variations in growth from one place to another derive from differences in the rate at which lost jobs are replaced, and that replacements originate in the formation of new firms and the growth of existing firms.*

Since we know that some locales are doing much better than others, it must be that there are enormous variations in the rates at which firms form and grow from one place to another. Our analysis of the 1981–1985 period suggests that some places have formation rates that are 10 times greater than others, and that the odds young firms will grow varies by a factor of 8. Some locales are obviously doing a much better job than others of riding the crest of the growth wave.

Which places are doing well, and why? In the good old days the key to success was low costs of labor, raw materials, and transportation. This often was wedded to a benign or friendly government offering all sorts of tax lures and related goodies, such as free or low-cost land, access roads, dredging, and, more recently, low-cost capital through one bonding scheme or another. The prize was a plant that offered hundreds, perhaps thousands of jobs, which in turn stimulated the rest of the local economy—the home builders, the car dealers, the stores, and so on down the line. Many communities and states still employ such tactics.

This approach worked best during the 1950s and 1960s, when on balance large, established corporations were still adding new workers. This came to an end in the early 1970s. Then, many communities, which in the past had simply assumed growth was the natural order of things, learned otherwise. Furthermore, with the completion of the interstate highway system and the advent of advanced telecommunications, many of the ancillary jobs that once formed around a new plant were likely to be elsewhere. In short, the odds are much lower—and the likely benefits much less—that a new plant will have the degree of impact on an area that once might have been the case.

Many parts of the country are undergoing traumatic change. The southeastern states—particularly the rural parts—that boomed in the 1960s and 1970s are now hurting. Very few southeastern states have as many manufacturing jobs today as they did back in 1970.

Yet the same kind of competition we have been talking about still exists. Let a large company announce it will build a major installation and it seems as though half the cities and towns in America compete to be the site. We saw it most dramatically in the jockeying to win the nod from Japanese car manufacturers. Tennessee won and may rival Michigan as the nation's car capital sometime in the 1990s. The reason given? Low labor costs and access to markets as good if not better than Detroit's. Yet relative to the overall employment picture in Tennessee, the plants are insignificant. In fact, they have not yet dented the state's net loss in the manufacturing sector. Even now, Tennessee has fewer manufacturing workers than it did in the early 1970s or in 1980, when the "auto hunt" began.

Perhaps the old game will work; apparently the politicos think so. We doubt it. After careful analysis of the relationship between factor costs and growth, we found that it is the *higher,* and not the lower, cost areas that are now exhibiting the greatest growth. Places like San Francisco and Orange County, Phoenix and Denver, Dallas and Boston, Atlanta and Miami, are not low-cost areas. They present businesses with higher costs for labor, land, housing, transportation, capital, energy, and taxes relative to their environs and, in most cases, relative to the country as a whole. Among the lowest cost-of-living areas in the United States are Terre Haute, Ind., Anniston, Florence, and Gadsden Ala., and Amarillo, Texas; Boston and New York are close to the top of the list. Yet the Boston and New York metropolitan areas are booming, while the low-cost areas are more or less stagnant. The average market value of a house in Amarillo is $37,000, the property taxes less than $600. Why aren't businesses rushing to Amarillo?

Think about it for a while and you'll see that a low-cost line of reasoning confuses cause and effect. We are not suggesting that the way to grow is to raise costs but rather that more appealing areas attract new businesses, causing the prices of production and living to rise. Firms do not locate around Boston because they crave high costs but rather their placement there results in higher prices for land and labor.

WHERE TO LOOK FOR INNOVATIVE COMPANIES

What we have called high-innovation firms are creating most of the growth in the American economy, so it makes sense to concentrate upon their development. High rates of innovation depend primarily on brains, not land or harbors or cheap labor. The key to attracting brains is to offer quality, not cheapness. The successful, innovation-based company will, in general, settle in an environment that bright, creative people find attractive. Otherwise these people won't come. Cost is no longer an absolute measure; it now is relative to the quality of the people and the environment that it provides. A high-cost area that attracts the best and the brightest through amenities it offers will, in general, do much better than a low-cost place that offers much less. Employers will pay an extra 25 or 30 percent to hire a CalTech computer programmer because they feel that by doing so they gain a significant competitive edge that more than compensates for the extra costs. Put enough of such firms in one place and you'll have a high-cost area.

This is not to denigrate those who prefer to live in low-cost areas. That these can be appealing is undeniable. The hard-driven New York or Boston executive, lawyer, or banker who earns $100,000 a year, lives in a cramped two-bedroom apartment, and has two children in private schools may find it difficult to make ends meet. Put the family down in a middle-sized town in the rural part of some southern or western state, slash his salary in half, and he will enjoy a higher standard of living. Indeed, the Innovation Revolution that has made some places centers for high technology has started to transform life in those low-cost areas too. At one time these were the so-called boondocks, away from the mainstream. Now, given cable television, inexpensive telecommunications, and feeder airlines, people living in out-of-the-way, low-tech areas can see and hear sophisticated entertainment; no one in the United States is more than a day away from New York, Chicago, or San Francisco, or two from London, Paris, or Tokyo.

Every year families do make the switch for that very reason. But they are outnumbered by those who are attracted to the high-innovation economy. So this is not a value judgement but simply a way of saying that those aggressive Yuppies you see in the nation's fastest-growing areas command high salaries because that's what it takes to get them. And the companies that pay those salaries do so because they feel the high-innovation workers are more than worth it. Quality costs. Quality pays.

Quality takes many forms. Five are especially important to innovative, entrepreneurial firms:

1. Educational resources, particularly higher education
2. Quality of labor
3. Quality of government
4. Telecommunications
5. Quality of life.

Universities—particularly those that concentrate upon research—are the wellspring of the high-innovation economy. These are the major "natural resource" in an economy that is based on constant innovation. Land, transportation, and energy costs are not important factors. The average energy consumption per worker in the service sectors (where most highly innovative firms are now located) is almost five times less than that per manufacturing worker. It is access to brains, not energy, that counts. We are not talking here about the fact that top universities attract top undergraduate students; these come from all parts of the world and after graduation tend to leave. Rather, the research-based universities have prize faculties and superb graduate students who can moonlight on business projects, while workers in highly innovative firms can attend the universities at night to receive not only graduate degrees, but exposure to ideas at the leading edge of change.

Consider the benefits of locating an innovation-based company within close range of such top-rated universities as MIT, Stanford, Columbia, the universities of Wisconsin and Michigan, Georgia Tech, Carnegie–Mellon, CalTech, and the like. A technologically oriented university is one of the most important government and private industry subsidies high-innovation industry could want. Whole new industries spring up around university laboratories. "Intelligence Alley," a small neighborhood in Cambridge, Mass., is literally within a stone's throw of the M.I.T. Artificial Intelligence Laboratory. That neighborhood now houses a major part of the world's artificial intelligence industry—an industry that will become a significant source of economic and job growth in the future. The sale of expert systems alone has grown from nothing to $140 million per year today and is predicted to expand to $810 million per year by 1990. Meanwhile, an estimated 80 percent of the *Fortune* 500 companies are engaged in expert system research.

The artificial intelligence industry does not appear at random locations in various parts of the country. Rather, it can be found adjacent to major AI laboratories in Boston, Pittsburgh, and San Francisco. Other makers and appliers of high technology in fields such as biotechnology and electronics components follow the same pattern. It is not natural resources or factor costs that determine where these new sectors of our economy grow. Rather, it is immediate access to the thinking and innovation upon which they are based that counts.

Local government officials with long time horizons, interested in developing their areas structurally rather than simply attracting relocations and trying to prevent moves, might consider that efforts spent in lobbying the state legislature to pour funds into local universities could be rewarding. Political leaders who fall over themselves seeking relocations are like shoppers going into a grocery store to purchase apples, when it might be wiser to plant a few apple trees and wait until they bear fruit. Of course, this is a long-term investment; but the sooner they start, the faster will the fruits be harvested.

Think of it in these terms and you will see why the technologically based university is to the waning years of the 20th century what the Mississippi River was to exporters of grain in America's midwest in the mid-19th century, the Mesabi Range to the steel industry in the late 19th century, and the oil fields to Texas in the early 20th century, namely a priceless resource.

IMPLICATIONS FOR LABOR

While the quality of labor is an important concern for most companies, it is crucial for those that are innovating. Not everyone who works for these firms has to be a genius with a Ph.D.; clearly most are not. But these companies require a great deal of many of their employees, who must possess more highly developed and honed skills than are found in the average factory or clerical office environment. They must have a deeper than usual understanding of the processes and equipment they work with and develop each day. At the same time the high-innovation worker must be flexible and adaptable. He or she must not only be able to keep up with the innovation occurring in firms at which they work but help generate change.

This means that high-innovation employees must possess a higher level of education than was needed by the vast majority of corporations in the past. Reread the qualifications sketched in the previous paragraph, and you will realize they were required in all burgeoning young American industries, from textiles in the early 19th century through automobiles in the early 20th century. Inspired entrepreneurs and tinkerers like Francis Cabot Lowell and Henry Ford could get by with self-education. Some of today's entrepreneur–engineers have trained themselves that way, too, but they are exceptions. Far more common in today's more innovative industries is the individual with a Ph.D. in engineering or biology who has recruited others with his or her background or an M.B.A. to start a firm in some exotic new field.

Workers in technologically advanced companies have to be broad as well as deep—broad in the sense that they have to be prepared to switch gears at turns in technology. The ability to adapt is vital. Without it, workers who today are prized will find themselves tomorrow's fossils.

Inexpensive labor is not required at this end of the business, but on the other hand high-innovation companies do generate jobs for the semiskilled. Go through the low-level buildings that dot the landscape throughout areas in which these companies are found and you will find armies of workers at shop benches. They may sit in front of a computer board with the components to be affixed to it in small containers by their sides. Workers press a button, and a light on the board shows them where to solder the next part. This done, another light goes on, and the procedure continues until the board is complete and sent on to be tested.

That assembly machine was designed by a highly skilled, highly paid engineer, while the worker using it might be semiskilled. In time, of course, another engineer will develop a machine to replace that worker. Or it might be that the company will shift its assembly work to Mexico, Taiwan, or Korea. The technological component will be done here, the assembly in low-cost parts of the world. And so it goes. The company expands its high-skilled cadre while reducing its low-skilled labor force. The net result either way will be expansion of high-innovation jobs and contraction of unskilled and semiskilled labor in the United States.

So cheap labor is not what is wanted. Rather, innovation-based firms need and are willing to pay for skilled and adaptable workers. Intelligence implies accuracy too, and given the tolerances required and the competitive nature of the businesses, this is of prime importance. We see it all about us. For example, a German manufacturer of sophisticated electrical connectors chose to locate its American plant in Connecticut after scanning the entire country for a site. Connecticut was selected because the total labor cost was lower there than most other places, even though hourly wages were much higher than elsewhere. Why? Because the number of defective connectors produced on exotic equipment by Connecticut workers was much lower than elsewhere, and the costs of rework for these commodities was very high. *Total* labor cost per deliverable connector was thus lower. The semiskilled and skilled Connecticut workers proved capable of adjusting quickly to the sophisticated equipment being used to produce the connectors.

It is no coincidence that the western states, starting from a base of only one-third of all American jobs, have consistently outgrown the rest of the country, and that the top 10 states, ranked in terms of the percent of their adult population with at least a high school education, are all western—Alaska, Utah, Colorado, Wyoming, Washington, Oregon, Nevada, Montana, Hawaii, and Idaho in that order. Many southern governors, who find their states at the bottom of the educational barrel, are directing their attention to this issue. The chief executives of Tennessee, Arkansas, and North and South Carolina have made the quality of elementary and secondary education in their states a top, if not the top, priority of their administrations. Tennessee's Ten-Point Better Schools Program is clearly right on target for a state whose labor force is among the least educated in the nation. It was inspired by that state's drive to attract not only automobile companies but high-innovation concerns, if not now then in the early 21st century. These governors are not only competing with each other and with the western states but with Europeans and Asians in a drive to create a labor force that can produce the products and services that a high-innovation economy demands.

THE QUALITY OF GOVERNMENT

"Quality of government" doesn't sound quite right at a time when so many public figures speak glowingly of "getting government off our backs." Yet, as we look across the country, we find growth is occurring in high-tax and not low-tax areas. Despite recent tax cuts, Massachusetts traditionally has been one of the more heavily taxed states and is flourishing. New York City and residents of nearby Nassau County are often cited as the most taxed individuals in America—and have the highest utilities bills to boot. They hardly are experiencing an outflow of residents. Indeed, both areas are in the midst of a long-term secular boom that shows no sign of slowing up.

We certainly aren't suggesting that the way to success is to raise taxes. Rather, the trick is to provide value for money, which is to say if taxes bring a higher quality of life, they are paid. Massachusetts offers a good example of the balance between quality and cost. The state has always provided extensive public services—but historically at a very high cost. Through public referenda and much better management, it has maintained its service delivery and significantly reduced cost. Perhaps a better way to describe Massachusetts today would be as a "tax-efficient" rather than "high-tax" state.

For more than a century, taxes have had a strong ideological base. The public—composed largely of workers—demanded services, and the way to get them seemed to be through taxing the fat cats—composed largely of big businesses. Besides looking upon new businesses as a source of employment and of demand for housing and other goods and services, political leaders view them as a tax source. True, abatements are offered, but every mayor and county executive who makes such concessions knows that down the road he will be able to levy stiff commercial rates and so take part of the burden of maintaining schools, roads, and social services "off the backs of the taxpayers."

But the typical innovation-based firm is not the same as the "big business" of the Industrial Revolution. The local property and sales taxes are not major items on most of their income statements, since they do not require large installations and heavy capital investment. The biggest issue would be the state and local personal income taxes simply because they raise the cost of labor, which is a more important consideration for innovative firms than it is for much of smokestack America.

What do the high-innovation firms want and get for their tax dollars? The smaller firms that now account for so many of the new jobs cannot afford to employ their own in-house lawyers, accountants, printing department, security guards, trash collectors, grounds keepers, etc. This kind of firm tends to locate in metropolitan areas where it can quickly and easily acquire the assistance of a lawyer or printing firm when it needs such help. It will also settle in a city that protects its facilities, picks up its trash, puts out its fires, and polices its streets.

Workers in innovation-based companies are a different breed from the men and women on the assembly line. They are less likely to be unionized, less concerned about workmans' compensation and unemployment benefits—many have no experience with either and no thought of them. They don't punch time clocks, and almost all but the semiskilled workers are paid salaries rather than hourly wages. Ask some of them what time and a half for overtime means and they'll return a blank stare. There are research labs dotting the countryside that are open twenty-four hours a day, seven days a week so that their employees can go there at any time an idea strikes them. These workers insist upon good recreational facilities and schools and will choose to settle in areas that offer such amenities.

Outrageous taxes with little visible return are not acceptable. Faced with them, the innovation-based companies will vote with their feet, namely move. Take the case of New York City during the 1960s and early 1970s. It had been said that New York was "a city with a heart." New York provided extensive services for the poorest of its citizens. Poor people from other parts of the country, who relocated there in search of work and became unemployed or underemployed, learned of and used comparatively generous social welfare programs. New York was one of the best places to reside if you were wealthy—or poor. Who paid for this? The middle class, which was taxed heavily without a commensurate return. Their reaction was to leave for the suburbs. The result was the erosion of the tax base and quality of life, which was the backdrop to the city's mid-decade fiscal crisis.

The answer isn't to slash taxes but to demonstrate concern for the desires of middle-class, high-innovation workers—in effect cater to their needs. Go through almost any area in which innovative firms are situated and study the school tax rates in different jurisdictions. In virtually all cases, there is a direct correlation between high taxes and high property values, the latter made possible by skilled workers anxious to provide the best education available to their offspring. Compare the relatively wealthy area of Anaheim–Santa Ana–Garden Grove, Calif., with Amarillo, Texas. The California community is the home for businesses that turn out computer components, electric meters, and aircraft parts; Amarillo is known for its flour, sorghum, lumber, and zinc products. The average household income in Amarillo in 1981 was just over $28,000, while that for Anaheim–Santa Ana–Garden Grove came to slightly more than $31,000. The local tax bite for the Amarillo family was $214, for the California community, $2,890.

Locales that do well offer more amenities than do others. Some, like Tennessee, have done so by increasing services while keeping taxes in line. Others, like Massachusetts, have maintained a "rich" service package while lowering the costs. Either way, they have struck a balance that growing firms seek.

THE ROLE OF TELECOMMUNICATIONS

Telecommunications are to the high-innovation economy what railroads, rivers, canals, and highways were and are to the industrial world. They are the central channel through which most of this economy flows. In general, innovation-based firms do not have much in the way of physical objects to move around, and their raw materials are few, compact, and easily transported. Manufacturers of computer chips don't concern themselves with being close to a source of silicon, a railroad, or port facility. Air parcel services, such as Federal Express, often serve all of their needs.

Most of what they move about is information—the kind contained on credit card slips, airline reservations, bank transactions, insurance claims, securities sales, personnel records, commercial credit reports, and mail orders.

Electronic mail and computers that communicate with one another through modems and telephones function as railroad cars, freight haulers, and barges do for the industrial economy. Indeed, even the central workplace can be disposed of. There is no reason for a stockbroker to work out of Wall Street, for example, or even his home in the suburbs. That is perhaps the reason Merrill Lynch moved most of its brokerage headquarters operations to Princeton, N.J. A condo in the Bahamas, Aruba—or anyplace in the world, for that matter—would do just as well, especially given the convenience of 800 numbers for clients to use in telephoning.

Locales that offer state-of-the-art communications facilities have a great advantage in this kind of economy. Memphis, Tenn., is a classic example of this. Because Federal Express and Holiday Inns are headquartered in Memphis, the local telephone companies have installed some of the most advanced switching gear in the world. Imagine the communications capacity required to keep track of all Holiday Inn reservations and the location and status of 350,000 separate Federal Express packages each day. These are akin to businesses that have a 100 percent inventory turnover every twenty-four hours, and communications are vital to keep things moving.

The availability of facilities to carry out the work have made Memphis the telecommunications capital of the South. More 800 and WATS calls go in and out of Memphis each day than any other city in the region. Firms that must process large numbers of calls or computer-to-computer transactions in the South take this into consideration when considering expansion possibilities. It is not a coincidence that Merrill Lynch located its regional processing center in that city, or that Williams–Sonoma, the large cookery firm that sells its products through mail order, has also located some of its facilities in Memphis.

THE QUALITY OF LIFE

If managers of innovative firms demand such services, their employees require even more to keep them content—more even than good schools, trash collection, and safe streets. They want an amorphous thing called quality of life. No one knows quite what it is, and each individual has a different personal agenda. For one it might be access to the theater and ballet, for another to hunting and fishing, a third to museums, a fourth to major league sports, and so on down the line. Nashville may be fine for those interested in country music, but opera devotees would prefer New York. Physical attractiveness is important too—some want to live among mountains, others near the sea or a lake, a third in a sky-scraper jungle, and so forth. Whatever it is, the quality of life has to do with "interesting pastimes" and an enjoyable atmosphere after work.

Which cities possess the quality of life that seems to appeal to high-innovation workers? The answer is not too difficult to find. Since, as we have seen, the companies can pretty well start up any-where, just look at the places they tend to cluster about. Boston and San Francisco clearly have it. So do Dallas, Phoenix, and Tuc-son. Seattle has lots of it. It now appears Pittsburgh has it too. So in fact do a large number of other places in a variety of different forms and mixes. Many smaller towns and cities have created unusually attractive environments relative to their size. Columbus, Indiana, is a good example. Lafayette, La., appears to have it as well. Some larger cities have created special enclaves in their midst—like the "festival marketplaces" the Rouse company has so brilliantly built in many cities, including Boston, Baltimore, Toledo, and now Miami. Whatever form it takes, "nice, exciting" places have decided advantages when it comes to appealing to executives of innovative firms for these are the areas where entre-preneurs and employees will want to settle and raise their families.

The growing importance of quality in its many forms rather than cost per se has already had a significant effect on where replacement of jobs—and hence growth—will take place. We found, for example, that the following states, in order of magni-tude, created the most new high-innovation jobs between 1977 and 1981:

1. California
2. Texas
3. Connecticut
4. Massachusetts
5. Illinois
6. New York

7. Ohio
8. Minnesota
9. Florida
10. New Jersey.

Many of the older, northern states with their great universities, their attractive countrysides and suburbs, and their rebuilding cities are at the top of the list.

Since the recession ended in 1982 and through 1985, we created about 8 million jobs in the American economy. The top ten states for job creation were:

1. California
2. Florida
3. New York
4. Georgia
5. New Jersey
6. Massachusetts
7. Texas
8. North Carolina
9. Virginia
10. Ohio.

You probably have noticed that seven states are on both lists— California, Texas, Massachusetts, New York, Ohio, Florida, and New Jersey. It is no coincidence; since high-innovation sectors are the most rapidly growing segment of the economy, one would expect this.

If we ignore the West and the Plains states for a minute and compare the states represented in the "Northeast-Midwest Coalition" (the Rust Belt) to the states represented in the Southern Governor's Association (including Texas), we find that the North actually outgrew the South in absolute terms during 1982–1985. Adding the West and Plains states, we get:

Area	Jobs-Created 1982–1985
RUST BELT	3,046,000
SOUTH	2,911,000
WEST AND PLAINS	2,178,000
TOTAL	8,135,000

Massachusetts created more jobs during the 1982–1985 recovery than did Texas, and Texas is two and a half times bigger. Indeed, Massachusetts added more jobs in 1984 than in any year since World War II and has consistently posted the lowest unemployment rate of the 10 largest states for the past few years. This is quite a performance for a state that in 1975 was flat on its back with a 10–12 percent unemployment rate. Clearly, Massachusetts has adapted splendidly to the Innovation Revolution.

The variations in performance are even greater at the metroplitan area level. Figures 6–1 and 6–2 summarize the propensity for new firms to form and young firms to grow for each of 239 areas in the United States from 1981 through 1985. These areas are defined as collections of counties that send most of their commuting workers to the largest nearby city or town. Thus the Portland, Maine, area includes those counties that send more commuting workers to Portland than to any other large city or town.

For each area, we have:

1. Computed the number of significant startups (defined as a firm that started between 1981 and 1985, and had a work force of 10 or more employees by the end of 1985)
2. Computed the number of young companies (defined as those started between 1977 and 1981) that grew significantly between 1981 and 1985
3. Converted the significant startups and young growers into percentages of the base population in their respective areas, so that the numbers for large and small places are comparable.

Following this procedure, we can determine the spread between the worst and best areas along each dimension and the relative position of all other areas in between.

The spreads are enormous. Austin has nine and a half times more significant startups as a percent of its base than rural Wisconsin. The Nashua–Manchester, N.H., area has over eight times as many significantly growing, younger companies as does rural eastern Nebraska. Many of the areas with a high percentage of startups and rapidly growing young companies are in states where we might expect to find them—Florida, Texas, California, Arizona, and Massachusetts. But attention has to be paid to other bubbling areas—Lafayette, La., shows up again, as do Charleston, Nashville, Norfolk, Fort Wayne, Memphis, Springfield (Missouri),

150

FIGURE 6-1. HIGH GROWTH STATISTICS BY FORECAST AREA, 1981–85

FORECAST AREA RANKED BY % SIGNIFICANT BIRTHS

RANK	FORECAST AREA	# BIRTHS	% BIRTHS	# HI GRO	% HI GRO
1	Austin, TX	782	7.33	131	4.72
2	Dallas–Ft Worth	3191	5.18	607	4.04
3	El Paso, TX	251	5.12	32	3.26
4	Phoenix, AZ	1272	4.92	254	3.62
5	San Antonio, TX	757	4.54	158	4.16
6	Houston–Galveston, TX	2722	4.45	597	3.34
7	Orlando, FL	598	4.20	142	3.65
8	Atlanta, GA	1676	3.87	382	3.56
9	Tucson, AZ	310	3.84	89	4.22
10	Denver–Boulder, CO	1275	3.73	2.73	3.08
11	San Diego, CA	1183	3.69	301	3.34
12	Huntsville, AL	102	3.68	20	3.12
13	Raleigh–Durham, NC	327	3.67	63	3.63
14	Lafayette, LA	146	3.62	29	2.33
15	Washington, DC/MD/VA	1935	3.54	411	3.60
16	Longview–Marshall–Tyler, TX	207	3.47	38	2.61
17	Las Vegas, NV	276	3.46	53	2.35
18	Tampa–St. Petersburg, FL	1035	3.37	202	2.43
19	Charleston, SC	183	3.33	51	3.84
20	Colorado Springs–Pueblo, CO	235	3.32	47	2.58
21	Baton Rouge, LA	260	3.26	66	3.24
22	Nashville, TN	434	3.25	110	3.82
23	Ft. Myers, FL	162	3.21	39	2.45
24	Pensacola, FL	135	3.18	24	2.58
25	Miami–Ft Lauderdale–W. Palm Beach, FL	2452	3.15	494	2.18
26	Odessa, Midland, TX	183	3.14	38	2.47
27	Norfolk–Portsmouth–VA Beach, VA	482	3.13	104	3.00
28	Corpus Christi, TX	180	3.07	29	2.22
29	S. Bend–Benton Harbor, IN/MI	295	3.06	56	3.36
30	Springfield, MO	130	3.03	15	1.61
31	Los Angeles, CA	6681	3.00	1590	2.96
32	Shreveport, LA	181	2.96	21	1.62
33	Tallahassee, FL	88	2.94	23	3.36
34	State of Alaska	293	2.92	72	3.23
35	Albuquerque, NM	223	2.92	75	3.80
36	Columbia, SC	181	2.91	31	2.43
37	Knoxville, TN	263	2.90	42	2.04
38	Waco-Killeen-Temple, TX	152	2.87	23	2.27
39	Jacksonville–Gainsville, FL	422	2.87	121	3.64
40	Brownsville–McAllen, TX	188	2.86	32	2.14
41	Sarasota, FL	160	2.83	40	2.40
42	Salt Lake City–Provo, UT	576	2.81	142	3.03

FIGURE 6–1. *(continued)*

FORECAST AREA RANKED BY % SIGNIFICANT BIRTHS

RANK	FORECAST AREA	# BIRTHS	% BIRTHS	# HI GRO	% HI GRO
43	Oklahoma City, OK	569	2.80	101	1.92
44	Northern Mtn Region, GA	185	2.77	28	1.88
45	Kansas City, MO/KS	755	2.74	166	2.86
46	Manchester–Nashua, NH	148	2.73	50	4.84
47	Sacramento, CA	568	2.73	127	2.38
48	Ft Smith–Fayettvl, AR/ OK	132	2.73	25	2.20
49	Eastern Rural SC	411	2.72	53	1.74
50	Lexington, KY	171	2.72	34	2.30
51	Northwestern FL	150	2.71	30	2.34
52	Topeka, KS	106	2.69	13	1.78
53	Boise, ID	100	2.69	20	2.25
54	Indianapolis, IN	520	2.68	86	2.41
55	Madison, WI	157	2.66	33	2.73
56	Greensboro–Wnstn–Slm, NC	362	2.65	70	2.63
57	Tulsa, OK	401	2.65	102	2.50
58	Melbourne–Titusville, FL	134	2.63	45	3.11
59	Charlotte, NC	419	2.63	72	2.30
60	Seattle, WA	946	2.61	228	2.59
61	Columbus, OH	483	2.56	103	2.88
62	San Francisco, CA	2748	2.55	780	3.34
63	Eastern TX	808	2.53	127	1.80
64	Memphis, TN/AR	351	2.53	107	3.49
65	Baltimore, MD	868	2.52	234	3.03
66	Reno, NV	131	2.51	28	2.14
67	Savannah, GA	88	2.48	26	3.32
68	Montgomery, AL	92	2.48	20	2.58
69	New Orleans, LA	556	2.44	115	2.18
70	Minneapolis–St Pl, MN/ WI	1073	2.44	259	2.88
71	Mobile, AL	170	2.43	27	1.68
72	Fort Wayne, IN	129	2.43	34	3.61
73	Spokane, WA	151	2.42	25	1.77
74	Beaumont–Port Arthur, TX	136	2.41	29	2.33
75	Louisville, KY/IN	382	2.40	71	2.19
76	Wichita, KS	205	2.40	41	2.42
77	Rural South FL	352	2.40	93	2.21
78	Chattanooga, TN/GA	150	2.39	24	1.80
79	Birmingham, AL	345	2.36	67	2.28
80	Greenville–Spartnbrg, SC	206	2.34	39	2.19
81	Jackson, MS	136	2.33	23	1.84
82	Omaha, NE/IA	251	2.33	54	2.35
83	Portsmth–Dover–Rchstr, NH	118	2.33	35	3.59
84	Green Bay–Appleton, WI	176	2.29	37	2.46
85	Boston, MA	1377	2.27	363	3.88

FIGURE 6-1. *(continued)*

FORECAST AREA RANKED BY % SIGNIFICANT BIRTHS

RANK	FORECAST AREA	# BIRTHS	% BIRTHS	# HI GRO	% HI GRO
86	Richmond, VA	279	2.26	75	2.81
87	Cincinnati, OH/KY/IN	562	2.26	120	2.39
88	Detroit, MI	1691	2.24	358	2.48
89	Amarillo, TX	84	2.23	21	2.41
90	Roanoke–Lynchburg, VA	135	2.23	21	1.77
91	New York, NY/NJ	7476	2.22	1591	2.53
92	Portland-Salem, OR	622	2.20	155	2.26
93	Lakeland-Winter Havn, FL	126	2.20	23	1.96
94	Southeast Rural KY	235	2.18	32	1.49
95	Brdgprt-Stmfrd-Nrwlk, CT	411	2.18	124	3.34
96	Santa Barbara, CA	143	2.15	48	3.01
97	Lubbock, TX	95	2.15	21	2.28
98	Dayton–Springfield, OH	319	2.14	55	2.02
99	Daytona Beach, FL	119	2.11	27	1.69
100	Charleston, WV	78	2.11	9	1.37
101	Wilmington, DE/NJ/MD	161	2.09	47	3.42
102	Little Rock-Pine Blf, AR	216	2.09	62	2.69
103	Youngstown-Warren, OH	162	2.08	29	2.08
104	Rural AZ	213	2.08	46	1.69
105	Bakersfield, CA	158	2.07	31	1.65
106	Rockford, IL	103	2.06	27	2.64
107	Philadelphia, PA/NJ	1779	2.06	437	2.94
108	Worcester, MA	216	2.05	53	3.39
109	Columbus, GA/AL	66	2.05	14	2.58
110	Rochester, NY	343	2.05	96	2.94
111	Macon, GA	78	2.05	10	1.41
112	Lincoln, NE	68	2.01	21	3.02
113	Northcentral TX	390	2.01	72	1.74
114	Augusta, GA/SC	90	2.00	34	3.35
115	Western NM	184	2.00	43	1.84
116	Chicago, IL/IN	2895	2.00	695	2.46
117	Lancaster, PA	132	1.99	28	2.54
118	Stockton–Modesto, CA	210	1.99	59	2.45
119	Appalachian Mtn Area, WV	193	1.98	23	1.28
120	Santa Crz–Sn Luis Ob, CA	154	1.98	45	2.12
121	Canton, OH	125	1.98	27	2.25
122	Tn River Valley, TN	202	1.96	32	1.42
123	Southern MS	274	1.96	43	1.50
124	Lansing–Jackson, MI	153	1.95	28	2.05
125	Flint, MI	108	1.94	16	1.55
126	State of Hawaii	364	1.93	81	1.88
127	Toledo, OH	194	1.93	51	2.66
128	Mountain Region, NC	318	1.92	56	1.72
129	Grand Rapids–Muskegn, MI	261	1.92	84	3.11
130	Northeastern Rural FL	174	1.92	34	1.44

Figure 6–1. (*continued*)

FORECAST AREA RANKED BY % SIGNIFICANT BIRTHS

Rank	Forecast Area	# Births	% Births	# Hi Gro	% Hi Gro
131	Milwaukee-Racine, WI	567	1.92	116	2.16
132	New Bedford–Fall Rvr, MA	145	1.92	36	2.93
133	Eastern NC	613	1.90	132	2.24
134	Cleveland–Akron, OH	863	1.89	202	2.31
135	Rural GA	537	1.89	89	1.55
136	Eastern NM	107	1.88	23	1.77
137	Northern Rural AL	246	1.87	34	1.27
138	Western CO	229	1.87	55	1.49
139	Pittsburgh, PA	684	1.86	134	2.23
140	Northern Rural LA	222	1.86	38	1.51
141	Southern LA	311	1.85	76	1.93
142	Northwestern WV	163	1.84	23	1.56
143	Tacoma, WA	141	1.84	25	1.37
144	Southeastern MA	216	1.83	61	2.86
145	Eastern CO	158	1.83	42	1.91
146	St. Lous, MO/IL	812	1.82	198	2.38
147	Salinas–Seasd-Montrey, CA	92	1.81	17	1.58
148	York, PA	112	1.80	20	2.04
149	State of Wyoming	205	1.80	43	1.41
150	Western Rural TN	235	1.79	39	1.40
151	Hartford, CT	402	1.79	79	2.03
152	Hntngtn–Ashlnd, WV/ KY/OH	78	1.78	11	1.35
153	Des Moines, IA	131	1.77	27	1.85
154	Southern Rural AL	183	1.77	23	1.25
155	Battle Crk-Kalamazoo, MI	94	1.76	27	2.74
156	New London–Norwich, CT	84	1.75	27	3.28
157	Jn C–Kgsprt–Brstl, TN/ VA	94	1.74	11	.96
158	Eastern MD	95	1.74	27	2.18
159	Eugene, OR	100	1.74	25	1.62
160	Rural New Hampshire	146	1.74	33	2.10
161	Mountain Region, VA	209	1.74	29	1.23
162	New Haven-Waterbury, CT	254	1.73	73	2.57
163	Evansville, IN/KY	109	1.73	28	2.45
164	Portland, ME	146	1.72	38	2.42
165	Southwestern TX	107	1.71	18	1.29
166	Bloomingtn–Champaign, IL	83	1.70	16	1.59
167	Western OK	249	1.70	45	1.33
168	Southern DE	56	1.68	17	2.76
169	Dvnprt–Rck I–Moln, IL/ IA	106	1.67	16	1.45
170	Buffalo, NY	372	1.65	96	2.34
171	Erie, PA	79	1.65	14	1.78

FIGURE 6–1. (*continued*)

		#	%	# HI	% HI
RANK	FORECAST AREA	BIRTHS	BIRTHS	GRO	GRO
172	Saginaw–Bay City, MI	89	1.61	20	2.09
173	Northwestern Rural SC	92	1.61	20	1.89
174	Fresno, CA	170	1.61	40	1.73
175	Syracuse, NY	183	1.61	54	2.60
176	Peoria, IL	100	1.61	11	.96
177	Northern Rural IN	482	1.60	80	1.58
178	Springfield, MA	155	1.60	33	2.05
179	Duluth, MN/WI	74	1.60	9	1.09
180	Northern MS	233	1.60	36	1.31
181	Allentown–Bthlhm, PA/ NJ	171	1.58	37	2.12
182	Western, WA	279	1.57	57	1.26
183	State of Rhode Island	311	1.56	93	2.85
184	Rural ID	228	1.54	39	1.17
185	Eastern OK	196	1.52	40	1.31
186	Rural UT	97	1.51	28	1.88
187	Johnstown–Altoona, PA	107	1.51	20	1.72
188	Western MT	147	1.50	34	1.25
189	Rural NV	56	1.50	9	.90
190	State of Vermont	159	1.50	53	2.66
191	Western AR	204	1.48	41	1.28
192	Western MD	49	1.47	9	1.48
193	Northwestern Rural KY	285	1.46	43	1.10
194	Springfield–Decatur, IL	79	1.45	11	1.11
195	Western OR	213	1.43	43	1.08
196	Eastern MT	138	1.42	26	1.10
197	Cedar Rapids–Ia City, IA	58	1.42	13	1.59
198	Albany–Schnctdy–Troy, NY	204	1.41	72	2.75
199	Eastern Rural VA	209	1.40	51	1.87
200	Southern Rural MO	309	1.40	47	1.02
201	State of North Dakota	187	1.38	31	1.16
202	Scrtn–Wlks Br–Hzltn, PA	192	1.38	35	1.79
203	Southern, Central WI	434	1.38	95	1.67
204	Eastern KS	243	1.38	35	1.12
205	Northwestern Rural OH	418	1.37	80	1.44
206	Rural Northwest, PA	220	1.35	41	1.55
207	Binghampton–Elmira, NY	73	1.35	21	2.41
208	Northern Rural MO	204	1.32	26	.94
209	Southeastern OH	229	1.31	51	1.72
210	Southern Rural IL	86	1.31	13	1.14
211	Atlantic City, NJ	131	1.31	42	2.06
212	Harrisburg, PA	122	1.30	28	1.82
213	North Panhandle TX	146	1.29	31	1.31
214	Eastern Rural AR	131	1.29	16	.75
215	Southern Rural MI	158	1.28	29	1.27
216	Reading, PA	64	1.26	11	1.46
217	Central Valley, CA	225	1.26	53	1.24
218	Northwest–East Rural CA	179	1.24	53	1.39

FORECAST AREA RANKED BY % SIGNIFICANT BIRTHS

FIGURE 6–1. (*continued*)

FORECAST AREA RANKED BY % SIGNIFICANT BIRTHS

RANK	FORECAST AREA	# BIRTHS	% BIRTHS	# HI GRO	% HI GRO
219	Northern Rural MI	232	1.24	46	1.20
220	State of South Dakota	177	1.23	38	1.32
221	Southern Rural IN	84	1.21	13	1.05
222	Eastern WA	166	1.21	36	1.07
223	Appalachia–Rural East PA	183	1.18	29	1.34
224	Rural Maine	125	1.16	40	2.15
225	Utica–Rome, NY	59	1.15	17	2.17
226	Finger Lakes Region, NY	142	1.12	22	.99
227	Catskill–Southeastern NY	137	1.10	32	1.65
228	Pittsfield, MA	41	1.08	16	2.63
229	Eastern OR	74	1.07	18	.95
230	Southern Rural MN	239	1.07	37	.86
231	Northwestern IA	182	1.04	41	1.27
232	Northern, Central IL	329	1.04	54	.96
233	Western NE	111	1.03	18	.79
234	Adirondack Region, NY	100	1.02	18	1.11
235	Southeastern IA	214	.95	40	1.00
236	Western KS	91	.95	25	1.33
237	Northern Rural MN	97	.94	18	.81
238	Eastern NE	89	.93	10	.58
239	Northern Rural WI	69	.77	21	1.18

FIGURE 6–2. HIGH GROWTH STATISTICS BY FORECAST AREA, 1981–85

FORECAST AREA RANKED BY % YOUNG HIGH-GROWERS

RANK	FORECAST AREA	# BIRTHS	% BIRTHS	# HI GRO	% HI GRO
1	Manchester–Nashua, NH	148	2.73	50	4.84
2	Austin, TX	782	7.33	131	4.72
3	Tucson, AZ	310	3.84	89	4.22
4	San Antonio, TX	757	4.54	158	4.16
5	Dallas–Ft Worth, TX	3191	5.18	607	4.04
6	Boston, MA	1377	2.27	363	3.88
7	Charleston, SC	183	3.33	51	3.84
8	Nashville, TN	434	3.25	110	3.82
9	Albuquerque, NM	223	2.92	75	3.80
10	Orlando, FL	598	4.20	142	3.65
11	Jacksonville–Gainsvl, FL	422	2.87	121	3.64
12	Raleigh–Durham, NC	327	3.67	63	3.63
13	Phoenix, AZ	1272	4.92	254	3.62
14	Fort Wayne, IN	129	2.43	34	3.61
15	Washington, DC–MD–VA	1935	3.54	411	3.60
16	Portsmth–Dvr–Rchstr, NH	118	2.33	35	3.59

FIGURE 6-2. *(continued)*

FORECAST AREA RANKED BY % YOUNG HIGH-GROWERS

RANK	FORECAST AREA	# BIRTHS	% BIRTHS	# HI GRO	% HI GRO
17	Atlanta, GA	1676	3.87	382	3.56
18	Memphis, TN–AR	351	2.53	107	3.49
19	Wilmington, DE–NJ–MD	161	2.09	47	3.42
20	Worcester, MA	216	2.05	53	3.39
21	S Bend–Bntn Hrbr, IN–MI	295	3.06	56	3.36
22	Tallahassee, FL	88	2.94	23	3.36
23	Augusta, GA–SC	90	2.00	34	3.35
24	San Francisco, CA	2748	2.55	780	3.34
25	Houston–Galveston, TX	2722	4.45	597	3.34
26	Brdgprt–Stmfrd–Nrwlk, CT	411	2.18	124	3.34
27	San Diego, CA	1183	3.69	301	3.34
28	Savannah, GA	88	2.48	26	3.32
29	New London–Norwich, CT	84	1.75	27	3.28
30	El Paso, TX	251	5.12	32	3.26
31	Baton Rouge, LA	260	3.26	66	3.24
32	State of Alaska	293	2.92	72	3.23
33	Huntsville, AL	102	3.68	20	3.12
34	Melbourne–Titusville, FL	134	2.63	45	3.11
35	Grand Rapids–Muskegn, MI	261	1.92	84	3.11
36	Denver–Boulder, CO	1275	3.73	273	3.08
37	Salt Lake City–Provo, UT	576	2.81	142	3.03
38	Baltimore, MD	868	2.52	234	3.03
39	Lincoln, NE	68	2.01	21	3.02
40	Santa Barbara, CA	143	2.15	48	3.01
41	Nrflk–Prtsmth–Va Bch, VA	482	3.13	104	3.00
42	Los Angeles, CA	6681	3.00	1590	2.96
43	Philadelphia, PA–NJ	1779	2.06	437	2.94
44	Rochester, NY	343	2.05	96	2.94
45	New Bedford–Fall Rvr, MA	145	1.92	36	2.93
46	Columbus, OH	483	2.56	103	2.88
47	Minneapolis–St Pl, MN–WI	1073	2.44	259	2.88
48	Kansas City, MO–KS	755	2.74	1.66	2.86
49	Southeastern MA	216	1.83	61	2.86
50	State of Rhode Island	311	1.56	93	2.85
51	Richmond, VA	279	2.26	75	2.81
52	Southern, DE	56	1.68	17	2.76
53	Albany–Schnctdy–Troy, NY	204	1.41	72	2.75
54	Battle Crk–Kalamazoo, MI	94	1.76	27	2.74

FIGURE 6–2. *(continued)*

FORECAST AREA RANKED BY % YOUNG HIGH-GROWERS

RANK	FORECAST AREA	# BIRTHS	% BIRTHS	# HI GRO	% HI GRO
55	Madison, WI	157	2.66	33	2.73
56	Little Rock–Pine Blf, AR	216	2.09	62	2.69
57	State of Vermont	159	1.50	53	2.66
58	Toledo, OH	194	1.93	51	2.66
59	Rockford, IL	103	2.06	27	2.64
60	Pittsfield, MA	41	1.08	16	2.63
61	Greensboro–Wnstn–Slm, NC	362	2.65	70	2.63
62	Longvw–Marshll–Tyler, TX	207	3.47	38	2.61
63	Syracuse, NY	183	1.61	54	2.60
64	Seattle, WA	946	2.61	228	2.59
65	Montgomery, AL	92	2.48	20	2.58
66	Columbus, GA–AL	66	2.05	14	2.58
67	Colorado Spgs–Pueblo, CO	235	3.32	47	2.58
68	Pensacola, FL	135	3.18	24	2.58
69	New Haven–Waterbury, CT	254	1.73	73	2.57
70	Lancaster, PA	132	1.99	28	2.54
71	New York, NY–NJ	7476	2.22	1591	2.53
72	Tulsa, OK	401	2.65	102	2.50
73	Detroit, MI	1691	2.24	358	2.48
74	Oldessa, Midland, TX	183	3.14	38	2.47
75	Chicago, IL–IN	2895	2.00	695	2.46
76	Green Bay–Appleton, WI	176	2.29	37	2.46
77	Evansville, IN–KY	109	1.73	28	2.45
78	Stockton–Modesto, CA	210	1.99	59	2.45
79	Ft Myers, FL	162	3.21	39	2.45
80	Tampa–St Petersburg, FL	1035	3.37	202	2.43
81	Columbia, SC	181	2.91	31	2.43
82	Wichita, KS	205	2.40	41	2.42
83	Portland, ME	146	1.72	38	2.42
84	Binghampton–Elmira, NY	73	1.35	21	2.41
85	Amarillo, TX	84	2.23	21	2.41
86	Indianapolis, IN	520	2.68	86	2.41
87	Sarasota, FL	160	2.83	40	2.40
88	Cincinnati, OH–KY–IN	562	2.26	120	2.39
89	St Louis, MO–IL	812	1.82	198	2.38
90	Sacramento, CA	568	2.73	127	2.38
91	Omaha, NE–IA	251	2.33	54	2.35
92	Las Vegas, NV	276	3.46	53	2.35
93	Northwestern FL	150	2.71	30	2.34
94	Buffalo, NY	372	1.65	96	2.34
95	Beaumont–Port Arthur, TX	136	2.41	29	2.33

FIGURE 6–2. *(continued)*

FORECAST AREA RANKED BY % YOUNG HIGH-GROWERS

RANK	FORECAST AREA	# BIRTHS	% BIRTHS	# HI GRO	% HI GRO
96	Lafayette, LA	146	3.62	29	2.33
97	Cleveland–Akron, OH	863	1.89	202	2.31
98	Charlotte, NC	419	2.63	72	2.30
99	Lexington, KY	171	2.72	34	2.30
100	Birmingham, AL	345	2.36	67	2.28
101	Lubbock, TX	95	2.15	21	2.28
102	Waco–Killeen–Temple, TX	152	2.87	23	2.27
103	Portland–Salem, OR	622	2.20	155	2.26
104	Canton, OH	125	1.98	27	2.25
105	Boise, ID	100	2.69	20	2.25
106	Eastern NC	613	1.90	132	2.24
107	Pittsburgh, PA	684	1.86	134	2.23
108	Corpus Christi, TX	180	3.07	29	2.22
109	Rural South FL	352	2.40	93	2.21
110	Ft Smith–Fayettvl, AR–OK	132	2.73	25	2.20
111	Greenville–Spartnbrg, SC	206	2.34	39	2.19
112	Louisville, KY–IN	382	2.40	71	2.19
113	Eastern MD	95	1.74	27	2.18
114	New Orleans, LA	556	2.44	115	2.18
115	Miami–Ft Ldrl–W Pm B, FL	2452	3.15	494	2.18
116	Utica–Rome, NY	59	1.15	17	2.17
117	Milwaukee–Racine, WI	567	1.92	116	2.16
118	Rural Maine	125	1.16	40	2.15
119	Brownsville–Mcallen, TX	188	2.86	32	2.14
120	Reno, NV	131	2.51	28	2.14
121	Allentown–Bthlhm, PA–NJ	171	1.58	37	2.12
122	Santa Crz–Sn Luis Ob, CA	154	1.98	45	2.12
123	Rural New Hampshire	146	1.74	33	2.10
124	Saginaw–Bay City, MI	89	1.61	20	2.09
125	Youngstown–Warren, OH	162	2.08	29	2.08
126	Atlantic City, NJ	131	1.31	42	2.06
127	Lansing–Jackson, MI	153	1.95	28	2.05
128	Springfield, MA	155	1.60	33	2.05
129	York, PA	112	1.80	20	2.04
130	Knoxville, TN	263	2.90	42	2.04
131	Hartford, CT	402	1.79	79	2.03
132	Dayton–Springfield, OH	319	2.14	55	2.02
133	Lakeland–Winter Havn, FL	126	2.20	23	1.96
134	Southern LA	311	1.85	76	1.93
135	Oklahoma City, OK	569	2.80	101	1.92

FIGURE 6-2. *(continued)*

FORECAST AREA RANKED BY % YOUNG HIGH-GROWERS

RANK	FORECAST AREA	# BIRTHS	% BIRTHS	# HI GRO	% HI GRO
136	Eastern CO	158	1.83	42	1.91
137	Northwestern Rural SC	92	1.61	20	1.89
138	Rural UT	97	1.51	28	1.88
139	State of Hawaii	364	1.93	81	1.88
140	Northern Mtn Region, GA	185	2.77	28	1.88
141	Eastern Rural VA	209	1.40	51	1.87
142	Des Moines, IA	131	1.77	27	1.85
143	Western NM	184	2.00	43	1.84
144	Jackson, MS	136	2.33	23	1.84
145	Harrisburg, PA	122	1.30	28	1.82
146	Chattanooga, TN–GA	150	2.39	24	1.80
147	Eastern, TX	808	2.53	127	1.80
148	Scrtn–Wlks Br–Hzltn, PA	192	1.38	35	1.79
149	Topeka, KS	106	2.69	13	1.78
150	Erie, PA	79	1.65	14	1.78
151	Roanoke–Lynchburg, VA	135	2.23	21	1.77
152	Eastern NM	107	1.88	23	1.77
153	Spokane, WA	151	2.42	25	1.77
154	Eastern Rural SC	411	2.72	53	1.74
155	Northcentral TX	390	2.01	72	1.74
156	Fresno, CA	170	1.61	40	1.73
157	Mountain Region, NC	318	1.92	56	1.72
158	Southeastern OH	229	1.31	51	1.72
159	Johnstown–Altoona, PA	107	1.51	20	1.72
160	Rural AZ	213	2.08	46	1.69
161	Daytona Beach, FL	119	2.11	27	1.69
162	Mobile, AL	170	2.43	27	1.68
163	Southern, Central WI	434	1.38	95	1.67
164	Catskill–Southeastern NY	137	1.10	32	1.65
165	Bakersfield, CA	158	2.07	31	1.65
166	Eugene, OR	100	1.74	25	1.62
167	Shreveport, LA	181	2.96	21	1.62
168	Springfield, MO	130	3.03	15	1.61
169	Cedar Rapids–IA City, IA	58	1.42	13	1.59
170	Bloomingtn–Champaign, IL	83	1.70	16	1.59
171	Northern Rural IN	482	1.60	80	1.58
172	Salinas–Seasd–Mntrey, CA	92	1.81	17	1.58
173	Northwestern WV	163	1.84	23	1.56
174	Rural GA	537	1.89	89	1.55
175	Rural Northwest, PA	220	1.35	41	1.55
176	Flint, MI	108	1.94	16	1.55
177	Northern Rural LA	222	1.86	38	1.51

FIGURE 6-2. *(continued)*

FORECAST AREA RANKED BY % YOUNG HIGH-GROWERS

RANK	FORECAST AREA	# BIRTHS	% BIRTHS	# HI GRO	% HI GRO
178	Southern MS	274	1.96	43	1.50
179	Southeast Rural KY	235	2.18	32	1.49
180	Western CO	229	1.87	55	1.49
181	Western MD	49	1.47	9	1.48
182	Reading, PA	64	1.26	11	1.46
183	Dvnprt–Rck I–Moln, IL–IA	106	1.67	16	1.45
184	Northeastern Rural FL	174	1.92	34	1.44
185	Northwestern Rural OH	418	1.37	80	1.44
186	Tn River Valley, TN	202	1.96	32	1.42
187	State of Wyoming	205	1.80	43	1.41
188	Macon, GA	78	2.05	10	1.41
189	Western Rural TN	235	1.79	39	1.40
190	Northwest–East Rural CA	179	1.24	53	1.39
191	Charleston, WV	78	2.11	9	1.37
192	Tacoma, WA	141	1.84	25	1.37
193	Hntngtn–Ashlnd, WV–KY–OH	78	1.78	11	1.35
194	Appalachia–Rural East PA	183	1.18	29	1.34
195	Western OK	249	1.70	45	1.33
196	Western KS	91	.95	25	1.33
197	State of South Dakota	177	1.23	38	1.32
198	Eastern OK	196	1.52	40	1.31
199	North Panhandle TX	146	1.29	31	1.31
200	Northern MS	233	1.60	36	1.32
201	Southwestern TX	107	1.71	18	1.29
202	Appalachlan Mtn Area, WV	193	1.98	23	1.28
203	Western AR	204	1.48	41	1.28
204	Northwestern IA	182	1.04	41	1.27
205	Southern Rural MI	158	1.28	29	1.27
206	Northern Rural AL	246	1.87	34	1.27
207	Western, WA	279	1.57	57	1.26
208	Southern Rural AL	183	1.77	23	1.25
209	Western MT	147	1.50	34	1.25
210	Central Valley, CA	225	1.26	53	1.24
211	Mountain Region, VA	209	1.74	29	1.23
212	Northern Rural MI	232	1.24	46	1.20
213	Northern Rural WI	69	.77	21	1.18
214	Rural ID	228	1.54	39	1.17
215	State of North Dakota	187	1.38	31	1.16
216	Southern Rural IL	86	1.31	13	1.14
217	Eastern KS	243	1.38	35	1.12
218	Adirondack Region, NY	100	1.02	18	1.11
219	Springfield–Decatur, IL	79	1.45	11	1.11
220	Northwestern Rural KY	285	1.46	43	1.10
221	Eastern MT	138	1.42	26	1.10

FIGURE 6–2. *(continued)*

		# BIRTHS	% BIRTHS	# HI GRO	% HI GRO
RANK	FORECAST AREA		FORECAST AREA RANKED BY % YOUNG HIGH-GROWERS		
222	Duluth, MN–WI	74	1.60	9	1.09
223	Western OR	213	1.43	43	1.08
224	Eastern WA	166	1.21	36	1.07
225	Southern Rural IN	84	1.21	13	1.05
226	Southern Rural MO	309	1.40	47	1.02
227	Southeastern IA	214	.95	40	1.00
228	Finger Lakes Region, NY	142	1.12	22	.99
229	Jn C–Kgsprt–Brstl, TN–VA	94	1.74	11	.96
230	Peoria, IL	100	1.61	11	.96
231	Northern, Central IL	329	1.04	54	.96
232	Eastern OR	74	1.07	18	.95
233	Northern Rural MO	204	1.32	26	.94
234	Rural NV	56	1.50	9	.90
235	Southern Rural MN	239	1.07	37	.86
236	Northern Rural MN	97	.94	18	.81
237	Western NE	111	1.03	18	.79
238	Eastern Rural AR	131	1.29	16	.75
239	Eastern NE	89	.93	10	.58

Benton Harbor (Michigan), and Fairfield county (Connecticut). The entrepreneurial process is not limited to a few hot-shot cities. It can emerge in some of the places one would consider unlikely at first blush.

THE ENVIRONMENT FOR HIGH-INNOVATION STARTUPS

What does it take for a locale to attract high-innovation entrepreneurs? The question puts us in mind of the tourist who, visiting an English castle, admired the lawn, and asked the groundskeeper how he managed to create such a marvel. "Well, you get the best seed, fertilize and water regularly, weed, roll whenever the need arises, and keep at it for 600 years."

This is to suggest that there are certain elements that cannot be created overnight—or even in a generation. Take those research facilities with their sophisticated faculties. Money and sheer will alone can't create MITs and Georgia Techs. But they do help. Some areas are giving it a try. For example, the State University of New York at Stony Brook was founded in 1957, but didn't really get going as a technology oriented institution until the late 1960s. Together with the nearby Brookhaven Laboratories, it provides a focus and breeding ground for high-tech companies in Suffolk County, one of the fastest-growing parts of the country.

A community can't alter its climate. We doubt that certain parts of the deep South or the Far North will ever be able to become major innovation capitals for any but industries that by their very nature deal with such environments. Cultural centers can be created, however, though like universities this takes time. Americans over the age of 50 can recall a period when Washington was close to being a cultural desert; such no longer is the case. Milwaukee as a center for the arts? The idea would have seemed absurd a few decades ago, but not today.

Much can be done, but it takes will—and a willingness to raise taxes to pay for the amenities. We know of scores of places in all parts of the country that have been endowed by nature with the raw materials from which an innovation-based center could be fashioned but that lack the desire to embark upon programs to bring it about.

In some cases, this results from a conscious decision to leave things the way they are. Such places import and grow businesses based upon the technologies of the old Industrial Revolution—furniture, plumbing supplies, processed agricultural products, clothing, and the like—and export not only these products but their bright, ambitious young people, who head to the innovation-based cities. Businesspeople and others there are aware of the situation and act knowingly. But there are many places that simply haven't thought the matter through.

Can people *really* make a difference? The answer might be no for industrial companies, so reliant upon raw materials and transportation. Not so for the high-innovation firms. We know of a drug company that has a research facility in the Caribbean—because some of its scientists enjoy scuba diving—and another with one in the Rockies—to accommodate skiers. As noted, express mail and telecommunications can eliminate all kinds of barriers.

Take the case of Seattle, a city that studied its pluses and minuses carefully and then acted. It has a fine climate—for those who don't mind a gentle rain, which, after all, produces lush greenery. Drive out of the city a few miles and you will be in the midst of some of the most spectacular forest in the world. Together with nearby Tacoma, it has a sizeable metropolitan area, which already is headquarters for several major corporations, among them

Boeing and Weyerhaeuser. Seattle possesses a good port and is ideally located for contacts with the Pacific basin, while Vancouver, Canada, is a short drive away and southern Alaska can be reached by ferry. In the University of Washington, Seattle has one of the nation's premier state universities. In short, much that is required to create a high-innovation complex is in place.

And one did come into being. Seattle finds that one out of every four new jobs created since 1980 are at firms that did not exist as recently as 1979 and that it now exports more services than goods. Boeing and Weyerhaueser are still there—but so are scores of smaller, growing innovation-based companies. We last counted 723 of them that were exhibiting significant growth—companies like Microsoft, Applied Microsystems, Meteor, McCaw Communications, Alaska Airlines, and Wondervisions.

East Cambridge, Massachusetts is an even more dramatic example of how it might be done. Sure, it is adjacent to some of the nation's most prestigious schools and has many other assets, but there were liabilities as well. East Cambridge is really a small neighborhood about two-thirds of a mile square in the eastern, most industrial, part of Cambridge. Twenty years ago the area consisted mainly of old, run-down factories built during the Industrial Revolution. Unless you lived there or knew the area well, you probably wouldn't have ventured into East Cambridge in the 1960s, and even then you wouldn't have felt safe after dark. Most people who lived in Boston had rarely been there, and many hadn't an idea of where it was located.

It did have those assets, however, and one more in the form of low rents at a time when rentals were starting to soar. So startup, highly innovative companies, needing to keep costs low, leased some of those old factories, renovated them, and became the nucleus for others. In this case little help was required from local political leaders; like Topsy, the area just grew. It continues to do so today. In the 1980s East Cambridge, by itself, *has created more jobs within its boundaries than have 13 states.* As noted earlier, it is one of the centers for computer software in general and artificial intelligence in particular. And it is no longer so grubby; over 4.5 million square feet of new or rehabilitated office space have been built in this tiny neighborhood, which houses the likes of Lotus Development, Index Systems, Symbolics, Thinking Machines, Lisp Machines, Applied Expert Systems, Gold Hill Computers, and Brattle Research.

East Cambridge is only one of several such centers in the area; there are over 1,200 software companies in Massachusetts, most within commuting distance of East Cambridge. These employ around 26,000 people, with 40 percent of them starting since 1980. The software industry is a classic example of a highly innovative service-sector industry that exports virtually all of its product.

You might be thinking that two decades ago East Cambridge was a diamond in the rough—but a diamond nonetheless, which is to say it had so many positive qualities that in time they were bound to surface. Other locales, not so fortunately endowed, made it on sheer will. We have to be impressed by the vision with which the state of Nebraska is forging a telecommunications policy. Urban revitalization, particularly around the water, has played a major role in increasing the perceived quality of living in such places as Baltimore, San Francisco, Toledo, and San Antonio. Good universities can be made better; the University of Texas is one such example. Other areas and states have done as much on a lesser scale.

We have seen, then, that high-innovation entrepreneurs have a much freer hand when it comes to location than did their Industrial Revolution counterparts. In most cases, however, they need assistance from farsighted political leaders. Pittsburgh has to be proud of being named the most livable city in the United States in a recent poll, given the fact that many of its residents can recall the time when it was dominated by steel mills, the dark smoke making living close to unbearable, the surrounding rivers polluted, and the very atmosphere oppressive. God did not turn Pittsburgh from one of the nation's ugliest cities into one of its more attractive places and a major center for robotics and artificial intelligence research. People did. People can do it in many places.

But will they? Will other cities and towns turn themselves around as have Boston and Pittsburgh? Or will they continue down the paths that were blazed in the 19th or the first half of the 20th century? The answer will have a significant effect on what happens to the people in these places. Will new job opportunities open to them, or will they be faced with a gradually declining share of the pie? In any case, how should the individual person cope with continuing transitions taking place and what advice should such persons offer their children? What should schools be preparing them for? These are the questions to which we shall next turn.

CHAPTER 7

What Does It Mean for Workers?

While the Innovation Revolution has brought many benefits to businesspeople and presented opportunities to entrepreneurs and investors, it has also been very hard on large numbers of workers. This was to have been expected. Every turn of the economic wheel throws some to the ground and raises others to the heights. There is no such thing as painless change, no matter how beneficial it may seem.

The Innovation Revolution is based upon the rapid obsolescence of products, services, and, in some instances, people as well. Firms rise and fall. Jobs are created and then vanish. Everyone in the labor force must constantly ask: Do I have the right job? How long will it last? What should I do next? Where will I live next? Am I secure (do I really want to be)? Do I have growth potential? We have touched upon all of this earlier and now will go into some detail and suggest answers.

Begin by noting that these are not "comfortable" questions. Also, reflect that they weren't asked as often and by so many people in the 1950s. Nor are they being asked as frequently in those parts of the economy and country relatively unaffected by the Innovation Revolution. The middle-aged manager of a saw mill catering to local markets in central Maine may not deem them important questions. Not so a computer programmer at a high-tech startup in a Washington suburb. In other words, they are the product of an economy competing in world markets on the basis of innovation.

CHANGING JOBS

In today's economy—in the aggregate—one out of every five workers leaves a job every year, and about one in ten switches careers every year. About half of those who leave a job are forced to do so when the firm they work for lays them off or goes out of business. The others quit for a variety of reasons, some to take up new careers. The number who change careers or jobs varies a great deal from one occupation to another. Figure 7–1, derived from Bureau of Labor Statistics releases, summarizes the odds of switching each year by occupation.

Note that doctors and lawyers are quite secure. Not so laborers and managers. Generally speaking, those with expertise that can be readily recycled are more likely to take on new careers than individuals who are less flexible. Also, satisfaction—a sense of accomplishment, excitement, money—can keep a person in a single occupation for life, while the lack of same would lead to switches. Observe that teachers have a high degree of occupational change, accountants a low level. Look the list over, and as with these two, try to imagine why they rank as they do. Then try to locate yourself, and give the matter some thought.

Changing occupations rarely is risk-free financially. Figure 7–2 shows the expected gains or losses (in 1980 dollars) realized by each career group as it made the changes in the past few years. You can see that far more people who change occupations take pay cuts than receive higher pay. Practical nurses, teachers, sales clerks, computer operators, food and health service workers, and laborers tend to do better for obvious reasons. On the other hand, a physician who leaves medicine to enter another occupation might expect to take a sharp pay cut, also for obvious reasons.

How does it all come out on balance? Do the gainers outweigh the losers? Are the rich getting richer, the poor poorer? Is the middle class shrinking, as some commentators seem to think? To answer these questions we took our forecast of employment change derived in Chapter 5 and converted it to occupations for 1984 and 1997 based on the mix of occupations in both of these years estimated by the Bureau of Labor Statistics. We then assigned dollar values to each occupation and divided the occupations into five equal groups: top, above average, middle, below average, and bottom. Figure 7–3 summarizes the share of total earnings taken home by each group. On balance, and despite the enormous mobil-

FIGURE 7-1. PERCENT CHANGING OCCUPATION EACH YEAR

1	Engineers	.024
2	Scientists	.049
3	Science Technicians	.066
4	Medical Workers	.017
5	Registered Nurses	.001
6	Physicians	.000
7	Health Technicians	.029
8	Practical Nurses	.019
9	Technicians nec	.148
10	Computer Specialists	.004
11	Social Scientists	.087
12	Teachers nec	.141
13	Teachers/Adult	.084
14	Teachers/College	.160
15	Teachers/Secondary	.027
16	Writers/Artists	.158
17	Professional Workers nec	.100
18	Accountants	.030
19	Buyers	.134
20	Lawyers	.003
21	Personnel Specialists	.116
22	Public Administrators	.227
23	Managers/Food/Lodge	.091
24	Managers/Administrative nec	.099
25	Sales/Insurance/Real Estate	.124
26	Sales nec	.110
27	Sales Clerks	.204
28	Secretaries	.122
29	Office Machine Operators	.077
30	Office Computer Operators	.089
31	Clerical	.106
32	Craft/Construction	.152
33	Craft/Supervisors	.238
34	Craft/Metalwork	.194
35	Craft/Mechanics	.150
36	Craft/Auto Mechanics	.111
37	Craft/Printing	.187
38	Craft/Public Utilities	.171
39	Crafts nec	.140
40	Operatives/Metal	.238
41	Operatives nec	.249
42	Operatives/Transportation	.159
43	Services/Bldg. Maintenance	.089
44	Services/Food	.053
45	Services/Health	.070
46	Services/Personal	.116
47	Services/Protection	.068
48	Services nec	.016
49	Laborers/Helpers	.251

NOTE: "nec" stands for "not elsewhere classified."

FIGURE 7–2. AVERAGE INCOME BEFORE AND AFTER OCCUPATIONAL SHIFTS, BY STARTING OCCUPATION

	OCCUPATION	ORIGINAL INCOME	INCOME AFTER SHIFT	DIFFERENCE
1	Engineers	$26,130	$24,187	$−1,943
2	Scientists	23,112	18,691	−4,421
3	Science Technicians	18,020	19,408	1,388
4	Medical Workers	17,803	14,968	−2,835
5	Registered Nurses	13,548	15,622	2,074
6	Physicians	47,870	16,096	−31,774
7	Health Technicians	12,608	13,541	933
8	Practical Nurses	9,446	13,579	4,133
9	Technicians nec	20,156	16,196	−3,960
10	Computer Specialists	20,474	19,799	−675
11	Social Scientists	24,204	27,860	3,656
12	Teachers nec	13,424	14,703	1,279
13	Teachers/Adult	13,371	15,227	1,856
14	Teachers/College	22,429	23,955	1,526
15	Teachers/Secondary	14,989	16,707	1,718
16	Writers/Artists	17,763	17,382	−381
17	Professional Workers nec	16,708	16,397	−311
18	Accountants	20,630	22,021	1,391
19	Buyers	18,453	18,798	345
20	Lawyers	34,712	30,498	−4,214
21	Personnel Specialists	20,841	21,726	885
22	Public Administrators	23,043	20,725	−2,318
23	Managers/Food/Lodge	11,719	16,160	4,441
24	Managers/Administrative nec	23,290	14,908	−8,382
25	Sales/Insurance/R.E.	25,016	18,286	−6,730
26	Sales nec	17,916	16,715	−1,201
27	Sales Clerks	9,101	13,691	4,590
28	Secretaries	10,587	14,293	3,706
29	Office Machine Oper.	11,144	11,624	480
30	Office Computer Oper.	12,669	17,674	5,005
31	Clerical	11,676	14,303	2,627
32	Craft/Construction	16,270	15,802	−468
33	Craft/Supervisors	21,322	16,829	−4,493
34	Craft/Metalwork	17,481	15,641	−1,840
35	Craft/Mechanics	17,497	16,609	−888
36	Craft/Auto Mechanics	14,604	15,694	1,090
37	Craft/Printing	14,678	15,045	367
38	Craft/Pub. Utilities	20,368	17,189	−3179
39	Crafts nec	15,248	16,872	1,624
40	Operatives/Metal	15,177	13,252	−1,925
41	Operatives nec	13,341	12,986	−355
42	Operatives/Transportation	16,997	14,165	−2,832
43	Services/Bldg. Maint.	10,182	12,775	2,593
44	Services/Food	7,804	13,253	5,449
45	Services/Health	8,606	12,321	3,715
46	Services/Personal	8,035	11,395	3,360

FIGURE 7-2. (*continued*)

	OCCUPATION	ORIGINAL INCOME	INCOME AFTER SHIFT	DIFFERENCE
47	Services/Protection	16,507	16,196	−311
48	Services nec	8,580	11,306	2,726
49	Laborers/Helpers	12,860	13,951	1,091

ity involved, the distribution of earning power will remain remarkably the same. The rich get slightly richer and the poor get slightly poorer, but only slightly. The middle stays just about the same.

So the transformation we are experiencing isn't likely to destroy any particular economic class or give one class an advantage over the others. Its main consequence is mobility. It demands that most people who aspire to the top rung on the ladder anticipate and be prepared for multiple jobs and serial careers. The days of joining the firm, putting in a solid lifetime of work and retiring with a gold watch may be over for an increasingly important segment of the population.

THE ROLE OF EDUCATION

How do you prepare for a fluid career of this sort? Where does your security come from? How do you minimize the constant (and justified) fear of losing your job? Large firms do not offer as much security as they once did. The *Fortune* 500 have reduced their work forces by about 3 million people in this decade alone. The small firm offers virtually no security. Investment banking rewards hot shots with six digit figures when the going is good—and throws

FIGURE 7-3. SHARE OF TOTAL EARNINGS BY GROUP, 1984–1997

GROUP	1984 SHARE	1997 SHARE
Rich	31.2	31.6
Above Average	22.8	23.1
Middle	18.4	18.4
Below Average	15.9	15.4
Poor	11.8	11.5

them into the streets when things turn sour. Even government, which once was a safe if not lucrative haven, is now subject to referenda and the kinds of massive layoffs several states have undergone in the 1970s. It is noteworthy that more and more unions are opting for the kind of settlements won by the United Auto Workers in recent contracts, namely giving up wages and fringe benefits in return for job security. Professor Milton Friedman, when challenged on a point, wryly grinned and said, "I am an aging tenured full professor at a major university. That is about as secure as you can get in our society." True enough. But security can bring sloth as well as freedom to speak out. That, incidentally, is one of the problems the high-innovation industries have to face.

Notwithstanding some auto workers, tenured professors, well-established sole proprietorship professionals, many civil service workers, and a number of others, in today's world security must flow from the individual not the job. Few jobs are secure; the only security derives from the ability to adapt and move, and these derive from the strength of the individual. By strength is meant the possession of a scarce resource in any period: general knowledge that can be quickly adapted to new circumstances. It is the ability to perform several jobs and concentrate on one or another when the need arises—to understand the basic principles involved rather than memorizing the manual that describes how something is done. In short, it is the strength derived from flexibility.

This confounds the conventional wisdom, which holds that workers—brain workers in particular—should attend colleges and major in concrete subjects such as accounting and engineering rather than "soft" ones like philosophy and literature. There is something to this, but it is a dangerous oversimplification. Engineers and accountants who memorize formulas and rules without an idea of the rationales behind them will be lost once the formulas are changed—as will philosophers and English majors who cannot reason and write well. All of them must be aware that much of the knowledge they gained in schools in year one will be obsolete in year five insofar as applications are concerned. An engineer with specific knowledge and an inability to adapt to changing ways will be out of a job. Meanwhile, philosophers and writers are in short supply, the former a prized resource in artificial intelligence research, the latter in demand to translate concepts and ideas formulated by innovation-based firms into language understandable by lay persons.

How do young students, and adults, become flexible? In general, how can you remain strong when what you know how to do is becoming obsolete? The obvious answer is that each member of the labor force must constantly reeducate himself or herself. The answer is not trivial because of the magnitudes and complexities involved.

There was a time when obsolescence rates were a relatively minor concern, when we could keep up with changes by modifying our educational system to produce a different mix of workers. Was there a shortage of elementary school teachers? The economy responded by raising their salaries and benefits, and districts would send recruiters to teachers' colleges seeking applicants. The word soon got around, the cadres of education majors would expand to meet the demand, and within a few years the shortage would be replaced by a generalized glut. A like process has answered needs for more petroleum technicians, computer programmers, auto mechanics, and so on down the occupational line. It still works today.

Yet the situation in the workplace, at least for high-innovation industries, has changed. The mix of occupations is being altered, and at the same time the growth of the labor force is slowing down. The good news for innovation-based workers knowledgeable about the environment is that they are scarce right now and will become more so in the future. The bad news for the entrepreneurs and managers of highly innovative concerns is that few entrants into their labor force possess the requisite skills and knowledge of how to change when the need presents itself.

TRAIN, RETRAIN, AND RETRAIN

Pat Choate, in his fascinating monograph *Retooling the American Workforce,* points out that about 90 percent of the labor force in 1990 will have held jobs in 1980. This implies that if all the schools did their jobs perfectly and produced exactly the right kinds of workers with exactly the right kinds of skills, they could only affect 10 percent of the work force in a single decade.

What about the other 90 percent? In the past, in not-so-innovative businesses, they might change slowly, perform their duties in pretty much the same ways as earlier, or be shifted to new tasks. Sometimes workers can still get away with it; in other situations their flaws become evident almost immediately. A professor of ancient history may fail to keep up with findings in the field, use the same lecture notes for years, and his shortcomings will be evident only to colleagues and brighter students. Not so a professor of computer science, who must change lectures not only every year but every semester and be prepared to alter them each time he reads a professional paper.

Put it this way: the work force used to be dominated by individuals like that teacher of ancient history; now, more and more people like that computer science professor are in demand. The rate at which people change careers (not jobs) is now 10 percent per year, not per decade as once it was.

Under these circumstances, we cannot possibly create a competitive labor force by simply improving the relevance and quality of what the schools teach, although even this would be difficult to accomplish. While the students can shift from major to major with comparative ease, recruiting the right kinds of faculty to meet their needs would be next to impossible. In the first place, such teachers, too, are scarce resources; there simply aren't enough of them to go around, even if salaries were competitive. Moreover, many schools have an abundance of faculty members in many subject areas akin to that professor of ancient history and can't easily get rid of them (Milton Friedman is right about tenured full professors). And if we can't do much as soon as is desirable about new workers, how can we hope to accomplish much with older ones, many of whom are fixed in their ways? This is the greatest challenge facing the new American industries.

This presents a dazzling opportunity for individuals who know the ground rules and can work within them—realizing all the while that rule number one is that the rules are always changing. It means that education must be constant, on the job, with much of it acquired through what passes for journalism. Books and articles in professional journals are still important, but their gestation periods often are so long that by the time they are printed, the information is partially obsolete. It takes nine months or so for a book to be transformed from a manuscript to a bound volume, and only slightly less than that for a journal article to be refereed, edited, and published.

Fortunately, high tech is coming to the rescue. Desk-top publishing, in which a writer can do what the compositor did what seems ages ago may solve the problem. Within a short period of time workers in innovation-based companies may be able to subscribe to a wide variety of journals put together in this fashion.

More important perhaps than the source of this new education will be its nature. Workers will have to learn to prize flexibility—their employers already do. Clerical workers, for example, should know the basic principles of computer science rather than how to operate a particular word processing system or spreadsheet. Word processors and spreadsheets become obsolete in about 16 months; basic computer science hasn't changed much in the past 16 years.

People who train mining technicians know that a mine safety engineer no longer simply memorizes the manual—how many timbers to use in what kind of a tunnel—but learns how to improvise solutions to new kinds of problems. Deeper and deeper mines are different environments than those to which engineers and technicians of, say, the 1950s were accustomed. Individuals making judgments in such circumstances must know as much about geology as stress points in timbering.

Think about the complex problems facing petroleum companies at Prudhoe Bay in the Arctic Circle. Consider the problems faced by petrologists and engineers relocated from Saudi Arabia. They had to adjust to totally different kinds of climate, devise new kinds of machinery, take into account radically different terrain, and worry about novel environmental problems. The companies had to erect entire cities under protective cover from which workers would not emerge for months. The problems involved in feeding and sleeping alone were enormous, to which were added those of recreation.

To be sure, all involved received high salaries, and there were plenty of workers eager for such jobs as truck driver, electrician, and the like. But there were shortages of able, experienced managers to make decisions and put them into practice. Putting together the Prudhoe Bay projects was more like establishing stations on the moon than in Saudi Arabia, and no one had that kind of experience. It had to be developed and learned. So it was. And such knowledge came from specialists who knew how to think generally and generalists capable of assimilating large amounts of specialized knowledge rapidly.

So it goes down the line. Welders have to know a great deal about metallurgy not simply welding techniques, because they are called upon to work with many different kinds of new metals. Hotel clerks must understand the basics of data-management sys-

174

tems. Some truck drivers have to know the fundamentals of tele-communications and computers. The typical Federal Express truck now carries an on-board computer driven by a mainframe in Memphis that tells the driver where to go next and what to pick up there. The manual to operate this equipment is over an inch thick and requires a fairly broad knowledge of how data-base systems operate if the driver is to exercise good judgment.

Unions have come to expect this kind of change, and many have already come to terms with it. When the workers at General Electric's Lynn, Mass. jet engine plant voted to accept the terms and conditions of the "factory of the future" as it was called, they agreed to go from some 300 job classifications to three. The person who once had to know only one kind of job now has to know dozens, perhaps scores, and be prepared to shift from one to another when the need arises, and must constantly upgrade knowledge. The worker in the plant capable of doing just that obviously will be in a much stronger position than the person who has comfortably settled in a narrow rut.

THE NEW PLAYING FIELD

More frequently than before, survival and advancement in the workplace requires changing employers and careers. This means workers must have a clear idea of the market for their skills and how that market is changing and is likely to change in the future. In Chapter 5 we presented some estimates of what kinds of jobs would be created in the next few years. These are "net jobs"—that is, the number of new jobs above and beyond those jobs already out there. Nothing was said then about job openings that might exist at any moment, and this is the crucial matter for those seeking employment.

A job opening can arise in a number of ways:

1. A net new job is created
2. Someone leaves the labor force (to go back to school, have a child, etc.)
3. Someone now holding a job retires
4. Someone now holding a job dies
5. Someone holding a job leaves it and looks for a new job elsewhere

The number of new jobs opening up due to people leaving the labor force or dying before retirement age is very much a function of the age of the workers. In general, the proportion of job openings (sometimes known as "slots") that are created by death and retirement is as follows:

AGE OF WORKER	PERCENT OF JOBS OPENING PER YEAR DUE TO DEATH AND RETIREMENT
18–24	.1
25–34	.1
35–54	.2
55+	2.5

It can be seen that relatively few jobs open up due to death and retirement—less than 3 percent in the aggregate. The real opportunities for work come from replacing those who for one reason or another quit or are fired and from job creation.

Millions of Americans are seeking work on any given day, but their talents, abilities, training, experience, desires, locales, and other factors narrow the field of potential competitors considerably. The recent law school graduate knows that he or she is not competing against all other LL.B.'s seeking posts. The competition narrows down to those who are newcomers plus a few with some little experience—lawyers with comparable skills who graduated in the same ranking from similarly regarded schools, who want to work in the same part of the country for the same salary range.

Here too flexibility is required. The individual who graduates in the bottom half of his class from a mediocre school should not be astonished if unable to settle in a place at a top New York or Washington firm. But he or she will find a job—if ready to be flexible on location, salary, and other factors. Individuals in any occupation who say "I can't find a job" generally mean they can't find one where they want to work, in the kind of work they want to perform, at the salary they hope to command.

Most job seekers have a pretty good idea of their talents and the problems to be surmounted, however. They know, for example, that they are competing against:

1. Recent graduates looking for the same kind of job
2. People reentering the labor force

3. Workers who have left a job and now are seeking the same one you want.

Figure 7–4 summarizes the number of people in terms of percentages of the base population entering or reentering the labor force by age and occupation. As might be expected, the reentry rate varies considerably by occupation. Usually there are many more younger entrants than older ones, though there are exceptions to the rule. As the growth of the labor force slows down, people rejoining it in later years can become a valuable resource. The returning mother and the returning retired person have become significant factors in the work force, and provide competition for new jobs.

Career switchers are also a major force in the labor market. From data provided by the Bureau of Labor Statistics, we can estimate who is switching from what job to what other job. One of the surprises is that not as many workers as might have been anticipated switch careers to make more money. Figure 7–5 summarizes the proportion of those who moved up and down financially. Workers at the top end of the scale, almost by definition, generally move down if they make switches. Physicians, lawyers, engineers, and managers have the most to give up when they make such career moves. Of course some can move up; lawyers become investment bankers, staff doctors become hospital administrators, engineers leave the salaried ranks and open their own businesses. But the majority take income cuts when they change careers in midstream. Conversely, those at the bottom of the economic ladder tend to move up. Able college instructors in computer science know they can improve their economic condition if they take a post in the private economy.

Whatever they do, *some* of them are competing for the job others want. The odds for a job seeker getting a position depends on the balance between the number of slots opening up and the number of available people seeking to fill them. If there are more slots than people, he or she will be in good shape. If the converse is true and the seekers outnumber the slots, the odds fall off, sometimes sharply. A prominent Wall Street bank offering $50,000 a year to trainees who know that within two or three years they will be making six-digit salaries may have 1,000 applicants—most of them superb—for 50 slots. An isolated rural community whose doctor dies or retires may spend years searching for a replacement at the same salary.

177

FIGURE 7–4. PERCENT NEW ENTRANTS (1980) BY OCCUPATION AND AGE

| | AGE | | | |
OCCUPATION	18–24	25–34	35–54	55+
Engineers	1.0	.2	.5	.5
Scientists	2.2	1.4	.6	.0
Science Technicians	4.6	.0	1.1	.9
Medical Workers	.0	.0	1.7	.0
Registered Nurses	.6	1.8	2.1	4.0
Physicians	9.1	.8	1.0	2.8
Health Technicians	3.1	2.0	3.2	2.2
Practical Nurses	5.2	2.2	4.5	1.5
Technicians nec	3.0	.5	.5	1.9
Computer Specialists	3.7	1.9	.0	.0
Social Scientists	.0	2.1	2.0	5.0
Teachers nec	6.5	5.0	1.7	2.3
Teachers/Adult	2.9	4.0	3.5	.0
Teachers/College	3.4	1.1	1.0	.0
Teachers/Secondary	3.7	2.4	1.4	3.5
Writers/Artists	3.5	3.2	2.7	4.0
Professional Workers nec	2.6	1.6	2.5	2.6
Accountants	1.3	.9	.9	1.3
Buyers	.0	1.5	.0	4.1
Lawyers	3.8	2.1	.4	1.9
Personnel Specialists	1.6	2.1	.8	2.3
Public Administrators	4.5	.5	1.0	2.1
Managers/Food/Lodge	1.5	4.9	1.1	.0
Managers/Admin nec	2.0	1.2	.8	1.7
Sales/Insurance/Real Estate	4.7	1.1	1.3	2.3
Sales nec	5.4	8.4	2.1	3.4
Sales Clerks	4.8	5.4	4.4	4.1
Secretaries	3.0	2.9	3.1	3.4
Office Machine Operators	5.1	2.9	.0	9.1
Office Comp Operators	2.2	1.9	.9	4.3
Clerical	3.8	3.3	3.0	3.7
Craft/Construction	3.5	1.5	2.0	4.3
Craft/Supervisors	.9	1.4	.8	1.8
Craft/Metalwork	1.7	.7	.8	.7
Craft/Mechanics	1.5	1.3	1.9	1.6
Craft/Auto Mechanics	3.1	1.2	1.3	4.2
Craft/Printing	4.6	1.7	1.1	3.1
Craft/Public Utilities	5.6	.7	.0	.0
Craft nec	8.8	3.7	2.9	1.8
Operatives/Metal	3.8	1.0	1.4	3.1
Operatives nec	4.1	2.8	2.6	3.0
Operatives/Transportation	3.6	1.8	1.8	3.3
Service/Bldg. Maintenance	7.2	5.2	4.8	5.4
Services/Food	7.5	7.9	4.2	5.6

FIGURE 7-4. (*continued*)

| | AGE | | | |
OCCUPATION	18–24	25–34	35–54	55+
Services/Health	5.3	4.1	3.8	5.4
Services/Personal	8.3	6.2	5.1	9.2
Services/Protection	6.7	.8	1.4	4.7
Services nec	11.7	.0	9.1	8.3
Laborers/Helpers	5.7	4.0	5.0	5.8

We already have noted that not everyone changes jobs to make more money. The old adage "money isn't everything" certainly appears to hold in the job market. Many do not want the extra stress and longer working hours associated with upward moves, or even in their present jobs. Others may gain a great deal of personal satisfaction from their occupations that is not measured in monetary terms. Kindergarten teachers may not feel comfortable selling cars, and nurses may turn down better-paid posts managing fast food outlets regardless of the financial stakes involved. Then, too, what one person perceives as an upward move another might consider the reverse. Department chairmanships are avoided at top universities and colleges, usually going to the person who has a knack for shuffling papers and soothing tempers, but is not engaged in research; such posts are prize plumbs at schools where research and related activities count for little.

Some people do not make shifts to significantly different occupations simply because they have never thought of themselves in these terms. The individual who looks in the mirror and sees a truck driver or a hair stylist may have difficulty imagining himself a bank clerk or a computer programmer. Perception is important, and can be a hurdle. But it can be overcome. After all, an over-the-hill actor who entered politics after retirement managed to become President of the United States.

MEASURING THE COSTS

To help you determine which occupations are comparable to the one you now have, a group working on an MIT project*

---

*David L. Birch, "Projections of Jobs, Occupations, and Career Opportunities for Connecticut" (Cambridge: MIT Program on Neighborhood and Regional Change, March, 1986).

FIGURE 7–5. PERCENT OF CAREER SWITCHERS MOVING UP AND DOWN IN SALARY, BY STARTING OCCUPATION

	STARTING OCCUPATION	PERCENT UP	PERCENT DOWN
1	Engineers	.320	.680
2	Scientists	.238	.762
3	Science Technicians	.409	.591
4	Medical Workers	.200	.800
5	Registered Nurses	.536	.464
6	Physicians	.000	1.000
7	Health Technicians	.550	.450
8	Practical Nurses	.961	.039
9	Technicians nec	.281	.719
10	Computer Specialists	.599	.401
11	Social Scientists	.440	.560
12	Teachers nec	.550	.450
13	Teachers/Adult	.603	.397
14	Teachers/College	.439	.561
15	Teachers/Secondary	.540	.460
16	Writers/Artists	.432	.568
17	Professionals Workers nec	.400	.600
18	Accountants	.499	.501
19	Buyers	.472	.528
20	Lawyers	.410	.590
21	Personnel Specialists	.472	.528
22	Public Administrators	.364	.636
23	Managers/Food/Lodge	.484	.516
24	Managers/Administrative nec	.091	.909
25	Sales/Insurance/Real Estate	.025	.975
26	Sales nec	.390	.610
27	Sales Clerks	.598	.402
28	Secretaries	.723	.277
29	Office Machine Operators	.586	.414
30	Office Computer Operators	.748	.252
31	Clerical	.596	.404
32	Craft/Construction	.417	.583
33	Craft/Supervisors	.317	6.83
34	Craft/Metalwork	.415	.585
35	Craft/Mechanics	.489	.511
36	Craft/Auto Mechanics	.564	.436
37	Craft/Printing	.518	.482
38	Craft/Public Utilities	.286	.714
39	Crafts nec	.490	.510
40	Operatives/Metal	.320	.680
41	Operatives nec	.363	.637
42	Operatives/Transportation	.288	.712

FIGURE 7–5.   (*continued*)

	STARTING OCCUPATION	PERCENT UP	PERCENT DOWN
43	Services/Bldg. Maintenance	.445	.555
44	Services/Food	1.000	.000
45	Services/Health	.809	.191
46	Services/Personal	.609	.391
47	Services/Protection	.426	.574
48	Services nec	.360	.640
49	Laborers Helpers	.493	.507

devised a method of describing a job in terms of five generalized kinds of competence needed to get the work done. We called these:

1. *Psychomotor* The manipulation of tools or processes to accomplish tasks.
2. *Intellectual/Cognitive* The kind of thinking and reasoning required.
3. *Interpersonal* The ways in which an individual must interact with others to complete a job.
4. *Motivational* The nature of the motivation required.
5. *Factual knowledge* The breadth and depth of knowledge required to perform effectively.

All jobs require different levels of each of these kinds of competence. Detailed descriptions of all the dimensions and their levels are to be found in Appendix 7–1. The values for each occupation are summarized in Figure 7–6. The utility of this exercise is that it permits comparisons between occupations that might seem quite different and enables people who are thinking of making changes to decide what might be suitable. For example, a manager of a store wouldn't be suited for work in personnel services—unless he had concluded that retail management was quite alien to his abilities and interests. But store managers might well consider technical sales or law. Likewise, it wouldn't be much of a change for a textile operator to become an office/computer operator, an office worker, or a truck driver. Similarly a school superintendent (classified as public administrators) whose job is threatened by a decline in the school-age population and the closing of his institu-

FIGURE 7–6. COMPETENCE LEVELS BY OCCUPATION

	OCCUPATION	PSYCHO-MOTOR	INTEL./COGNITIVE	INTER-PERSONAL	MOTIVA-TIONAL	FACT. KNOWL-EDGE
1	Engineers	3	5	2	3	4
2	Scientists	4	5	2	3	4
3	Science Technicians	4	3	2	3	3
4	Medical Workers	5	4	3	3	3
5	Regist. Nurses	4	4	4	3	3
6	Physicians	5	5	3	3	4
7	Health Technicians	4	3	2	3	3
8	Practical Nurses	4	3	4	2	2
9	Technicians nec	4	3	2	3	3
10	Computer Specialists	2	5	2	3	3
11	Social Scientists	2	5	3	6	4
12	Teachers nec	3	5	4	4	3
13	Teachers/Adult	2	5	4	4	3
14	Teachers/College	2	5	4	6	4
15	Teach/Secondary	2	5	4	4	3
16	Writers/Artists	4	5	5	6	3
17	Prof. Workers nec	2	5	4	4	3
18	Accountants	2	3	3	3	3
19	Buyers	2	2	4	5	3
20	Lawyers	2	4	4	3	4
21	Personnel Specs.	2	5	4	4	3
22	Public Admin.	2	4	5	6	3
23	Managers/Food/Lodge	2	4	3	4	3
24	Managers/Admin. nec	2	4	4	4	4
25	Sales/Ins./R.E.	2	4	4	5	3
26	Sales nec	2	3	4	5	3
27	Sales Clerks	2	2	3	1	2
28	Secretaries	3	2	2	3	2
29	Office Machine Oper.	3	1	1	1	1
30	Office Comp. Oper.	3	1	1	1	2
31	Clerical	2	2	2	2	2
32	Craft/Construct.	4	4	2	3	3
33	Craft/Supervisor	2	4	4	4	3
34	Craft/Metalwork	5	3	1	3	3

FIGURE **7–6.** (*continued*)

	OCCUPATION	PSYCHO-MOTOR	INTEL./ COGNITIVE	INTER-PERSONAL	MOTIVA-TIONAL	FACTUAL KNOWL-EDGE
35	Craft/Mechanics	4	4	1	3	3
36	Craft/Auto Mech.	4	4	1	3	3
37	Craft/Printing	4	3	1	3	3
38	Craft/Pub. Util.	4	3	1	3	3
39	Crafts nec	5	3	1	3	3
40	Operatives/ Metal	3	1	1	1	2
41	Operatives nec	3	1	1	1	2
42	Operatives/ Trans.	4	2	1	1	2
43	Serv./Bldg. Main.	1	1	1	1	1
44	Serv./Food	2	2	2	2	2
45	Serv./Health	2	1	3	2	2
46	Serv./Personal	2	1	2	2	2
47	Serv./Protection	3	3	2	4	2
48	Services nec	2	1	1	3	2
49	Laborers/ Helpers	1	1	1	1	1

tion should consider carefully, a career in technical sales, store management, or that of buyer—remote from what he was doing as they may at first appear.

Switching careers is not simply a matter of identifying an interesting and opening slot, applying for it, being hired, and starting to work. There usually are costs, sometimes prohibitive ones, associated with making the switch. You can't just "be" a computer technician; you have to have an aptitude for the work and then learn how to become one. Learning takes time and money—lost income while the new competencies are being acquired and, in some cases, actual tuition payments to some form of training institution.

We can think of the costs of switching careers in terms of the percentage of a year's salary on the new job that, on average, one must "pay" to get there. In this context, pay may mean actual payment and unrealized wages. It may also involve an indirect cost incurred by employers who have to put up with the fact that new workers don't know what they are doing when they first show up and have to be taught. Estimating such costs—direct and indirect—is one of the most difficult parts of the career-switching calculation for both employee and employer. The costs are not written down anywhere and have to be estimates. Drawing upon data gathered during the MIT project, I have attempted to estimate the cost of obtaining the five different types of competence, and Figure 7–7 presents the results.

Of course, not all of these costs will be incurred in the first year. For example, it frequently takes several years of training and on-the-job experience to obtain a significant jump in interpersonal or motivational competence. It can be done, however, and the cost estimates in Figure 7–7 measure the total cost over several years as a percent of one year's salary.

So switching careers is a delicate balancing act. The would-be switcher must consider the availability of slots, the odds of getting one, the costs of making the switch, and the financial and psychic gains to be made by the switching. The psychic gains are difficult to measure, since they involve individual and personal judgments. The other parts of the balance are knowable, however. Given our knowledge of job creation, entry and exit rates from the labor force, likely career-switching patterns, the competence required to perform each job (and the costs required to obtain competence), and

FIGURE 7–7. COSTS OF OBTAINING COMPETENCE

COMPETENCE	PERCENT OF A YEAR'S SALARY ON A NEW JOB REQUIRED TO OBTAIN ONE INCREMENT OF COMPETENCE
Psychomotor	9%
Intellectual/Cognitive	25%
Interpersonal	50%
Motivational	33%

The factual knowledge dimension is more complex, and depends on the starting and ending point:

		ENDING COMPETENCE LEVEL			
		1	2	3	4
	1	0	.5	3	8
Starting	2	0	.5	2	7
Competence	3	0	.5	1.5	6
Level	4	0	.5	1.0	6

the expected earnings for each job, we can calculate the "expected value" of switching.

Expected value is an important concept, very precise though not easily understood. For one thing, the costs are paid out in the present and immediate future, while the benefits tend to be reaped in the more distant future. This involves what economists call "the future costs of money," which simply means that a dollar in the hand today is worth more than a dollar in hand a year from now, because you could put today's dollar in a bank and in a year receive, say, $1.08 because of interest accumulated. Put another way, $1.00 a year from now is worth $0.92 today. Therefore, to make a proper evaluation of a career switch, we must "discount" future dollars so we can weigh them against near-term costs.

Perhaps an example would be best at this point. Take an individual who works in an office operating a copier, sorter, or some other kind of machine and who is considering becoming a truck driver. The reason might be that by-now familiar one—due to office automation, the prospects for such office workers are bleak. And from a competence standpoint, the shift to truck driving doesn't look too bad:

COMPETENCE	OFFICE MACHINE OPERATOR	TRUCK DRIVER	INCREMENT
Psychomotor	3	4	1
Intellectual/cognitive	1	2	1
Interpersonal	1	1	0
Motivational	1	1	0
Factual knowledge	1	2	1

The total cost of switching (derived from Figure 7–7) would be:

COMPETENCE	INCREMENTS	PERCENT OF 1 YEAR'S SALARY	TOTAL COST
Psychomotor	1	.09	.09
Intellectual/cognitive	1	.25	.25
Interpersonal	0	.50	0
Motivational	0	.33	0
Factual knowledge	1	.50	.50
Total portion of 1 year's salary			.84

Assume the average truck driver's first year salary is $16,997. Then the total switching cost would be .84 times $16,997, or $14,277.

The gain to be made from switching is the gain of the salary increase (over the present salary) in future years, discounted by the fact that the gains are deferred. In this case, if we assume the office worker is making $11,144 a year, the gain would be $5,853 for the first year. While there is no way of knowing how fast or slow salary increases would be made for each profession, let us assume that during the person's working life the same $5,853 differential between office workers and truck drivers continues. While we are at it, also assume that the shift is made when the worker is 30 years old, so that he has 35 more years to go until retirement. The net gain in today's dollars, after all the discounting is done, assuming an interest rate of 8 percent, would be $56,447 ($5,853 × .92 in year one, plus $5,853 × .85 in year two, plus 5,853 × .78 in year three, and so on). Dollars in more distant years become worth much less. For example, a dollar 15 years from now, assuming that same 8 percent interest rate, would be 29 cents today.

Other people become truck drivers also. After adding up all the slots and job seekers we find that anyone wanting to enter that field will not have too much competition. Our national calculations suggest that about 340,000 people will be looking for jobs as truck drivers, and there will be about 686,000 openings. So the odds of job seekers finding work are pretty good—we estimate about 91 percent based on past experience.

The total expected value of the switch is thus the net gain (gains minus costs) times the odds of getting a job—in this case ($56,447 − $14,277) × .91 = $38,241. We have made these calculations for all occupations in terms of all other occupations to which an individual might switch as a function of the age of the person in the present occupation. Figure 7–8 summarizes the results for office machine operators nationally. As can be seen, they have many profitable opportunities for switching.

Figure 7–9 summarizes the results of similar detailed analyses for many occupations. As might have been expected, the opportunities for improvement are limited for those at the top of the ladder and for those approaching retirement age, since this latter group does not have sufficient working years left to capitalize upon the opportunities available. For a significant number of occupations, however, we must conclude that either (1) the satisfactions

FIGURE 7-8 LABOR FORCE OCCUPATION: OFFICE WORKER

LABOR FORCE AGE GROUP: 18–24

PREFERENCE	OCCUPATION	VALUE
1	Operatives/Transportation	38833.
2	Operatives/Metal	30386.
3	Laborers/Helpers	14597.
4	Operatives nec	14070.
5	Services/Protection	5992.
6	Craft/Public Utilities	3559.
7	Office Computer Operators	1492.
8	Office Machine Operators	0.
9	Computer Specialists	−518.
10	Lawyers	−619.

LABOR FORCE AGE GROUP: 25–34

PREFERENCE	OCCUPATION	VALUE
1	Operatives/Transportation	38241.
2	Operatives/Metal	29832.
3	Laborers/Helpers	15019.
4	Operatives nec	13571.
5	Services/Protection	5723.
6	Craft/Public Utilities	2254.
7	Office Computer Operators	1466.
8	Office Machine Operators	0.
9	Computer Specialists	−589.
10	Lawyers	−634.

LABOR FORCE AGE GROUP: 35–54

PREFERENCE	OCCUPATION	VALUE
1	Operatives/Transportation	35231.
2	Operatives/Metal	27653.
3	Laborers/Helpers	14135.
4	Operatives nec	12406.
5	Services/Protection	4084.
6	Office Computer Operator	1314.
7	Office Machine Operator	0.
8	Lawyers	−690.
9	Computer Specialists	−788.
10	Physicians	−1454.

LABOR FORCE AGE GROUP: 55+

PREFERENCE	OCCUPATION	VALUE
1	Operatives/Metal	7337.
2	Operatives/Transportation	7173.
3	Laborers/Helpers	5903.
4	Operatives nec	1550.
5	Office Machine Operators	0.
6	Office Computer Operators	−97.
7	Lawyers	−1212.
8	Service/Bldg. Maintenance	−2314.
9	Computer Specialists	−2643.
10	Physicians	−2974.

FIGURE 7-9. MAXIMUM GAINS AND BEST OPTIONS FOR CAREER SWITCHERS AGED 25–34, BY PRESENT OCCUPATION

PRESENT OCCUPATION	MAXIMUM GAIN	THREE BEST OPTIONS		
		1	2	3
Engineers	−670	Lawyers	Physicians	Computer Specs.
Scientists	−548	Lawyers	Physicians	Computer Specs.
Science Techs.	−379	Lawyers	Physicians	Computer Specs.
Medical Workers	1907	Sales/Ins./R.E.	Physicians	Lawyers
Register. Nurses	35719	Sales/Ins./R.E.	Craft/Pub. Util.	Craft/Supervisor
Physicians	−1475	Lawyers	Physicians	Computer Specs.
Health Techs.	41701	Craft/Pub. Util.	Operatives/Trans.	Sales/Ins./R.E.
Practical Nurses	58332	Operatives/Trans.	Craft/Pub. Util.	Craft/Supervisor
Techs. nec	−465	Lawyers	Physicians	Computer Specs.
Computer Specs.	−441	Lawyers	Physicians	Computer Specs.
Social Sci.	−519	Lawyers	Physicians	Computer Specs.
Teachers nec	41687	Sales/Ins./R.E.	Craft/Supervisor	Craft/Pub. Util.
Teachers/Adult	42010	Sales/Ins./R.E.	Craft/Supervisor	Craft/Pub. Util.
Teachers/College	−41	Sales/Ins./R.E.	Lawyers	Physicians
Teachers/Second.	32156	Sales/Ins./R.E.	Craft/Supervisor	Craft/Pub. Util.
Writers/Artists	20476	Sales/Ins./R.E.	Craft/Supervisor	Public Admin.
Prof. Workers nec	21688	Sales/Ins./R.E.	Craft/Supervisor	Craft/Pub. Util.
Accountants	−411	Lawyers	Physicians	Computer Specs.
Buyers	8375	Sales/Ins./R.E.	Lawyers	Physicians
Lawyers	−871	Lawyers	Physicians	Computer Specs.
Personnel Specs.	−308	Physicians	Lawyers	Computer Specs.
Public Admin.	−400	Lawyers	Physicians	Public Admin.
Mgrs./Food/Lodge	46321	Craft/Pub. Util.	Sales/Ins./R.E.	Craft/Supervisor

Mgrs./Admin. nec	−410	Lawyers	Physicians	Computer Specs.
Sales/Ins./R.E.	−480	Lawyers	Physicians	Computer Specs.
Sales nec	15594	Sales/Ins./R.E.	Lawyers	Physicians
Sales Clerks	58575	Operatives/Trans.	Operatives/Metal	Craft/Pub. Util.
Secretaries	46966	Operatives/Trans.	Craft/Pub. Util.	Operatives/Metal
Office Mach. Oper.	38241	Operatives/Trans.	Operatives/Metal	Laborers/Helpers
Office Comp. Oper.	24904	Operatives/Trans.	Operatives/Metal	Craft/Pub. Util.
Clerical	36055	Operatives/Trans.	Craft/Pub. Util.	Operatives/Metal
Craft/Construct.	8446	Craft/Pub. Util.	Sales/Ins./R.E.	Techs. nec
Craft/Supervisor	−330	Lawyers	Physicians	Computer Specs.
Craft/Metalwork	−430	Lawyers	Physicians	Computer Specs.
Craft/Mechanics	−394	Lawyers	Physicians	Computer Specs.
Craft/Auto Mech.	23575	Craft/Pub. Util.	Operatives/Trans.	Sales/Ins./R.E.
Craft/Printing	22903	Craft/Pub. Util.	Operatives/Trans.	Techs. nec
Craft/Pub. Util.	−546	Lawyers	Physicians	Computer Specs.
Crafts nec	17727	Craft/Pub. Util.	Operatives/Trans.	Techs. nec
Operatives/Metal	2970	Operatives/Trans.	Lawyers	Physicians
Operatives nec	19027	Operatives/Trans.	Operatives/Metal	Craft/Pub. Util.
Operatives/Trans.	−688	Lawyers	Physicians	Computer Specs.
Serv./Bldg. Main.	43880	Operatives/Trans.	Operatives/Metal	Laborers/Helpers
Serv./Food	69918	Operatives/Trans.	Craft/Pub. Util.	Operatives/Metal
Serv./Health	59051	Operatives/Trans.	Operatives/Metal	Craft/Pub. Util.
Serv./Personal	64045	Operatives/Trans.	Operatives/Metal	Craft/Pub. Util.
Serv./Protection	−463	Lawyers	Computer Specs.	Physicians
Services nec	59278	Operatives/Trans.	Craft/Pub. Util.	Operatives/Metal
Laborers/Helpers	20459	Operatives/Trans.	Operatives/Metal	Laborers/Helpers

Interpersonal Dimension

It is assumed that there are five fundamental levels of the interpersonal skill dimension. They are:

TO DO THE JOB EFFECTIVELY, IN MOST CASES, A PERSON MUST AT LEAST BE ABLE TO:

1. Work relatively alone, or merely in the presence of others
2. Work with others on tasks requiring interaction, coordination, or interdependence of activities.
3. Work with others requiring influencing specific individuals to do something
4. Work with others requiring influencing specific individuals who are strangers *or* a group in an established pattern
5. Work with others requiring influencing a group of people as a whole

Motivational Dimension

It is assumed that there are six somewhat unique motivational orientations, or dispositions, relating to this dimension. They are:

TO DO THE JOB EFFECTIVELY, IN MOST CASES, A PERSON MUST AT LEAST BE CONCERNED WITH BEING:

1. Secure (i.e., having subsistence money, etc.)
2. Affiliative, desiring to be with others, working alongside or with others, getting to know people, and being able to interact with individuals on other than task-related matters
3. Precise, desiring to be accurate, conscientious, and placing a great deal of attention to detail
4. Integrative, desiring to coordinate and orchestrate the work of numerous other individuals or groups
5. Entrepreneurial, desiring to do new and innovative things, do things better than ever done before, seek opportunities to innovate
6. Influential, desiring to lead, inspire, or stimulate others to do things

Note that there are two themes co-mingled in this dimension. One theme is level of psychosocial maturity as found in developmental personality theories. The other theme involves the likelihood of putting extra effort into the job (i.e., what turns you on). Remember this dimension refers to intent, not necessarily behavior.

Factual-Knowledge Dimension

It is assumed that there are four fundamental levels of the factual-knowledge skill dimension. This does not refer to what field of knowledge or body of knowledge is involved, but merely to the degree of factual knowledge. Factual knowl-

192

edge refers to knowledge of a discipline such as economics or chemistry; knowledge related to an organizational function, such as manufacturing; knowledge related to a product or process, such as high-energy physics; and so forth. The four levels are:

TO DO THE JOB EFFECTIVELY, IN MOST CASES, A PERSON MUST AT LEAST HAVE:

1. No particular field or body of factual knowledge
2. Some specialized knowledge in a particular field
3. In-depth knowledge of a particular field or body of information
4. In-depth knowledge of several fields or bodies of information (i.e., you would have to go to multiple university departments to get formal background in the area)

CHAPTER 8

Thinking About Choices

Innovation is the key to economic growth.

Of course the idea is not unusual; economists have been saying as much since the time of Adam Smith. Also, we know that the American culture supports innovation—it is written across the national experience. It would be foolish to attempt to generalize about a nation with over 240 million people, but there clearly are more innovators and risk takers per capita in the United States than elsewhere.

While Americans are slow to recognize this, foreigners are not. Ask European and Asian businesspeople what they deem the outstanding characteristics of their American counterparts and one of the top two or three will be the knack for innovation. We encourage striving for success and tolerate failure more than they do. Throughout our history, Americans have held up entrepreneurs as role models for children; it's a theme that runs from Benjamin Franklin to Lee Iacocca and Steve Jobs. Furthermore, at a very practical level, America permits its entrepreneurs to hold on to the rewards that flow from their efforts.

As has been iterated and reiterated, our country's basic approach to business has worked well for job creation. But can we sustain the pace? Capital appears in ample supply, flowing in from all over the world. Domestic critics complain that American business is going into debt by sucking in capital from Europe and Asia. Meanwhile writers overseas are worried that earnings gained from exports to the United States are going right back there, because foreign investors recognize the lure of the American markets. Natural resources are becoming less important than before as the Innovation Revolution progresses. Of course, the United States remains richly endowed with a wide variety of raw materials, even energy; it often is forgotten that even while petroleum imports account for an important part of the U.S. trade deficit, this country is the world's second largest producer of oil after the U.S.S.R.

Transportation and communications present no important problem. The former infrastructure is in place, while the latter is rapidly being renovated, renewed, and updated. Lack of entrepreneurs to put it all together is not the kind of problem here that it is in so many other parts of the world. We seem to be experiencing an explosion of entrepreneurship, recognizable by others even if American Cassandras ignore it. When in the summer of 1986 Mitch Kapor decided to leave Lotus Development, the startlingly successful software company he had started in 1982 and shepherded into a $225 million company in four years, the *British Economist* took note of his departure by writing, "Lotus Development is one of those business successes that seem peculiar to America." So it is. The United States grows Lotuses by the carload.

THE PROBLEM IS PEOPLE

The problem will be people. Our present system chews them up. One in ten workers is fired each year. One in five changes jobs each year. Some of this mobility is self-inflicted, but much of it is not. Rather, it flows from the enormous turbulence within our corporate population—the replacement of the old with the new. And of course, turbulence creates insecurity.

Most people who work for a living are coping with this challenge. They are shifting jobs, remaining flexible, and permitting the kind of growth that keeps capital and concepts flowing into and around America. Others are not doing so well. Our magazines are filled with depressing tales about dislocated factory workers—especially elderly workers who are relatively unadaptable and don't want to leave their hometowns or neighborhoods even if they could. From such articles one might easily conclude that the nation is populated by large numbers of such jobless people and that they constitute a major problem.

That this is something about which to be concerned is generally agreed, but the magnitude of the problem isn't formidable. Remember that if roughly 10 percent of our work force actually works in factories and 10 percent of that number is unemployed and half of these are elderly, that makes about one-half of one percent of the labor force "older, dislocated factory workers."

Compassion has an important place in making decisions, but we cannot shape national thinking on the basis of one-half of one percent of the work force. The elderly, dislocated worker might be compensated generously, on an individual basis, to alleviate strains; it is through no fault of their own they have been dislocated by a rapid technological change. But you don't halt the locomotive of progress and necessary change for that reason.

The problem goes beyond the dislocated factory worker, however—it is the dislocated *every* worker. We know that large corporations are laying off thousands of managerial and white collar employees and that small companies come and go at a rapid rate, also dislocating their work forces. Only slightly more subtle is the pressure on the worker who is not laid off, but forced to learn new skills, and sometimes a whole new trade, in order to hold on to an existing position. Dislocation is a phenomenon that is creeping into everyone's job.

Several years ago in a panel discussion between American and Soviet undergraduates, the participants exchanged views on their respective career paths. The Americans were getting the better of it until one Soviet engineering student remarked that he knew he would have a position upon being awarded his degree, that it would be provided for and guaranteed by the state, and that for the rest of his life job insecurity would not be a problem. The Americans hesitated for a moment, looking a trifle uneasy, and then one of them shot back that freedom meant opportunities and that was an exciting prospect. For a fleeting moment, however, you could catch a glimpse of envy in the Americans' eyes. True enough, American college students *do* face an uncertain future. It *can* be exciting, but it also is a fearful thing to contemplate.

Can we have a larger measure of job security? Yes, but at a price. We can slow down the rate of change and thereby relieve some of the pressure. We can have job guarantees—such as those of tenured professors—written into labor contracts. It is the practice in Europe, and one of the reasons for the difficulties companies there have in innovation and change. Even so, we really don't have that option. At one time, when we were much more the masters of our own fate, we might have been able to deliberately choose to slow things down. But we are no longer calling the tune. We no more can halt technology than could our ancestors opt for the pony express once the telegraph was available, the horsecart when the railroad made its appearance, vaudeville when radio became widespread, and calculators when computers could be purchased or leased.

Technology has a compelling logic that cannot be denied. And it usually works out well for the labor force. Henry Ford put a lot of buggy whip manufacturers out of business, but that hardly was an argument against the automobile. Moreover, he helped create far more positions on the assembly lines than were lost. Was there dislocation? Of course. Did workers suffer? They did. Was there an alternative given the goal of economic efficiency and growth? Yes. The agonies of change can be mitigated. But they can be eliminated only at a price no enterprising economy can afford.

Even if we could halt or even slow down the pace of change the choice is out of our hands. The rest of the world is calling the tune—or at least playing a few of the notes. We compete in a global economy in which our well-being is based on the rate at which we can innovate and accommodate change. The automated factory, the fifth-generation computer, the automated office, and the automated farm are all crucial to our long-term competitiveness. It's what we are good at and what helps keep us ahead of the pack.

Put it another way: should we slow down, as Europe did, we will simply be substituting macro for micro instability. We will offer greater short-term job security but only by decreasing the likelihood that there will be jobs enough to go around when the next generation comes to the labor market. Remember that one of the reasons those Soviet students have assured jobs is that they will be entering a sluggish economy in which innovation is frowned upon, even discouraged. We can have that too, but do we want it? Return to that point about buggy whips. Imagine a situation where the owner of a factory turning them out rejects the thought that his offspring one day might not head the operation and enlists government and unions to make certain the firm is around, intact, through the 20th century. Such situations develop when we permit those with a stake in the past to dictate the future.

Those American students were uneasy, perhaps, because they realized they will have to develop and market the kinds of skills that the market will require not only upon graduation but that will evolve during the next half century or so. Certainly, it is a worrisome thing, but what is the alternative? If we do not remain competitive through innovation and change, we will eventually transfer jobs held by Americans to workers in other countries. To complete the analogy, the buggy whip manufacturer's son or daughter may take over the business, but who will buy its products?

This is not as far-fetched as might appear. The Japanese captured the American television receiver market by licensing American technology and then producing transistorized sets when most American firms were trying to squeeze the last bit of profit from the vacuum tube models. They did the same with autos, in part by developing new manufacturing techniques while Detroit continued on as it had for the past quarter of a century. Was there micro stability at RCA, Magnavox, General Motors, and Chrysler? Of course. But you know what happened in the 1970s and beyond.

SECURE BRIDGES

We are *not* suggesting a rampant laissez-faire approach, a return to predatory capitalism. Nor do we have a craving to throw displaced workers into the job pool to sink or swim. Rather, we believe the best way to go would be to erect "secure bridges" over which workers can safely traverse the path from one job or occupation to the next. A sense of well-being and security, necessary for most workers, would then derive from the knowledge that the bridge is there, rather than from assurances that their jobs are for life. If you know that there is in place a well-defined procedure by which you can move from one job to another without significant sacrifice, you will be just as secure as if granted some form of permanency. In fact, workers would be more secure, they would have more self-esteem, because they would know that their services would always be of value and that their jobs were not provided simply out of raw political or union pressure.

Building these secure bridges is a new challenge for Americans. Traditionally we have not thought of the problem in such terms, nor have our institutions focused upon it. We offer security at the beginning of a career (guaranteed public education) and at the end (in the form of Social Security) but nothing in the middle. If we are to hold our present pace and remain competitive, we must now concentrate on the middle.

Several creative approaches to building these bridges have been suggested. Knowledge of what's "out there" is a good start. The building trades, for example, have been experimenting in their now highly mobile industry with a computerized job-listing service that permits a laid-off carpenter in one part of the country to learn where individuals with his skills are in demand—perhaps in his own backyard.

The aforementioned Pat Choate has developed a more comprehensive approach, which he calls the Individual Training Account (ITA). The ITA is patterned after the Individual Retirement Account (IRA) to which many Americans contribute. Rather than a cushion for retirement, the ITA is one for those crucial middle years. In one form or another employees (perhaps together with employers) would create a fund vested in the individual, not the job, which can be used for retraining or relocation if and when the need arises. The fund would have a specified cap, at which point contributions would cease. Should the fund be used, it would be replenished once the worker obtained a new post. Whatever balance remains upon retirement could be transferred to an IRA.

The ITA concept should be attractive to employees. It offers the possibility of tax-sheltered income that can be used as a secure bridge in a period of retraining or relocation. Employers should like it because the ITA would take a great deal of the onus off them when layoffs are necessary and it would encourage and facilitate retraining. It would also benefit the macro economy by providing a further source of savings for investment purposes.

The Educational Malaise

Job-listing services and ITAs are themselves only a small part of what must be created to give workers that sense of security in a time of accelerating change. More important perhaps is a reconfiguration of the educational system, and the problems here are so deep-rooted as to lead one to suspect that perhaps nothing can be done after all.

For decades—ever since the 1930s, in fact—teaching has been a poorly rewarded and regarded occupation. Even during the 1950s, when salaries were boosted thanks to teacher shortages, the work conditions in most elementary and secondary schools inhibited innovation. Classroom teachers were so entrapped in bureaucratic rules as to discourage the ablest undergraduates from seeking careers in education. The decline in discipline and standards during the 1960s exacerbated the situation. Finally, tenure rules meant that while excellent teachers are secure in their positions, many less qualified ones become time-servers, who stifle rather than encourage their better students. In other words, the high schools are positioning in a way similar to the auto industry in the 1970s, namely, turning out shoddy goods. But, of course, there are differences. For one thing, Detroit had competition and had to adapt to survive. Your local public high school doesn't have to face this problem. Moreover, when a car stops running or a fender rusts, we know there were problems in manufacture. How can we tell whether or not a school system is doing its job? All are self-congratulatory. Put another way: if graduating classes were like cars, there would be massive recalls throughout the United States.

Sadly, educators today seem more concerned with granting diplomas than anything else. Their traditional view of the world is that their jobs depend upon producing graduates who will go on to college or build careers upon the base the schools provide. This is fine in theory but not in practice.

College instructors complain that not only do students lack a base in factual and analytical knowledge but too often are deficient in such basic skills as reading and writing; the expansion of remedial work at the college level indicates that a breakdown may be near. At a time when more skills and knowledge are required, our public schools are graduating students with less of them. It puts one in mind of the scarecrow in *The Wizard of Oz,* who becomes smart after receiving a diploma. Young people receive their diplomas and are unqualified not only for jobs but even training programs, especially for industries of the future. Sixty-five percent of the job applicants at one of Boston's largest banks cannot even complete the application form.

The dry rot has reached many of the colleges and universities as well. To be sure, the high-quality institutions are still doing well by skimming off the cream of the high school seniors, but what is left is of a lower quality than once was the case. It now is possible to receive B.A.'s and B.B.A.'s from accredited colleges without the kind of knowledge and accumulation of skills that marked the high school graduate of two generations ago.

Here, too, years of neglect have created problems in the form of faculties with secure jobs unable or unwilling to face the reality of a new kind of job market. English departments seem more interested in turning out students who will go to graduate schools and become scholars in 16th-century poetry than people able to research and write a report for a marketing or management operation. Individuals capable of translating technical prose into workaday English are scarce and well remunerated. Yet subjects under the rubric of "business English" are despised and are usually taught be junior faculty, when there is a shortage in the labor force of people who are skilled in just that area.

This isn't to say that an appreciation of Shakespeare is to be scorned but rather that such knowledge will nourish the soul of a student for life but do precious little for his body. If the English departments of America could teach their students how to write press releases, speeches, articles on contemporary issues, and the like, they would provide them with marketable skills. There is a cottage industry comprised of free-lance writers who churn out software manuals for programs used by personal computers, because those written by the companies are so opaque. The company's manuals often are written by technicians who developed the software, while the manuals sold in bookstores and computer outlets come from the word processors of liberal arts graduates with an ability to absorb technical data and relate it in an understandable fashion. As has been seen, this is just the kind of person who will ride the crest of the Innovation Revolution.

Sloth has mired schools of education in the same mind lock. Administrators there concentrate on recruiting, educating, and training students who will be classroom teachers in the 1990s, and this certainly is an important mission. But teaching is far more than important. Indeed, in the high-innovation age it has become crucial. Knowledge is of little value unless it is spread and understood, and that is the role of teachers.

We know of one disillusioned elementary school teacher who applied for a post at ROLM, the telecommunications company now part of IBM, hoping to get a trainee post in personnel. After her interview she found herself part of a team that trained customers in the use of private branch exchanges. "If you can teach kids to read, you should be able to teach secretaries how to switch calls, place them on hold, arrange conference calls, and the like," she was told. Within one year she was heading a team that was doing just that at a major university that had just installed a ROLM system, feeling more useful—and being better paid, with more responsibility—than before.

Then there is a lawyer who started a small operation geared to training executives to make and use computer-generated spreadsheets. It was done through total immersion over a weekend at a Manhattan hotel, where 30 "students" working in pairs at computers together with 15 instructors went at it for a total of 30 hours. After that the executives were better fitted to survive in the offices of the future (which happen to exist today).

Where did those 15 instructors come from? "For the most part they are moonlighting high school social science and English teachers who came to me with almost no knowledge of computers," said the lawyer. "It isn't too difficult to train a born teacher in computers," he said, "but it's almost impossible to get a computer whiz to speak in ways businessmen can understand."

Today that lawyer is a full-time educator attempting to franchise his techniques, while some of those moonlighters are full-time business machine teachers working for corporations, schools, sales outlets, or themselves.

It has been said that a poor teacher is worthless, a good one priceless, but the meaning has changed since the thought was first uttered. There is a shortage of teachers today, a manageable one in the public schools, a severe one in business. And no institution of higher education is doing anything about it.

So education must shift its focus more to the reeducation and retraining of the existing labor force. If it does not, then surely this function will be taken over by the private sector. At a time when the nation's corporations spend more than $30 billion a year on training (IBM alone earmarks more than $1 billion a year on educational pursuits) and there is a crying shortage of teachers in nonacademic areas, the schools of education are silent.

While it is encouraging to see market forces at work in this way, it is discouraging in another sense. Corporations do not offer equal access to all who come. Their programs are designed to educate and train those who already have come through the door. The executive training programs at such firms as General Electric, Procter & Gamble, Macy's, and General Motors are world-famous for their excellence. These companies use the undergraduate and graduate schools as "screens," admitting those who performed well, knowing they have the basic skills but also that they will have to be carefully trained before they are of use on the job.

Smaller companies often have no formal training program,

relying instead upon mentor-and-student relationships and a catch-as-catch-can form of apprenticeship. As we now know, most of our new jobs are being created in small companies and startups, which means that their workers gain their knowledge in this unstructured fashion—or are expected to generate it on their own. Occasionally the informal approach works out fine, but the times it does are the exceptions. We simply can't continue on a trial-and-error basis; much is gained, but more is lost.

Sooner or later we must offer a public option to which all workers can gain access if we are to keep pace with training practices in other nations. This may have to occur outside of the public schools, which due to entrenched interests and simple ignorance often prepare students for jobs that don't exist. Failure here is especially hard on students for whom high school is terminal education. Unprepared for jobs that require an ability to learn fast, change rapidly, and demonstrate basic skills, they increasingly turn to jobs in the older part of the economy—manual labor, hairdressing, lawn services, and for a few, apprenticeships.

The time when a mechanically adept young man could get a job pumping gas and then proceed to become a mechanic is passing. Today's cars are rolling electronic shops, and mechanics who service them have to know how to use complicated testing machines. They have to learn how to learn—something that should have come but often does not in the high schools. So most will change oil and filters and mufflers but never work on motors and transmissions. Likewise, armies of young women have left high school to work as typists in offices. Some will continue to do so, but increasingly typists are being replaced by word, data, and information processors. Typing is a relatively simple skill; not so the new ones. So those high school graduates also will be left at a low level of employment—unless they are taught how to learn.

Little wonder, then, that the Armed Forces is an increasingly popular choice for those students not planning to go on to college. The Army and Navy stress educational possibilities in their advertisements, which attract young people awakening to the fact that they have a diploma and no marketable skills. Consider the Army recruiting slogan: "Be all that you can be." The words must have been carefully thought out and chosen, in recognition of the fact that the present school system isn't creating that opportunity for its graduates.

MOBILITY AND SECURITY: ARE THEY POSSIBLE?

However we go about creating security, it must foster, not inhibit, mobility and do so in a way that provides the individual worker with a sense of control over his or her own destiny. Moreover, we have to get on with it quickly, for events have a way of overtaking us. As increasing numbers of workers are threatened by the process of change, more will demand that we either slow the pace or create more secure bridges for them to cross. Since we cannot win by slowing down, the alternative is clear enough.

As we have been saying throughout, this means changing the rules of the game. In a sense, it isn't fair to do so in the middle of a person's career and upset their lives, when they did all that was required of them under the old rules. The situation is placing great pressure on workers, companies, and governments, even while it is straining our international balance of payments as we struggle to substitute new kinds of exports for old.

Yet we argue and debate—in the press, on television, and in the political arena—concepts and problems that either are outmoded or are slightly beside the real issue. Should we have less or more government? Should we raise or lower taxes? Are workers getting a fair share of the economic pie? Should we resort to higher or lower tariffs? We know the litany.

This isn't to suggest that these are trivial questions, but rather that they ignore the underlying developments attendant upon what we have been calling the Innovation Revolution—what most others consider the rise of a high-tech economy—and the impact it will have upon American workers and companies. Debate if we will the proper role of government, but while doing so we also might think of *what* functions government should perform as well as its size. Restudy the social safety net, but be aware of the need to foster an atmosphere of flexibility and mobility and of the perils of too much security. The Individual Training Account is an idea thrown out to indicate the directions in which we have to be heading; it is not necessarily a blueprint for the future. If we are going to change the rules of the game, we must be prepared to alter the way we umpire the game as well.

Our saving grace is that the process of change does not depend fundamentally upon any major structural reforms undertaken by concerted government-business-labor action. Rather, the process is based upon the actions of millions of creative people taking millions of new initiatives each year. Some politicians are racing to understand what is going on, to catch up with it, and assume positions of leadership. But it is not leadership that is mostly needed. Rather, the proper function of politicians under the present circumstances would be to facilitate change, not direct it. Government's primary role is to clear the path. Its key role will be to provide access and knowledge, not direction. This is one of those situations where our cultural traditions transcend our law.

Our culture is one of multiple paths, not a single superhighway. Over a million people start some kind of enterprise each year. Our future strength will flow from imagination and enterprise—computers named after fruits and software named after flowers. We appear to have ample measures of creativity and diversity, which places us in a strong position for the future.

Definitions of 239
Forecast Areas

Identification Number of Geographic Market	Geographic Markets		
1	**Rural Maine**		
	Aroostook, ME	Franklin, ME	Hancock, ME
	Kennebec, ME	Knox, ME	Lincoln, ME
	Oxford, ME	Penobscot, ME	Piscataquis, ME
	Sagadahoc, ME	Somerset, ME	Waldo, ME
	Washington, ME		
2	**Portland, Maine**		
	Androscoggin, ME	Cumberland, ME	York, ME
3	**Portsmouth-Dover-Rochester, New Hampshire**		
	Rockingham, NH	Strafford, NH	
4	**Manchester-Nashua, New Hampshire**		
	Hillsborough, NH		
5	**Rural New Hampshire**		
	Belknap, NH	Carroll, NH	Cheshire, NH
	Coos, NH	Grafton, NH	Merrimack, NH
	Sullivan, NH		
6	**State of Vermont**		
	Addison, VT	Bennington, VT	Caledonia, VT
	Chittenden, VT	Essex, VT	Franklin, VT
	Grand Isle, VT	Lamoille, VT	Orange, VT
	Orleans, VT	Rutland, VT	Washington, VT
	Windham, VT	Windsor, VT	
7	**Pittsfield, Massachusetts**		
	Berkshire, MA	Franklin, MA	
8	**Springfield, Massachusetts**		
	Hampden, MA	Hampshire, MA	
9	**Worcester, Massachusetts**		
	Worcester, MA		
10	**Boston, Massachusetts**		
	Essex, MA	Middlesex, MA	Norfolk, MA
	Suffolk, MA		
11	**Southeastern, Massachusetts**		
	Barnstable, MA	Dukes, MA	Nantucket, MA
	Plymouth, MA		
12	**New Bedford-Fall River, Massachusetts**		
	Bristol, MA		
13	**State of Rhode Island**		
	Bristol, RI	Kent, RI	Newport, RI
	Providence, RI	Washington, RI	
14	**New London-Norwich, Connecticut**		
	New London, CT	Windham, CT	
15	**New Haven-Waterbury, Connecticut**		
	New Haven, CT		
16	**Bridgeport-Stamford-Norwalk, Connecticut**		
	Fairfield, CT		

208

Identification Number of Geographic Market	Geographic Markets		
17	**Hartford, Connecticut**		
	Hartford, CT	Litchfield, CT	Middlesex, CT
	Tolland, CT		
18	**Albany-Schenectady-Troy, New York**		
	Albany, NY	Greene, NY	Montgomery, NY
	Resselaer, NY	Saratoga, NY	Schenectady, NY
19	**Adirondack Region, New York**		
	Clinton, NY	Essex, NY	Franklin, NY
	Fulton, NY	Hamilton, NY	Jefferson, NY
	Lewis, NY	Saint Lawrence, NY	Warren, NY
	Washington, NY		
20	**Utica-Rome, New York**		
	Herkimer, NY	Oneida, NY	
21	**Syracuse, New York**		
	Madison, NY	Onondaga, NY	Oswego, NY
22	**Rochester, New York**		
	Livingston, NY	Monroe, NY	Ontario, NY
	Orleans, NY	Wayne, NY	
23	**Buffalo, New York**		
	Erie, NY	Niagara, NY	
24	**Finger Lakes Region, New York**		
	Allegany, NY	Cattaraugus, NY	Cayuga, NY
	Chautauqua, NY	Cortland, NY	Genesee, NY
	Schuyler, NY	Seneca, NY	Steuben, NY
	Tompkins, NY	Wyoming, NY	Yates, NY
25	**Binghampton-Elmira, New York**		
	Broome, NY	Chemung, NY	Tioga, NY
26	**Catskill-Southeastern New York**		
	Chenango, NY	Columbia, NY	Delaware, NY
	Dutchess, NY	Otsego, NY	Schoharie, NY
	Sullivan, NY	Ulster, NY	
27	**New York, New York/New Jersey**		
	Bergen, NJ	Essex, NJ	Hudson, NJ
	Hunterdon, NJ	Middlesex, NJ	Monmouth, NJ
	Morris, NJ	Ocean, NJ	Passaic, NJ
	Somerset, NJ	Sussex, NJ	Union, NJ
	Bronx, NY	Kings, NY	Nassau, NY
	New York, NY	Orange, NY	Putnam, NY
	Queens, NY	Richmond, NY	Rockland, NY
	Suffolk, NY	Westchester, NY	
28	**Atlantic City, New Jersey**		
	Atlantic, NJ	Cape May, NJ	Cumberland, NJ
29	**Philadelphia, Pennsylvania/New Jersey**		
	Burlington, NJ	Camden, NJ	Gloucester, NJ
	Mercer, NJ	Bucks, PA	Chester, PA
	Delaware, PA	Montgomery, PA	Philadelphia, PA
30	**Lancaster, Pennsylvania**		
	Lancaster, PA		

209

Identification Number of Geographic Market	Geographic Markets		
31	**York, Pennsylvania** Adams, PA	York, PA	
32	**Harrisburg, Pennsylvania** Cumberland, PA Perry, PA	Dauphin, PA	Lebanon, PA
33	**Reading, Pennsylvania** Berks, PA		
34	**Allentown-Bethlehem, Pennsylvania/New Jersey** Warren, NJ Northampton, PA	Carbon, PA	Lehigh, PA
35	**Scranton-Wilkes-Barre-Hazelton, Pennsylvania** Columbia, PA Monroe, PA	Lackawanna, PA Wyoming, PA	Luzerne, PA
36	**Appalachia-Rural Eastern Pennsylvania** Bedford, PA Franklin, PA Juniata, PA Montour, PA Schuylkill, PA Susquehanna, PA Wayne, PA	Bradford, PA Fulton, PA Lycoming, PA Northumberland, PA Snyder, PA Tioga, PA	Clinton, PA Huntingdon, PA Mifflin, PA Pike, PA Sullivan, PA Union, PA
37	**Johnstown-Altoona, Pennsylvania** Blair, PA Somerset, PA	Cambria, PA	Centre, PA
38	**Pittsburgh, Pennsylvania** Allegheny, PA Washington, PA	Beaver, PA Westmoreland, PA	Fayette, PA
39	**Rural Northwestern Pennsylvania** Armstrong, PA Clarion, PA Elk, PA Indiana, PA McKean, PA Venango, PA	Butler, PA Clearfield, PA Forest, PA Jefferson, PA Mercer, PA Warren, PA	Cameron, PA Crawford, PA Greene, PA Lawrence, PA Potter, PA
40	**Erie, Pennsylvania** Erie, PA		
41	**Southeastern Ohio** Adams, OH Belmont, OH Columbiana, OH Gallia, OH Highland, OH Jackson, OH Monroe, OH Noble, OH Ross, OH Vinton, OH	Ashtabula, OH Brown, OH Coshocton, OH Guernsey, OH Hocking, OH Jefferson, OH Morgan, OH Perry, OH Scioto, OH Washington, OH	Athens, OH Clinton, OH Fayette, OH Harrison, OH Holmes, OH Meigs, OH Muskingum, OH Pike, OH Tuscarawas, OH
42	**Youngstown-Warren, Ohio** Mahoning, OH	Trumbull, OH	

Identification Number of Geographic Market	Geographic Markets		
43	**Cleveland-Akron, Ohio**		
	Cuyahoga, OH	Geauga, OH	Lake, OH
	Medina, OH	Portage, OH	Summit, OH
44	**Canton, Ohio**		
	Carroll, OH	Stark, OH	
45	**Columbus, Ohio**		
	Delaware, OH	Fairfield, OH	Franklin, OH
	Licking, OH	Madison, OH	Pickaway, OH
	Union, OH		
46	**Dayton-Springfield, Ohio**		
	Clark, OH	Greene, OH	Miami, OH
	Montgomery, OH		
47	**Cincinnati, Ohio/Kentucky/Indiana**		
	Dearborn, IN	Boone, KY	Campbell, KY
	Kenton, KY	Clermont, OH	Hamilton, OH
	Warren, OH		
48	**Northwestern Rural Ohio**		
	Allen, OH	Ashland, OH	Auglaize, OH
	Butler, OH	Champaign, OH	Crawford, OH
	Darke, OH	Defiance, OH	Erie, OH
	Hancock, OH	Hardin, OH	Henry, OH
	Huron, OH	Knox, OH	Logan, OH
	Lorain, OH	Marion, OH	Mercer, OH
	Morrow, OH	Ottawa, OH	Paulding, OH
	Preble, OH	Putnam, OH	Richland, OH
	Sandusky, OH	Seneca, OH	Shelby, OH
	Van Wert, OH	Wayne, OH	Williams, OH
	Wyandot, OH		
49	**Toledo, Ohio**		
	Fulton, OH	Lucas, OH	Wood, OH
50	**Detroit, Michigan**		
	Lapeer, MI	Livingston, MI	Macomb, MI
	Monroe, MI	Oakland, MI	Saint Clair, MI
	Washtenaw, MI	Wayne, MI	
51	**Flint, Michigan**		
	Genesee, MI		
52	**Saginaw-Bay City, Michigan**		
	Bay, MI	Midland, MI	Saginaw, MI
53	**Lansing-Jackson, Michigan**		
	Clinton, MI	Eaton, MI	Ingham, MI
	Jackson, MI		
54	**Battle Creek-Kalamazoo, Michigan**		
	Calhoun, MI	Kalamazoo, MI	
55	**Grand Rapids-Muskegon, Michigan**		
	Kent, MI	Muskegon, MI	Ottawa, MI

211

Identification Number of Geographic Market	Geographic Markets		
56	**Northern Rural Michigan**		
	Alcona, MI	Alger, MI	Alpena, MI
	Antrim, MI	Arenac, MI	Baraga, MI
	Benzie, MI	Charlevoix, MI	Cheboygan, MI
	Chippewa, MI	Clare, MI	Crawford, MI
	Delta, MI	Dickinson, MI	Emmet, MI
	Gladwin, MI	Gogebic, MI	Grand Traverse, M
	Houghton, MI	Iosco, MI	Iron, MI
	Kalkaska, MI	Keweenaw, MI	Lake, MI
	Leelanau, MI	Luce, MI	Mackinac, MI
	Manistee, MI	Marquette, MI	Mason, MI
	Mecosta, MI	Menominee, MI	Missaukee, MI
	Montmorency, MI	Newaygo, MI	Oceana, MI
	Ogemaw, MI	Ontonagon, MI	Osceola, MI
	Oscoda, MI	Otsego, MI	Presque Isle, MI
	Roscommon, MI	Schoolcraft, MI	Wexford, MI
57	**Southern Rural Michigan**		
	Allegan, MI	Barry, MI	Branch, MI
	Cass, MI	Gratiot, MI	Hillsdale, MI
	Huron, MI	Ionia, MI	Isabella, MI
	Lenawee, MI	Montcalm, MI	Saint Joseph, MI
	Sanilac, MI	Shiawassee, MI	Tuscola, MI
	Van Buren, MI		
58	**South Bend-Benton Harbor, Indiana/Michigan**		
	Elkhart, IN	Saint Joseph, IN	Berrien, MI
59	**Fort Wayne, Indiana**		
	Allen, IN	De Kalb, IN	Whitley, IN
60	**Indianapolis, Indiana**		
	Boone, IN	Hamilton, IN	Hancock, IN
	Hendricks, IN	Johnson, IN	Marion, IN
	Morgan, IN	Shelby, IN	
61	**Northern Rural Indiana**		
	Adams, IN	Bartholomew, IN	Benton, IN
	Blackford, IN	Brown, IN	Carroll, IN
	Cass, IN	Clay, IN	Clinton, IN
	Decatur, IN	Delaware, IN	Fayette, IN
	Fountain, IN	Franklin, IN	Fulton, IN
	Grant, IN	Greene, IN	Henry, IN
	Howard, IN	Huntington, IN	Jasper, IN
	Jay, IN	Kosciusko, IN	La Porte, IN
	Lagrange, IN	Madison, IN	Marshall, IN
	Miami, IN	Monroe, IN	Montgomery, IN
	Newton, IN	Noble, IN	Owen, IN
	Parke, IN	Pulaski, IN	Putnam, IN
	Randolph, IN	Rush, IN	Starke, IN
	Steuben, IN	Sullivan, IN	Tippecanoe, IN
	Tipton, IN	Union, IN	Vermillion, IN
	Vigo, IN	Wabash, IN	Warren, IN
	Wayne, IN	Wells, IN	White, IN
62	**Southern Rural Indiana**		
	Crawford, IN	Daviess, IN	Dubois, IN
	Gibson, IN	Jackson, IN	Jefferson, IN
	Jennings, IN	Knox, IN	Lawrence, IN
	Martin, IN	Ohio, IN	Orange, IN
	Perry, IN	Pike, IN	Ripley, IN
	Scott, IN	Spencer, IN	Switzerland, IN
	Washington, IN		

Identification Number of Geographic Market	Geographic Markets		
63	**Evansville, Indiana/Kentucky**		
	Posey, IN	Vanderburgh, IN	Warrick, IN
	Daviess, KY	Henderson, KY	
64	**Southern Rural Illinois**		
	Alexander, IL	Franklin, IL	Gallatin, IL
	Hardin, IL	Jackson, IL	Jefferson, IL
	Johnson, IL	Massac, IL	Perry, IL
	Pope, IL	Pulaski, IL	Randolph, IL
	Saline, IL	Union, IL	Washington, IL
	Williamson, IL		
65	**Northern, Central Illinois**		
	Adams, IL	Bond, IL	Brown, IL
	Bureau, IL	Calhoun, IL	Carroll, IL
	Cass, IL	Christian, IL	Clark, IL
	Clay, IL	Coles, IL	Crawford, IL
	Cumberland, IL	DeKalb, IL	DeWitt, IL
	Douglas, IL	Edgar, IL	Edwards, IL
	Effingham, IL	Fayette, IL	Ford, IL
	Fulton, IL	Greene, IL	Hamilton, IL
	Hancock, IL	Henderson, IL	Iroquois, IL
	Jasper, IL	Jo Daviess, IL	Knox, IL
	LaSalle, IL	Lawrence, IL	Lee, IL
	Livingston, IL	Logan, IL	Macoupin, IL
	Marion, IL	Marshall, IL	Mason, IL
	McDonough, IL	Mercer, IL	Montgomery, IL
	Morgan, IL	Moultrie, IL	Ogle, IL
	Piatt, IL	Pike, IL	Putnam, IL
	Richland, IL	Schuyler, IL	Scott, IL
	Shelby, IL	Stark, IL	Stephenson, IL
	Vermilion, IL	Wabash, IL	Warren, IL
	Wayne, IL	White, IL	Whiteside, IL
66	**Springfield-Decatur, Illinois**		
	Macon, IL	Menard, IL	Sangamon, IL
67	**Bloomington-Champaign, Illinois**		
	Champaign, IL	McLean, IL	
68	**Peoria, Illinois**		
	Peoria, IL	Tazewell, IL	Woodford, IL
69	**Davenport-Rock Island-Moline, Illinois/Iowa**		
	Scott, IA	Henry, IL	Rock Island, IL
70	**Chicago, Illinois/Indiana**		
	Cook, IL	DuPage, IL	Grundy, IL
	Kane, IL	Kankakee, IL	Kendall, IL
	Lake, IL	McHenry, IL	Will, IL
	Lake, IN	Porter, IN	
71	**Rockford, Illinois**		
	Boone, IL	Winnebago, IL	
72	**Milwaukee-Racine, Wisconsin**		
	Kenosha, WI	Milwaukee, WI	Ozaukee, WI
	Racine, WI	Washington, WI	Waukesha, WI

213

Identification Number of Geographic Market	Geographic Markets		
73	**Madison, Wisconsin**		
	Dane, WI		
74	**Green Bay-Appleton, Wisconsin**		
	Brown, WI	Calumet, WI	Outagamie, WI
	Winnebago, WI		
75	**Southern, Central Wisconsin**		
	Adams, WI	Buffalo, WI	Chippewa, WI
	Clark, WI	Columbia, WI	Crawford, WI
	Dodge, WI	Door, WI	Dunn, WI
	Eau Claire, WI	Fond Du Lac, WI	Grant, WI
	Green, WI	Green Lake, WI	Iowa, WI
	Jackson, WI	Jefferson, WI	Juneau, WI
	Kewaunee, WI	La Crosse, WI	Lafayette, WI
	Manitowoc, WI	Marathon, WI	Marquette, WI
	Menominee, WI	Monroe, WI	Pepin, WI
	Pierce, WI	Portage, WI	Richland, WI
	Rock, WI	Sauk, WI	Shawano, WI
	Sheboygan, WI	Trempealeau, WI	Vernon, WI
	Walworth, WI	Waupaca, WI	Waushara, WI
	Wood, WI		
76	**Northern Rural Wisconsin**		
	Ashland, WI	Barron, WI	Bayfield, WI
	Burnett, WI	Florence, WI	Forest, WI
	Iron, WI	Langlade, WI	Lincoln, WI
	Marinette, WI	Oconto, WI	Oneida, WI
	Polk, WI	Price, WI	Rusk, WI
	Sawyer, WI	Taylor, WI	Vilas, WI
	Washburn, WI		
77	**Duluth, Minnesota/Wisconsin**		
	Saint Louis, MN	Douglas, WI	
78	**Northern Rural Minnesota**		
	Aitkin, MN	Becker, MN	Beltrami, MN
	Carlton, MN	Cass, MN	Clearwater, MN
	Cook, MN	Crow Wing, MN	Hubbard, MN
	Itasca, MN	Kanabec, MN	Kittson, MN
	Koochiching, MN	Lake, MN	Lake of Woods, MN
	Mahnomen, MN	Marshall, MN	Mille Lacs, MN
	Morrison, MN	Norman, MN	Pennington, MN
	Pine, MN	Polk, MN	Red Lake, MN
	Roseau, MN	Todd, MN	Wadena, MN
79	**Minneapolis-St. Paul, Minnesota/Wisconsin**		
	Anoka, MN	Benton, MN	Carver, MN
	Chisago, MN	Dakota, MN	Hennepin, MN
	Isanti, MN	Ramsey, MN	Scott, MN
	Sherburne, MN	Stearns, MN	Washington, MN
	Wright, MN	Saint Croix, WI	

Identification Number of Geographic Market	Geographic Markets		
80	**Southern Rural Minnesota**		
	Big Stone, MN	Blue Earth, MN	Brown, MN
	Chippewa, MN	Clay, MN	Cottonwood, MN
	Dodge, MN	Douglas, MN	Faribault, MN
	Fillmore, MN	Freeborn, MN	Goodhue, MN
	Grant, MN	Houston, MN	Jackson, MN
	Kandiyohi, MN	Lac Qui Parle, MN	Le Sueur, MN
	Lincoln, MN	Lyon, MN	Martin, MN
	McLeod, MN	Meeker, MN	Mower, MN
	Murray, MN	Nicollet, MN	Nobles, MN
	Olmsted, MN	Otter Tail, MN	Pipestone, MN
	Pope, MN	Redwood, MN	Renville, MN
	Rice, MN	Rock, MN	Sibley, MN
	Steele, MN	Stevens, MN	Swift, MN
	Traverse, MN	Wabasha, MN	Waseca, MN
	Watonwan, MN	Wilkin, MN	Winona, MN
	Yellow Medicine, MN		
81	**State of North Dakota**		
	Adams, ND	Barnes, ND	Benson, ND
	Billings, ND	Bottineau, ND	Bowman, ND
	Burke, ND	Burleigh, ND	Cass, ND
	Cavalier, ND	Dickey, ND	Divide, ND
	Dunn, ND	Eddy, ND	Emmons, ND
	Foster, ND	Golden Valley, ND	Grand Forks, ND
	Grant, ND	Griggs, ND	Hettinger, ND
	Kidder, ND	LaMoure, ND	Logan, ND
	McHenry, ND	McIntosh, ND	McKenzie, ND
	McLean, ND	Mercer, ND	Morton, ND
	Mountrail, ND	Nelson, ND	Oliver, ND
	Pembina, ND	Pierce, ND	Ramsey, ND
	Ransom, ND	Renville, ND	Richland, ND
	Rolette, ND	Sargent, ND	Sheridan, ND
	Sioux, ND	Slope, ND	Stark, ND
	Steele, ND	Stutsman, ND	Towner, ND
	Traill, ND	Walsh, ND	Ward, ND
	Wells, ND	Williams, ND	
82	**State of South Dakota**		
	Aurora, SD	Beadle, SD	Bennett, SD
	Bon Homme, SD	Brookings, SD	Brown, SD
	Brule, SD	Buffalo, SD	Butte, SD
	Campbell, SD	Charles Mix, SD	Clark, SD
	Clay, SD	Codington, SD	Corson, SD
	Custer, SD	Davison, SD	Day, SD
	Deuel, SD	Dewey, SD	Douglas, SD
	Edmunds, SD	Fall River, SD	Faulk, SD
	Grant, SD	Gregory, SD	Haakon, SD
	Hamlin, SD	Hand, SD	Hanson, SD
	Harding, SD	Hughes, SD	Hutchinson, SD
	Hyde, SD	Jackson, SD	Jerauld, SD
	Jones, SD	Kingsbury, SD	Lake, SD
	Lawrence, SD	Lincoln, SD	Lyman, SD
	Marshall, SD	McCook, SD	McPherson, SD
	Meade, SD	Mellette, SD	Miner, SD
	Minnehaha, SD	Moody, SD	Pennington, SD
	Perkins, SD	Potter, SD	Roberts, SD
	Sanborn, SD	Shannon, SD	Spink, SD
	Stanley, SD	Sully, SD	Todd, SD
	Tripp, SD	Turner, SD	Union, SD
	Walworth, SD	Washabaugh, SD	Yankton, SD
	Ziebach, SD		

Identification Number of Geographic Market	Geographic Markets		
83	**Northwestern Iowa**		
	Audubon, IA	Boone, IA	Buena Vista,
	Butler, IA	Calhoun, IA	Carroll, IA
	Cerro Gordo, IA	Cherokee, IA	Clay, IA
	Crawford, IA	Dickinson, IA	Emmet, IA
	Floyd, IA	Franklin, IA	Greene, IA
	Grundy, IA	Hamilton, IA	Hancock, IA
	Hardin, IA	Harrison, IA	Humboldt, IA
	Ida, IA	Kossuth, IA	Lyon, IA
	Mitchell, IA	Monoma, IA	O'Brien, IA
	Osceola, IA	Palo Alto, IA	Plymouth, IA
	Pocahontas, IA	Sac, IA	Shelby, IA
	Sioux, IA	Story, IA	Webster, IA
	Winnebago, IA	Woodbury, IA	Worth, IA
	Wright, IA		
84	**Cedar Rapids-Iowa City, Iowa**		
	Johnson, IA	Linn, IA	
85	**Des Moines, Iowa**		
	Dallas, IA	Polk, IA	Warren, IA
86	**Southeastern Iowa**		
	Adair, IA	Adams, IA	Allamakee, IA
	Appanoose, IA	Benton, IA	Black Hawk,
	Bremer, IA	Buchanan, IA	Cass, IA
	Cedar, IA	Chickasaw, IA	Clarke, IA
	Clayton, IA	Clinton, IA	Davis, IA
	Decatur, IA	Delaware, IA	Des Moines,
	Dubuque, IA	Fayette, IA	Fremont, IA
	Guthrie, IA	Henry, IA	Howard, IA
	Iowa, IA	Jackson, IA	Jasper, IA
	Jefferson, IA	Jones, IA	Keokuk, IA
	Lee, IA	Louisa, IA	Lucas, IA
	Madison, IA	Mahaska, IA	Marion, IA
	Marshall, IA	Mills, IA	Monroe, IA
	Montgomery, IA	Muscatine, IA	Page, IA
	Poweshiek, IA	Ringgold, IA	Tama, IA
	Taylor, IA	Union, IA	Van Buren, IA
	Wapello, IA	Washington, IA	Wayne, IA
	Winneshiek, IA		
87	**Omaha, Nebraska/Iowa**		
	Pottawattamie, IA	Douglas, NE	Sarpy, NE
	Washington, NE		
88	**Lincoln, Nebraska**		
	Lancaster, NE		
89	**Eastern Nebraska**		
	Antelope, NE	Boone, NE	Boyd, NE
	Brown, NE	Burt, NE	Butler, NE
	Cass, NE	Cedar, NE	Colfax, NE
	Cuming, NE	Dakota, NE	Dixon, NE
	Dodge, NE	Fillmore, NE	Gage, NE
	Holt, NE	Jefferson, NE	Johnson, NE
	Keya Paha, NE	Knox, NE	Madison, NE
	Nemaha, NE	Otoe, NE	Pawnee, NE
	Pierce, NE	Platte, NE	Polk, NE
	Richardson, NE	Rock, NE	Saline, NE
	Saunders, NE	Seward, NE	Stanton, NE
	Thayer, NE	Thurston, NE	Wayne, NE
	York, NE		

216

Identification Number of Geographic Market	Geographic Markets		
90	**Western Nebraska**		
	Adams, NE	Arthur, NE	Banner, NE
	Blaine, NE	Box Butte, NE	Buffalo, NE
	Chase, NE	Cherry, NE	Cheyenne, NE
	Clay, NE	Custer, NE	Dawes, NE
	Dawson, NE	Deuel, NE	Dundy, NE
	Franklin, NE	Frontier, NE	Furnas, NE
	Garden, NE	Garfield, NE	Gosper, NE
	Grant, NE	Greeley, NE	Hall, NE
	Hamilton, NE	Harlan, NE	Hayes, NE
	Hitchcock, NE	Hooker, NE	Howard, NE
	Kearney, NE	Keith, NE	Kimball, NE
	Lincoln, NE	Logan, NE	Loup, NE
	McPherson, NE	Merrick, NE	Morrill, NE
	Nance, NE	Nuckolls, NE	Perkins, NE
	Phelps, NE	Red Willow, NE	Scotts Bluff, NE
	Sheridan, NE	Sherman, NE	Sioux, NE
	Thomas, NE	Valley, NE	Webster, NE
	Wheeler, NE		
91	**Western Kansas**		
	Barber, KS	Barton, KS	Cheyenne, KS
	Clark, KS	Comanche, KS	Decatur, KS
	Edwards, KS	Ellis, KS	Finney, KS
	Ford, KS	Gove, KS	Graham, KS
	Grant, KS	Gray, KS	Greeley, KS
	Hamilton, KS	Harper, KS	Haskell, KS
	Hodgeman, KS	Jewell, KS	Kearny, KS
	Kiowa, KS	Lane, KS	Logan, KS
	Meade, KS	Morton, KS	Ness, KS
	Norton, KS	Osborne, KS	Pawnee, KS
	Phillips, KS	Pratt, KS	Rawlins, KS
	Rooks, KS	Rush, KS	Russell, KS
	Scott, KS	Seward, KS	Sheridan, KS
	Sherman, KS	Smith, KS	Stafford, KS
	Stanton, KS	Stevens, KS	Thomas, KS
	Trego, KS	Wallace, KS	Wichita, KS
92	**Wichita, Kansas**		
	Butler, KS	Sedgwick, KS	
93	**Eastern Kansas**		
	Allen, KS	Anderson, KS	Atchison, KS
	Bourbon, KS	Brown, KS	Chase, KS
	Chautauqua, KS	Cherokee, KS	Clay, KS
	Cloud, KS	Coffey, KS	Cowley, KS
	Crawford, KS	Dickinson, KS	Doniphan, KS
	Elk, KS	Ellsworth, KS	Franklin, KS
	Geary, KS	Greenwood, KS	Harvey, KS
	Jackson, KS	Jefferson, KS	Kingman, KS
	Labette, KS	Lincoln, KS	Linn, KS
	Lyon, KS	Marion, KS	Marshall, KS
	McPherson, KS	Mitchell, KS	Montgomery, KS
	Morris, KS	Nemaha, KS	Neosho, KS
	Osage, KS	Ottawa, KS	Pottawatomie, KS
	Reno, KS	Republic, KS	Rice, KS
	Riley, KS	Saline, KS	Sumner, KS
	Wabaunsee, KS	Washington, KS	Wilson, KS
	Woodson, KS		
94	**Topeka, Kansas**		
	Douglas, KS	Shawnee, KS	

Identification Number of Geographic Market	Geographic Markets		
95	**Kansas City, Missouri/Kansas**		
	Johnson, KS	Leavenworth, KS	Miami, KS
	Wyandotte, KS	Cass, MO	Clay, MO
	Jackson, MO	Lafayette, MO	Platte, MO
	Ray, MO		
96	**Northern Rural Missouri**		
	Adair, MO	Andrew, MO	Atchison, MO
	Audrain, MO	Boone, MO	Buchanan, MO
	Caldwell, MO	Callaway, MO	Carroll, MO
	Chariton, MO	Clark, MO	Clinton, MO
	Cole, MO	Cooper, MO	Daviess, MO
	DeKalb, MO	Gasconade, MO	Gentry, MO
	Grundy, MO	Harrison, MO	Holt, MO
	Howard, MO	Johnson, MO	Knox, MO
	Lewis, MO	Lincoln, MO	Linn, MO
	Livingston, MO	Macon, MO	Marion, MO
	Mercer, MO	Moniteau, MO	Monroe, MO
	Montgomery, MO	Nodaway, MO	Osage, MO
	Pettis, MO	Pike, MO	Putnam, MO
	Ralls, MO	Randolph, MO	Saline, MO
	Schuyler, MO	Scotland, MO	Shelby, MO
	Sullivan, MO	Warren, MO	Worth, MO
97	**St. Louis, Missouri/Illinois**		
	Clinton, IL	Jersey, IL	Madison, IL
	Monroe, IL	Saint Clair, IL	Franklin, MO
	Jefferson, MO	Saint Charles, MO	Saint Louis, MO
	Saint Louis City, MO		
98	**Springfield, Missouri**		
	Christian, MO	Greene, MO	
99	**Southern Rural Missouri**		
	Barry, MO	Barton, MO	Bates, MO
	Benton, MO	Bollinger, MO	Butler, MO
	Camden, MO	Cape Girardeau, MO	Carter, MO
	Cedar, MO	Crawford, MO	Dade, MO
	Dallas, MO	Dent, MO	Douglas, MO
	Dunklin, MO	Henry, MO	Hickory, MO
	Howell, MO	Iron, MO	Jasper, MO
	Laclede, MO	Lawrence, MO	Madison, MO
	Maries, MO	McDonald, MO	Miller, MO
	Mississippi, MO	Morgan, MO	New Madrid, MO
	Newton, MO	Oregon, MO	Ozark, MO
	Pemiscot, MO	Perry, MO	Phelps, MO
	Polk, MO	Pulaski, MO	Reynolds, MO
	Ripley, MO	Saint Clair, MO	Saint Francois, MO
	Sainte Genevieve, MO	Scott, MO	Shannon, MO
	Stoddard, MO	Stone, MO	Taney, MO
	Texas, MO	Vernon, MO	Washington, MO
	Wayne, MO	Webster, MO	Wright, MO
100	**Huntington-Ashland, West Virginia/Kentucky/Ohio**		
	Boyd, KY	Carter, KY	Greenup, KY
	Lawrence, OH	Cabell, WV	Wayne, WV
101	**Charleston, West Virginia**		
	Kanawha, WV	Putnam, WV	

Identification Number of Geographic Market	Geographic Markets		
102	**Northwestern West Virginia**		
	Braxton, WV	Brooke, WV	Calhoun, WV
	Clay, WV	Doddridge, WV	Gilmer, WV
	Hancock, WV	Harrison, WV	Jackson, WV
	Lewis, WV	Marion, WV	Marshall, WV
	Mason, WV	Monongalia, WV	Ohio, WV
	Pleasants, WV	Preston, WV	Ritchie, WV
	Roane, WV	Taylor, WV	Tyler, WV
	Wetzel, WV	Wirt, WV	Wood, WV
103	**Appalachian Mountain Area, West Virginia**		
	Barbour, WV	Berkeley, WV	Boone, WV
	Fayette, WV	Grant, WV	Greenbrier, WV
	Hampshire, WV	Hardy, WV	Jefferson, WV
	Lincoln, WV	Logan, WV	McDowell, WV
	Mercer, WV	Mineral, WV	Mingo, WV
	Monroe, WV	Morgan, WV	Nicholas, WV
	Pendleton, WV	Pocahontas, WV	Raleigh, WV
	Randolph, WV	Summers, WV	Tucker, WV
	Upshur, WV	Webster, WV	Wyoming, WV
104	**Western Maryland**		
	Allegany, MD	Garrett, MD	Washington, MD
105	**Baltimore, Maryland**		
	Anne Arundel, MD	Baltimore, MD	Baltimore City, MD
	Carroll, MD	Harford, MD	Howard, MD
	Queen Annes, MD		
106	**Eastern Maryland**		
	Caroline, MD	Dorchester, MD	Kent, MD
	Saint Marys, MD	Somerset, MD	Talbot, MD
	Wicomico, MD	Worcester, MD	
107	**Southern Delaware**		
	Kent, DE	Sussex, DE	
108	**Wilmington, Delaware/New Jersey/Maryland**		
	New Castle, DE	Cecil, MD	Salem, NJ
109	**Washington, District of Columbia/Maryland/Virginia**		
	District of Columbia	Calvert, MD	Charles, MD
	Frederick, MD	Montgomery, MD	Prince Georges, MD
	Alexandria City, VA	Arlington, VA	Fairfax, VA
	Fairfax City, VA	Falls Church City, VA	Loudoun, VA
	Manasses City, VA	Manasses Park City, VA	Prince William, VA
	Stafford, VA		
110	**Mountain Region, Virginia**		
	Alleghany, VA	Augusta, VA	Bath, VA
	Bland, VA	Buchanan, VA	Buena Vista City, VA
	Carroll, VA	Clarke, VA	Clifton Forge City, VA
	Covington City, VA	Craig, VA	Dickenson, VA
	Floyd, VA	Frederick, VA	Galax City, VA
	Giles, VA	Grayson, VA	Harrisonburg City, VA
	Highland, VA	Lee, VA	Lexington City, VA
	Montgomery, VA	Norton City, VA	Page, VA
	Pulaski, VA	Radford City, VA	Rockbridge, VA
	Rockingham, VA	Russell, VA	Shenandoah, VA
	Smyth, VA	Staunton City, VA	Tazewell, VA
	Warren, VA	Waynesboro City, VA	Winchester City, VA
	Wise, VA	Wythe, VA	

Identification Number of Geographic Market	Geographic Markets		
111	**Roanoke-Lynchburg, Virginia**		
	Amherst, VA	Botetourt, VA	Campbell, VA
	Lynchburg City, VA	Roanoke, VA	Roanoke City, VA
	Salem City, VA		
112	**Eastern Rural Virginia**		
	Accomack, VA	Albemarle, VA	Amelia, VA
	Appomattox, VA	Bedford, VA	Bedford City, VA
	Brunswick, VA	Buckingham, VA	Caroline, VA
	Charlotte, VA	Charlottesville City, VA	Culpeper, VA
	Cumberland, VA	Danville City, VA	Emporia City, VA
	Essex, VA	Fauquier, VA	Fluvanna, VA
	Franklin VA	Franklin City, VA	Fredericksburg City,
	Greene, VA	Greensville, VA	Halifax, VA
	Henry, VA	Isle of Wight, VA	King and Queen, VA
	King George, VA	King William, VA	Lancaster, VA
	Louisa, VA	Lunenberg, VA	Madison, VA
	Martinsville City, VA	Mathews, VA	Mecklenburg, VA
	Middlesex, VA	Nansemond, VA	Nelson, VA
	Northhampton, VA	Northumberland, VA	Nottoway, VA
	Orange, VA	Patrick, VA	Pittsylvania, VA
	Prince Edward, VA	Rappahannock, VA	Richmond, VA
	South Boston City, VA	Southampton, VA	Spotsylvania, VA
	Surry, VA	Sussex, VA	Westmoreland, VA
113	**Richmond, Virginia**		
	Charles City, VA	Chesterfield, VA	Colonial Heights City
	Dinwiddie, VA	Goochland, VA	Hanover, VA
	Henrico, VA	Hopewell City, VA	New Kent, VA
	Petersburg City, VA	Powhatan, VA	Prince George, VA
	Richmond City, VA		
114	**Norfolk-Portsmouth-Virginia Beach, Virginia**		
	Chesapeake City, VA	Gloucester, VA	Hampton City, VA
	James City, VA	Newport News City, VA	Norfolk City, VA
	Poquoson City, VA	Portsmouth City, VA	Suffolk City, VA
	Virginia Beach City, VA	Williamsburg City, VA	York, VA
115	**Eastern North Carolina**		
	Alamance, NC	Anson, NC	Beaufort, NC
	Bertie, NC	Bladen, NC	Brunswick, NC
	Camden, NC	Carteret, NC	Caswell, NC
	Chatham, NC	Chowan, NC	Columbus, NC
	Craven, NC	Cumberland, NC	Currituck, NC
	Dare, NC	Duplin, NC	Edgecombe, NC
	Gates, NC	Granville, NC	Greene, NC
	Halifax, NC	Harnett, NC	Hertford, NC
	Hoke, NC	Hyde, NC	Johnston, NC
	Jones, NC	Lee, NC	Lenoir, NC
	Martin, NC	Montgomery, NC	Moore, NC
	Nash, NC	New Hanover, NC	Northampton, NC
	Onslow, NC	Pamlico, NC	Pasquotank, NC
	Pender, NC	Perquimans, NC	Person, NC
	Pitt, NC	Richmond, NC	Robeson, NC
	Rockingham, NC	Sampson, NC	Scotland, NC
	Stanly, NC	Tyrrell, NC	Vance, NC
	Warren, NC	Washington, NC	Wayne, NC
	Wilson, NC		

Identification Number of Geographic Market	Geographic Markets		
116	**Raleigh-Durham, North Carolina**		
	Durham, NC	Franklin, NC	Orange, NC
	Wake, NC		
117	**Greensboro-Winston-Salem, North Carolina**		
	Davidson, NC	Davie, NC	Forsyth, NC
	Guilford, NC	Randolph, NC	Stokes, NC
	Yadkin, NC		
118	**Charlotte, North Carolina**		
	Cabarrus, NC	Gaston, NC	Lincoln, NC
	Mecklenburg, NC	Rowan, NC	Union, NC
	York, SC		
119	**Mountain Region, North Carolina**		
	Alexander, NC	Alleghany, NC	Ashe, NC
	Avery, NC	Buncombe, NC	Burke, NC
	Caldwell, NC	Catawba, NC	Cherokee, NC
	Clay, NC	Cleveland, NC	Graham, NC
	Haywood, NC	Henderson, NC	Iredell, NC
	Jackson, NC	Macon, NC	Madison, NC
	McDowell, NC	Mitchell, NC	Polk, NC
	Rutherford, NC	Surry, NC	Swain, NC
	Transylvania, NC	Watauga, NC	Wilkes, NC
	Yancey, NC		
120	**Greenville-Spartanburg, South Carolina**		
	Greenville, SC	Pickens, SC	Spartanburg, SC
121	**Eastern Rural South Carolina**		
	Allendale, SC	Bamberg, SC	Barnwell, SC
	Beaufort, SC	Calhoun, SC	Chester, SC
	Chesterfield, SC	Clarendon, SC	Colleton, SC
	Darlington, SC	Dillon, SC	Fairfield, SC
	Florence, SC	Georgetown, SC	Hampton, SC
	Horry, SC	Jasper, SC	Kershaw, SC
	Lancaster, SC	Lee, SC	Marion, SC
	Marlboro, SC	Orangeburg, SC	Sumter, SC
	Williamsburg, SC		
122	**Charleston, South Carolina**		
	Berkeley, SC	Charleston, SC	Dorchester, SC
123	**Columbia, South Carolina**		
	Lexington, SC	Richland, SC	
124	**Northwestern Rural South Carolina**		
	Abbeville, SC	Anderson, SC	Cherokee, SC
	Edgefield, SC	Greenwood, SC	Laurens, SC
	McCormick, SC	Newberry, SC	Oconee, SC
	Saluda, SC	Union, SC	
125	**Augusta, Georgia/South Carolina**		
	Columbia, GA	McDuffie, GA	Richmond, GA
	Aiken, SC		

Identification Number of Geographic Market	Geographic Markets		
126	**Northern Mountain Region, Georgia**		
	Banks, GA	Chattooga, GA	Dawson, GA
	Fannin, GA	Franklin, GA	Gilmer, GA
	Gordon, GA	Habersham, GA	Hall, GA
	Hart, GA	Lumpkin, GA	Murray, GA
	Pickens, GA	Rabun, GA	Stephens, GA
	Towns, GA	Union, GA	White, GA
	Whitfield, GA		
127	**Atlanta, Georgia**		
	Barrow, GA	Butts, GA	Cherokee, GA
	Clayton, GA	Cobb, GA	Coweta, GA
	DeKalb, GA	Douglas, GA	Fayette, GA
	Forsyth, GA	Fulton, GA	Gwinnett, GA
	Henry, GA	Newton, GA	Paulding, GA
	Rockdale, GA	Spalding, GA	Walton, GA
128	**Columbus, Georgia/Alabama**		
	Russell, AL	Chattahoochee, GA	Muscogee, GA
129	**Macon, Georgia**		
	Bibb, GA	Houston, GA	Jones, GA
	Peach, GA		
130	**Savannah, Georgia**		
	Chatham, GA	Effingham, GA	
131	**Rural Georgia**		
	Appling, GA	Atkinson, GA	Bacon, GA
	Baker, GA	Baldwin, GA	Bartow, GA
	Ben Hill, GA	Berrien, GA	Bleckley, GA
	Brantley, GA	Brooks, GA	Bryan, GA
	Bulloch, GA	Burke, GA	Calhoun, GA
	Camden, GA	Candler, GA	Carroll, GA
	Charlton, GA	Clarke, GA	Clay, GA
	Clinch, GA	Coffee, GA	Colquitt, GA
	Cook, GA	Crawford, GA	Crisp, GA
	Decatur, GA	Dodge, GA	Dooly, GA
	Dougherty, GA	Early, GA	Echols, GA
	Elbert, GA	Emanuel, GA	Evans, GA
	Floyd, GA	Glascock, GA	Glynn, GA
	Grady, GA	Greene, GA	Hancock, GA
	Haralson, GA	Harris, GA	Heard, GA
	Irwin, GA	Jackson, GA	Jasper, GA
	Jeff Davis, GA	Jefferson, GA	Jenkins, GA
	Johnson, GA	Lamar, GA	Lanier, GA
	Laurens, GA	Lee, GA	Liberty, GA
	Lincoln, GA	Long, GA	Lowndes, GA
	Macon, GA	Madison, GA	Marion, GA
	McIntosh, GA	Meriwether, GA	Miller, GA
	Mitchell, GA	Monroe, GA	Montgomery, GA
	Morgan, GA	Oconee, GA	Oglethorpe, GA
	Pierce, GA	Pike, GA	Polk, GA
	Pulaski, GA	Putnam, GA	Quitman, GA
	Randolph, GA	Schley, GA	Screven, GA
	Seminole, GA	Stewart, GA	Sumter, GA
	Talbot, GA	Taliaferro, GA	Tattnall, GA
	Taylor, GA	Telfair, GA	Terrell, GA
	Thomas, GA	Tift, GA	Toombs, GA
	Treutlen, GA	Troup, GA	Turner, GA
	Twiggs, GA	Upson, GA	Ware, GA
	Warren, GA	Washington, GA	Wayne, GA
	Webster, GA	Wheeler, GA	Wilcox, GA
	Wilkes, GA	Wilkinson, GA	Worth, GA

Identification Number of Geographic Market	Geographic Markets		
132	**Jacksonville/Gainesville, Florida**		
	Alachua, FL	Bradford, FL	Clay, FL
	Duval, FL	Nassau, FL	Saint Johns, FL
133	**Daytona Beach, Florida**		
	Volusia, FL		
134	**Melbourne-Titusville, Florida**		
	Brevard, FL		
135	**Miami-Ft. Lauderdale-West Palm Beach, Florida**		
	Broward, FL	Dade, FL	Palm Beach, FL
136	**Rural Southern Florida**		
	Charlotte, FL	Collier, FL	De Soto, FL
	Glades, FL	Hardee, FL	Hendry, FL
	Highlands, FL	Indian River, FL	Manatee, FL
	Martin, FL	Monroe, FL	Okeechobee, FL
	Saint Lucie, FL		
137	**Ft. Myers, Florida**		
	Lee, FL		
138	**Sarasota, Florida**		
	Sarasota, FL		
139	**Tampa-St. Petersburg, Florida**		
	Hernando, FL	Hillsborough, FL	Pasco, FL
	Pinnellas, FL		
140	**Lakeland-Winter Haven, Florida**		
	Polk, FL		
141	**Orlando, Florida**		
	Orange, FL	Osceola, FL	Seminole, FL
142	**Northeastern Rural Florida**		
	Baker, FL	Citrus, FL	Columbia, FL
	Dixie, FL	Flagler, FL	Gilchrist, FL
	Hamilton, FL	Jefferson, FL	Lafayette, FL
	Lake, FL	Levy, FL	Madison, FL
	Marion, FL	Putnam, FL	Sumter, FL
	Suwannee, FL	Taylor, FL	Union, FL
143	**Tallahassee, Florida**		
	Gadsden, FL	Leon, FL	
144	**Northwestern Florida**		
	Bay, FL	Calhoun, FL	Franklin, FL
	Gulf, FL	Holmes, FL	Jackson, FL
	Liberty, FL	Okaloosa, FL	Wakulla, FL
	Walton, FL	Washington, FL	
145	**Pensacola, Florida**		
	Escambia, FL	Santa Rosa, FL	
146	**Mobile, Alabama**		
	Baldwin, AL	Mobile, AL	

223

Identification Number of Geographic Market	Geographic Markets		
147	**Southern Rural Alabama**		
	Barbour, AL	Bullock, AL	Butler, AL
	Chambers, AL	Choctaw, AL	Clarke, AL
	Coffee, AL	Conecuh, AL	Covington, AL
	Crenshaw, AL	Dale, AL	Dallas, AL
	Escambia, AL	Geneva, AL	Greene, AL
	Hale, AL	Henry, AL	Houston, AL
	Lee, AL	Lowndes, AL	Macon, AL
	Marengo, AL	Monroe, AL	Perry, AL
	Pike, AL	Randolph, AL	Sumter, AL
	Tallapoosa, AL	Washington, AL	Wilcox, AL
148	**Montgomery, Alabama**		
	Autauga, AL	Elmore, AL	Montgomery, AL
149	**Birmingham, Alabama**		
	Blount, AL	Jefferson, AL	Saint Clair, AL
	Shelby, AL	Tuscaloosa, AL	Walker, AL
150	**Huntsville, Alabama**		
	Madison, AL		
151	**Northern Rural Alabama**		
	Bibb, AL	Calhoun, AL	Cherokee, AL
	Chilton, AL	Clay, AL	Cleburne, AL
	Colbert, AL	Coosa, AL	Cullman, AL
	De Kalb, AL	Etowah, AL	Fayette, AL
	Franklin, AL	Jackson, AL	Lamar, AL
	Lauderdale, AL	Lawrence, AL	Limestone, AL
	Marion, AL	Marshall, AL	Morgan, AL
	Pickens, AL	Talladega, AL	Winston, AL
152	**Memphis, Tennessee/Arkansas**		
	Crittenden, AR	Shelby, TN	Tipton, TN
153	**Western Rural Tennessee**		
	Bedford, TN	Benton, TN	Carroll, TN
	Chester, TN	Coffee, TN	Crockett, TN
	Decatur, TN	Dyer, TN	Fayette, TN
	Franklin, TN	Gibson, TN	Giles, TN
	Hardeman, TN	Hardin, TN	Haywood, TN
	Henderson, TN	Henry, TN	Hickman, TN
	Houston, TN	Humphreys, TN	Lake, TN
	Lauderdale, TN	Lawrence, TN	Lewis, TN
	Lincoln, TN	Madison, TN	Marshall, TN
	Maury, TN	McNairy, TN	Montgomery, TN
	Moore, TN	Obion, TN	Perry, TN
	Stewart, TN	Wayne, TN	Weakley, TN
154	**Nashville, Tennessee**		
	Cheatham, TN	Davidson, TN	Dickson, TN
	Robertson, TN	Rutherford, TN	Sumner, TN
	Williamson, TN	Wilson, TN	
155	**Chattanooga, Tennessee/Georgia**		
	Catoosa, GA	Dade, GA	Walker, GA
	Hamilton, TN	Marion, TN	Sequatchie, TN

Identification Number of Geographic Market	Geographic Markets		
156	**Tennessee River Valley, Tennessee**		
	Bledsoe, TN	Bradley, TN	Campbell, TN
	Cannon, TN	Claiborne, TN	Clay, TN
	Cocke, TN	Cumberland, TN	De Kalb, TN
	Fentress, TN	Greene, TN	Grundy, TN
	Hamblen, TN	Hancock, TN	Jackson, TN
	Johnson, TN	Loudon, TN	Macon, TN
	McMinn, TN	Meigs, TN	Monroe, TN
	Morgan, TN	Overton, TN	Pickett, TN
	Polk, TN	Putnam, TN	Rhea, TN
	Roane, TN	Scott, TN	Smith, TN
	Trousdale, TN	Van Buren, TN	Warren, TN
	White, TN		
157	**Knoxville, Tennessee**		
	Anderson, TN	Blount, TN	Grainger, TN
	Jefferson, TN	Knox, TN	Sevier, TN
	Union, TN		
158	**Johnson City-Kingsport-Bristol, Tennessee/Virginia**		
	Carter, TN	Hawkins, TN	Sullivan, TN
	Unicoi, TN	Washington, TN	Bristol City, VA
	Scott, VA	Washington, VA	
159	**Southeastern Rural Kentucky**		
	Bath, KY	Bell, KY	Breathitt, KY
	Clay, KY	Clinton, KY	Elliott, KY
	Estill, KY	Floyd, KY	Harlan, KY
	Jackson, KY	Johnson, KY	Knott, KY
	Knox, KY	Laurel, KY	Lawrence, KY
	Lee, KY	Leslie, KY	Letcher, KY
	Magoffin, KY	Martin, KY	McCreary, KY
	Menifee, KY	Montgomery, KY	Morgan, KY
	Owsley, KY	Perry, KY	Pike, KY
	Powell, KY	Pulaski, KY	Rockcastle, KY
	Rowan, KY	Russell, KY	Wayne, KY
	Whitley, KY	Wolfe, KY	
160	**Lexington, Kentucky**		
	Bourbon, KY	Clark, KY	Fayette, KY
	Jessamine, KY	Scott, KY	Woodford, KY
161	**Louisville, Kentucky/Indiana**		
	Clark, IN	Floyd, IN	Harrison, IN
	Bullitt, KY	Jefferson, KY	Oldham, KY
	Shelby, KY		

Identification Number of Geographic Market	Geographic Markets		
162	**Northwestern Rural Kentucky**		
	Adair, KY	Allen, KY	Anderson, KY
	Ballard, KY	Barren, KY	Boyle, KY
	Bracken, KY	Breckinridge, KY	Butler, KY
	Caldwell, KY	Calloway, KY	Carlisle, KY
	Carroll, KY	Casey, KY	Christian, KY
	Crittenden, KY	Cumberland, KY	Edmonson, KY
	Fleming, KY	Franklin, KY	Fulton, KY
	Gallatin, KY	Garrard, KY	Grant, KY
	Graves, KY	Grayson, KY	Green, KY
	Hancock, KY	Hardin, KY	Harrison, KY
	Hart, KY	Henry, KY	Hickman, KY
	Hopkins, KY	Larue, KY	Lewis, KY
	Lincoln, KY	Livingston, KY	Logan, KY
	Lyon, KY	Madison, KY	Marion, KY
	Marshall, KY	Mason, KY	McCracken, KY
	McLean, KY	Meade, KY	Mercer, KY
	Metcalfe, KY	Monroe, KY	Muhlenberg, KY
	Nelson, KY	Nicholas, KY	Ohio, KY
	Owen, KY	Pendleton, KY	Robertson, KY
	Simpson, KY	Spencer, KY	Taylor, KY
	Todd, KY	Trigg, KY	Trimble, KY
	Union, KY	Warren, KY	Washington, KY
	Webster, KY		
163	**Northern Mississippi**		
	Alcorn, MS	Attala, MS	Benton, MS
	Bolivar, MS	Calhoun, MS	Carroll, MS
	Chickasaw, MS	Choctaw, MS	Clay, MS
	Coahoma, MS	De Soto, MS	Grenada, MS
	Holmes, MS	Humphreys, MS	Issaquena, MS
	Itawamba, MS	Kemper, MS	Lafayette, MS
	Leake, MS	Lee, MS	Leflore, MS
	Lowndes, MS	Marshall, MS	Monroe, MS
	Montgomery, MS	Neshoba, MS	Noxubee, MS
	Oktibbeha, MS	Panola, MS	Pontotoc, MS
	Prentiss, MS	Quitman, MS	Sharkey, MS
	Sunflower, MS	Tallahatchie, MS	Tate, MS
	Tippah, MS	Tishomingo, MS	Tunica, MS
	Union, MS	Washington, MS	Webster, MS
	Winston, MS	Yalobusha, MS	Yazoo, MS
164	**Jackson, Mississippi**		
	Hinds, MS	Madison, MS	Rankin, MS
165	**Southern Mississippi**		
	Adams, MS	Amite, MS	Claiborne, MS
	Clarke, MS	Copiah, MS	Covington, MS
	Forrest, MS	Franklin, MS	George, MS
	Greene, MS	Hancock, MS	Harrison, MS
	Jackson, MS	Jasper, MS	Jefferson, MS
	Jefferson Davis, MS	Jones, MS	Lamar, MS
	Lauderdale, MS	Lawrence, MS	Lincoln, MS
	Marion, MS	Newton, MS	Pearl River, MS
	Perry, MS	Pike, MS	Scott, MS
	Simpson, MS	Smith, MS	Stone, MS
	Walthall, MS	Warren, MS	Wayne, MS
	Wilkinson, MS		
166	**New Orleans, Louisiana**		
	Jefferson, LA	Orleans, LA	Saint Bernard, LA
	Saint Charles, LA	Saint John Baptist, LA	Saint Tammany, L

Identification Number of Geographic Market	Geographic Markets		
167	**Baton Rouge, Louisiana**		
	Ascension, LA	East Baton Rouge, LA	Livingston, LA
	West Baton Rouge, LA		
168	**Lafayette, Louisiana**		
	Lafayette, LA	Saint Martin, LA	
169	**Southern Louisiana**		
	Acadia, LA	Allen, LA	Assumption, LA
	Beauregard, LA	Calcasieu, LA	Cameron, LA
	East Feliciana, LA	Evangeline, LA	Iberia, LA
	Iberville, LA	Jefferson Davis, LA	Lafourche, LA
	Plaquemines, LA	Pointe Coupee, LA	Saint Helena, LA
	Saint James, LA	Saint Landry, LA	Saint Mary, LA
	Tangipahoa, LA	Terrebonne, LA	Vermilion, LA
	Washington, LA	West Feliciana, LA	
170	**Northern Rural Louisiana**		
	Avoyelles, LA	Bienville, LA	Caldwell, LA
	Catahoula, LA	Claiborne, LA	Concordia, LA
	De Soto, LA	East Carroll, LA	Franklin, LA
	Grant, LA	Jackson, LA	La Salle, LA
	Lincoln, LA	Madison, LA	Morehouse, LA
	Natchitoches, LA	Ouachita, LA	Rapides, LA
	Red River, LA	Richland, LA	Sabine, LA
	Tensas, LA	Union, LA	Vernon, LA
	Webster, LA	West Carroll, LA	Winn, LA
171	**Shreveport, Louisiana**		
	Bossier, LA	Caddo, LA	
172	**Eastern Rural Arkansas**		
	Arkansas, AR	Ashley, AR	Bradley, AR
	Chicot, AR	Clay, AR	Cleveland, AR
	Craighead, AR	Cross, AR	Desha, AR
	Drew, AR	Greene, AR	Independence, AR
	Jackson, AR	Lawrence, AR	Lee, AR
	Lincoln, AR	Mississippi, AR	Monroe, AR
	Phillips, AR	Poinsett, AR	Prairie, AR
	Randolph, AR	Saint Francis, AR	Sharp, AR
	White, AR	Woodruff, AR	
173	**Little Rock-Pine Bluff, Arkansas**		
	Faulkner, AR	Jefferson, AR	Lonoke, AR
	Pulaski, AR	Saline, AR	
174	**Western Arkansas**		
	Baxter, AR	Benton, AR	Boone, AR
	Calhoun, AR	Carroll, AR	Clark, AR
	Cleburne, AR	Columbia, AR	Conway, AR
	Dallas, AR	Franklin, AR	Fulton, AR
	Garland, AR	Grant, AR	Hempstead, AR
	Hot Spring, AR	Howard, AR	Izard, AR
	Johnson, AR	Lafayette, AR	Little River, AR
	Logan, AR	Madison, AR	Marion, AR
	Miller, AR	Montgomery, AR	Nevada, AR
	Newton, AR	Ouachita, AR	Perry, AR
	Pike, AR	Polk, AR	Pope, AR
	Scott, AR	Searcy, AR	Sevier, AR
	Stone, AR	Union, AR	Van Buren, AR
	Yell, AR		

Identification Number of Geographic Market	Geographic Markets		
175	**Ft. Smith-Fayetteville, Arkansas/Oklahoma**		
	Crawford, AR	Sebastian, AR	Washington, AR
	Sequoyah, OK		
176	**Eastern Oklahoma**		
	Adair, OK	Atoka, OK	Bryan, OK
	Carter, OK	Cherokee, OK	Choctaw, OK
	Coal, OK	Craig, OK	Delaware, OK
	Garvin, OK	Haskell, OK	Hughes, OK
	Johnston, OK	Latimer, OK	Le Flore, OK
	Love, OK	Marshall, OK	Mayes, OK
	McCurtain, OK	McIntosh, OK	Murray, OK
	Muskogee, OK	Nowata, OK	Okfuskee, OK
	Okmulgee, OK	Ottawa, OK	Pittsburg, OK
	Pontotoc, OK	Pushmataha, OK	Seminole, OK
	Washington, OK		
177	**Tulsa, Oklahoma**		
	Creek, OK	Osage, OK	Rogers, OK
	Tulsa, OK	Wagoner, OK	
178	**Oklahoma City, Oklahoma**		
	Canadian, OK	Cleveland, OK	Lincoln, OK
	Logan, OK	McClain, OK	Oklahoma, OK
	Pottawatomie, OK		
179	**Western Oklahoma**		
	Alfalfa, OK	Beaver, OK	Beckham, OK
	Blaine, OK	Caddo, OK	Cimarron, OK
	Comanche, OK	Cotton, OK	Custer, OK
	Dewey, OK	Ellis, OK	Garfield, OK
	Grady, OK	Grant, OK	Greer, OK
	Harmon, OK	Harper, OK	Jackson, OK
	Jefferson, OK	Kay, OK	Kingfisher, OK
	Kiowa, OK	Major, OK	Noble, OK
	Pawnee, OK	Payne, OK	Roger Mills, OK
	Stephens, OK	Texas, OK	Tillman, OK
	Washita, OK	Woods, OK	Woodward, OK
180	**Amarillo, Texas**		
	Potter, TX	Randall, TX	
181	**Lubbock, Texas**		
	Lubbock, TX		
182	**Odessa, Midland, Texas**		
	Ector, TX	Midland, TX	

Identification Number of Geographic Market	Geographic Markets		
183	**North Panhandle Texas**		
	Andrews, TX	Armstrong, TX	Bailey, TX
	Borden, TX	Briscoe, TX	Carson, TX
	Castro, TX	Childress, TX	Cochran, TX
	Collingsworth, TX	Cottle, TX	Crane, TX
	Crosby, TX	Dallam, TX	Dawson, TX
	Deaf Smith, TX	Dickens, TX	Donley, TX
	Floyd, TX	Gaines, TX	Garza, TX
	Glasscock, TX	Gray, TX	Hale, TX
	Hall, TX	Hansford, TX	Hartley, TX
	Hemphill, TX	Hockley, TX	Howard, TX
	Hutchinson, TX	Kent, TX	King, TX
	Lamb, TX	Lipscomb, TX	Lynn, TX
	Martin, TX	Moore, TX	Motley, TX
	Ochiltree, TX	Oldham, TX	Parmer, TX
	Reagan, TX	Roberts, TX	Scurry, TX
	Sherman, TX	Stonewall, TX	Swisher, TX
	Terry, TX	Upton, TX	Ward, TX
	Wheeler, TX	Winkler, TX	Yoakum, TX
184	**Northcentral Texas**		
	Archer, TX	Baylor, TX	Blanco, TX
	Brown, TX	Burnet, TX	Callahan, TX
	Clay, TX	Coke, TX	Coleman, TX
	Comanche, TX	Concho, TX	Cooke, TX
	Eastland, TX	Erath, TX	Fisher, TX
	Foard, TX	Gillespie, TX	Hamilton, TX
	Hardeman, TX	Haskell, TX	Irion, TX
	Jack, TX	Jones, TX	Kendall, TX
	Kerr, TX	Kimble, TX	Knox, TX
	Lampasas, TX	Llano, TX	Mason, TX
	McCulloch, TX	Menard, TX	Mills, TX
	Mitchell, TX	Montague, TX	Nolan, TX
	Palo Pinto, TX	Runnels, TX	San Saba, TX
	Shackelford, TX	Stephens, TX	Sterling, TX
	Taylor, TX	Throckmorton, TX	Tom Green, TX
	Wichita, TX	Wilbarger, TX	Wise, TX
	Young, TX		
185	**Dallas-Ft. Worth, Texas**		
	Collin, TX	Dallas, TX	Denton, TX
	Ellis, TX	Johnson, TX	Kaufman, TX
	Parker, TX	Rockwall, TX	Tarrant, TX
186	**Longview-Marshall-Tyler, Texas**		
	Gregg, TX	Harrison, TX	Smith, TX
187	**Beaumont-Port Arthur, Texas**		
	Hardin, TX	Jefferson, TX	Orange, TX
188	**Houston-Galveston, Texas**		
	Brazoria, TX	Fort Bend, TX	Galveston, TX
	Harris, TX	Liberty, TX	Montgomery, TX
	Waller, TX		

Identification Number of Geographic Market	Geographic Markets		
189	**Eastern Texas**		
	Anderson, TX	Angelina, TX	Aransas, TX
	Atascosa, TX	Austin, TX	Bastrop, TX
	Bee, TX	Bosque, TX	Bowie, TX
	Brazos, TX	Burleson, TX	Caldwell, TX
	Calhoun, TX	Camp, TX	Cass, TX
	Chambers, TX	Cherokee, TX	Colorado, TX
	De Witt, TX	Delta, TX	Falls, TX
	Fannin, TX	Fayette, TX	Franklin, TX
	Freestone, TX	Goliad, TX	Gonzales, TX
	Grayson, TX	Grimes, TX	Henderson, TX
	Hill, TX	Hood, TX	Hopkins, TX
	Houston, TX	Hunt, TX	Jackson, TX
	Jasper, TX	Jim Wells, TX	Karnes, TX
	Kenedy, TX	Kleberg, TX	Lamar, TX
	Lavaca, TX	Lee, TX	Leon, TX
	Limestone, TX	Live Oak, TX	Madison, TX
	Marion, TX	Matagorda, TX	Milam, TX
	Morris, TX	Nacogdoches, TX	Navarro, TX
	Newton, TX	Panola, TX	Polk, TX
	Rains, TX	Red River, TX	Refugio, TX
	Robertson, TX	Rusk, TX	Sabine, TX
	San Augustine, TX	San Jacinto, TX	Shelby, TX
	Somervell, TX	Titus, TX	Trinity, TX
	Tyler, TX	Upshur, TX	Van Zandt, TX
	Victoria, TX	Walker, TX	Washington, TX
	Wharton, TX	Willacy, TX	Wilson, TX
	Wood, TX		
190	**Waco-Killeen-Temple, Texas**		
	Bell, TX	Coryell, TX	McLennan, TX
191	**Austin, Texas**		
	Hays, TX	Travis, TX	Williamson, TX
192	**San Antonio, Texas**		
	Bexar, TX	Comal, TX	Guadalupe, TX
193	**Corpus Christi, Texas**		
	Nueces, TX	San Patricio, TX	
194	**Brownsville-McAllen, Texas**		
	Cameron, TX	Hidalgo, TX	
195	**Southwestern Texas**		
	Bandera, TX	Brewster, TX	Brooks, TX
	Crockett, TX	Culberson, TX	Dimmit, TX
	Duval, TX	Edwards, TX	Frio, TX
	Hudspeth, TX	Jeff Davis, TX	Jim Hogg, TX
	Kinney, TX	LaSalle, TX	Loving, TX
	Maverick, TX	McMullen, TX	Medina, TX
	Pecos, TX	Presidio, TX	Real, TX
	Reeves, TX	Schleicher, TX	Starr, TX
	Sutton, TX	Terrell, TX	Uvalde, TX
	Val Verde, TX	Webb, TX	Zapata, TX
	Zavala, TX		

Identification Number of Geographic Market	Geographic Markets		
196	**El Paso, Texas**		
	El Paso, TX		
197	**Western New Mexico**		
	Catron, NM	Dona Ana, NM	Grant, NM
	Hidalgo, NM	Lincoln, NM	Los Alamos, NM
	Luna, NM	McKinley, NM	Otero, NM
	Rio Arriba, NM	San Juan, NM	Sandoval, NM
	Santa Fe, NM	Sierra, NM	Socorro, NM
	Taos, NM	Torrance, NM	Valencia, NM
198	**Albuquerque, New Mexico**		
	Bernalillo, NM		
199	**Eastern New Mexico**		
	Chaves, NM	Colfax, NM	Curry, NM
	DeBaca, NM	Eddy, NM	Guadalupe, NM
	Harding, NM	Lea, NM	Mora, NM
	Quay, NM	Roosevelt, NM	San Miguel, NM
	Union, NM		
200	**Eastern Colorado**		
	Baca, CO	Bent, CO	Cheyenne, CO
	Crowley, CO	Elbert, CO	Kiowa, CO
	Kit Carson, CO	Larimer, CO	Las Animas, CO
	Lincoln, CO	Logan, CO	Morgan, CO
	Otero, CO	Phillips, CO	Prowers, CO
	Sedgwick, CO	Washington, CO	Weld, CO
	Yuma, CO		
201	**Colorado Springs-Pueblo, Colorado**		
	El Paso, CO	Pueblo, CO	
202	**Denver-Boulder, Colorado**		
	Adams, CO	Arapahoe, CO	Boulder, CO
	Clear Creek, CO	Denver, CO	Douglas, CO
	Gilpin, CO	Jefferson, CO	
203	**Western Colorado**		
	Alamosa, CO	Archuleta, CO	Chaffee, CO
	Conejos, CO	Costilla, CO	Custer, CO
	Delta, CO	Dolores, CO	Eagle, CO
	Fremont, CO	Garfield, CO	Grand, CO
	Gunnison, CO	Hinsdale, CO	Huerfano, CO
	Jackson, CO	La Plata, CO	Lake, CO
	Mesa, CO	Mineral, CO	Moffat, CO
	Montezuma, CO	Montrose, CO	Ouray, CO
	Park, CO	Pitkin, CO	Rio Blanco, CO
	Rio Grande, CO	Routt, CO	Saguache, CO
	San Juan, CO	San Miguel, CO	Summit, CO
	Teller, CO		
204	**State of Wyoming**		
	Albany, WY	Big Horn, WY	Campbell, WY
	Carbon, WY	Converse, WY	Crook, WY
	Fremont, WY	Goshen, WY	Hot Springs, WY
	Johnson, WY	Laramie, WY	Lincoln, WY
	Natrona, WY	Niobrara, WY	Park, WY
	Platte, WY	Sheridan, WY	Sublette, WY
	Sweetwater, WY	Teton, WY	Uinta, WY
	Washakie, WY	Weston, WY	Yellowstone National Park, WY

Identification Number of Geographic Market	Geographic Markets		
205	**Eastern Montana**		
	Big Horn, MT	Blaine, MT	Carbon, MT
	Carter, MT	Cascade, MT	Chouteau, MT
	Custer, MT	Daniels, MT	Dawson, MT
	Fallon, MT	Fergus, MT	Garfield, MT
	Golden Valley, MT	Hill, MT	Judith Basin, MT
	Liberty, MT	McCone, MT	Musselshell, MT
	Petroleum, MT	Phillips, MT	Pondera, MT
	Powder River, MT	Prairie, MT	Richland, MT
	Roosevelt, MT	Rosebud, MT	Sheridan, MT
	Stillwater, MT	Sweet Grass, MT	Teton, MT
	Toole, MT	Treasure, MT	Valley, MT
	Wheatland, MT	Wibaux, MT	Yellowstone, MT
	Yellowstone National Park, MT		
206	**Western Montana**		
	Beaverhead, MT	Broadwater, MT	Deer Lodge, MT
	Flathead, MT	Gallatin, MT	Glacier, MT
	Granite, MT	Jefferson, MT	Lake, MT
	Lewis and Clark, MT	Lincoln, MT	Madison, MT
	Meagher, MT	Mineral, MT	Missoula, MT
	Park, MT	Powell, MT	Ravalli, MT
	Sanders, MT	Silver Bow, MT	
207	**Rural Idaho**		
	Adams, ID	Bannock, ID	Bear Lake, ID
	Benewah, ID	Bingham, ID	Blaine, ID
	Boise, ID	Bonner, ID	Bonneville, ID
	Boundary, ID	Butte, ID	Camas, ID
	Canyon, ID	Caribou, ID	Cassia, ID
	Clark, ID	Clearwater, ID	Custer, ID
	Elmore, ID	Franklin, ID	Fremont, ID
	Gem, ID	Gooding, ID	Idaho, ID
	Jefferson, ID	Jerome, ID	Kootenai, ID
	Latah, ID	Lemhi, ID	Lewis, ID
	Lincoln, ID	Madison, ID	Minidoka, ID
	Nez Perce, ID	Oneida, ID	Owyhee, ID
	Payette, ID	Power, ID	Shoshone, ID
	Teton, ID	Twin Falls, ID	Valley, ID
	Washington, ID	Yellowstone National Park, ID	
208	**Boise, Idaho**		
	Ada, ID		
209	**Salt Lake City-Provo, Utah**		
	Davis, UT	Salt Lake, UT	Utah, UT
	Weber, UT		
210	**Rural Utah**		
	Beaver, UT	Box Elder, UT	Cache, UT
	Carbon, UT	Daggett, UT	Duchesne, UT
	Emery, UT	Garfield, UT	Grand, UT
	Iron, UT	Juab, UT	Kane, UT
	Millard, UT	Morgan, UT	Piute, UT
	Rich, UT	San Juan, UT	Sanpete, UT
	Sevier, UT	Summit, UT	Tooele, UT
	Uintah, UT	Wasatch, UT	Washington, UT
	Wayne, UT		
211	**Rural Nevada**		
	Carson City, NV	Churchill, NV	Douglas, NV
	Elko, NV	Esmeralda, NV	Eureka, NV
	Humboldt, NV	Lander, NV	Lincoln, NV
	Lyon, NV	Mineral, NV	Nye, NV
	Pershing, NV	Storey, NV	White Pine, NV

Identification Number of Geographic Market	Geographic Markets		
212	**Reno, Nevada** Washoe, NV		
213	**Las Vegas, Nevada** Clark, NV		
214	**Rural Arizona** Apache, AZ Gila, AZ Mohave, AZ Santa Cruz, AZ	Cochise, AZ Graham, AZ Navajo, AZ Yavapai, AZ	Coconino, AZ Greenlee, AZ Pinal, AZ Yuma, AZ
215	**Phoenix, Arizona** Maricopa, AZ		
216	**Tucson, Arizona** Pima, AZ		
217	**Northwestern-Eastern Rural California** Alpine, CA Del Norte, CA Inyo, CA Mendocino, CA Nevada, CA Siskiyou, CA	Amador, CA Humboldt, CA Lake, CA Modoc, CA Plumas, CA Trinity, CA	Calaveras, CA Imperial, CA Lassen, CA Mono, CA Sierra, CA Tuolumne, CA
218	**San Diego, California** San Diego, CA		
219	**Los Angeles, California** Los Angeles, CA San Bernardino, CA	Orange, CA Ventura, CA	Riverside, CA
220	**Santa Barbara, California** Santa Barbara, CA		
221	**Santa Cruz-San Luis Obispo, California** San Benito, CA	San Luis Obispo, CA	Santa Cruz, CA
222	**Salinas-Seaside-Monterey, California** Monterey, CA		
223	**Bakersfield, CA** Kern, CA		
224	**Central Valley, California** Butte, CA Kings, CA Merced, CA Tehama, CA	Colusa, CA Madera, CA Shasta, CA Tulare, CA	Glenn, CA Mariposa, CA Sutter, CA Yuba, CA
225	**Fresno, California** Fresno, CA		
226	**Stockton-Modesto, California** San Joaquin, CA	Stanislaus, CA	
227	**San Francisco, California** Alameda, CA Napa, CA Santa Clara, CA	Contra Costa, CA San Francisco, CA Solano, CA	Marin, CA San Mateo, CA Sonoma, CA
228	**Sacramento, California** El Dorado, CA Yolo, CA	Placer, CA	Sacramento, CA

233

Identification Number of Geographic Market	Geographic Markets		
229	**Western Oregon**		
	Benton, OR	Clatsop, OR	Columbia, OR
	Coos, OR	Curry, OR	Douglas, OR
	Jackson, OR	Josephine, OR	Klamath, OR
	Lincoln, OR	Linn, OR	Tillamook, OR
230	**Eugene, Oregon**		
	Lane, OR		
231	**Portland-Salem, Oregon**		
	Clackamas, OR	Marion, OR	Multnomah, OR
	Polk, OR	Washington, OR	Yamhill, OR
232	**Eastern Oregon**		
	Baker, OR	Crook, OR	Deschutes, OR
	Gilliam, OR	Grant, OR	Harney, OR
	Hood River, OR	Jefferson, OR	Lake, OR
	Malheur, OR	Morrow, OR	Sherman, OR
	Umatilla, OR	Union, OR	Wallowa, OR
	Wasco, OR	Wheeler, OR	
233	**Spokane, Washington**		
	Spokane, WA		
234	**Eastern Washington**		
	Adams, WA	Asotin, WA	Benton, WA
	Chelan, WA	Columbia, WA	Douglas, WA
	Ferry, WA	Franklin, WA	Garfield, WA
	Grant, WA	Island, WA	Kittitas, WA
	Klickitat, WA	Lincoln, WA	Okanogan, WA
	Pend Oreille, WA	San Juan, WA	Stevens, WA
	Walla Walla, WA	Whitman, WA	Yakima, WA
235	**Seattle, Washington**		
	King, WA	Snohomish, WA	
236	**Tacoma, Washington**		
	Pierce, WA		
237	**Western, Washington**		
	Clallam, WA	Clark, WA	Cowlitz, WA
	Grays Harbor, WA	Jefferson, WA	Kitsap, WA
	Lewis, WA	Mason, WA	Pacific, WA
	Skagit, WA	Skamania, WA	Thurston, WA
	Wahkiakum, WA	Whatcom, WA	
238	**State of Alaska**		
	Aleutian Islands, AK	Anchorage, AK	Bethel, AK
	Bristol Bay, AK	Dillingham, AK	Fairbanks-North Star,
	Haines, AK	Juneau, AK	Kenai Peninsula, AK
	Ketchikan-Gateway, AK	Kobuk, AK	Kodiak, AK
	Matanuska-Susitna, AK	Nome, AK	North Slope, AK
	Prince of Wales-Outer Ketchikan, AK		Sitka, AK
	Skagway-Yakutat-Angoon, AK	Southeast Fairbanks, AK	Valdez-Cordova, AK
	Wade Hampton, AK	Wrangell-Petersburg, AK	Yukon/Koyukuk, AK
239	**State of Hawaii**		
	Hawaii, HI	Honolulu, HI	Kauai, HI
	Maui/Kalawao, HI		

Index